Designing and Renovating Larger Gardens

Designing and Renovating Larger Gardens

Douglas Coltart

All illustrations and photographs by Douglas Coltart except pages 30, 37, 41, 42, 43, 52, 59, 65, 95 (bottom), 96, 110 (top) and 118 by John Brookes; pages 12, 128 and 129 by Raymond Jungles; pages 13 (lower), 18 (lower), 44 (bottom left) and 92 (top right) by Doug Hoerr; pages 20 (upper and lower), 38, 63, 68 (bottom left), 74 (bottom), 80 (bottom), 87 (left), 89, 115 (right), 116, 122 (top and bottom), 127 (bottom), 131–134, 136 and 138 (top left) by Debbie Roberts and Ian Smith; and page 124 by Ron Sutherland.

Published in 2007 by
Timber Press, Inc.
The Haseltine Building
133 S.W. Second Avenue, Suite 450
Portland, Oregon 97204-3527, U.S.A.
www.timberpress.com
For contact information regarding editorial, marketing, sales, and distribution in the United Kingdom, see
www.timberpress.co.uk.

Design by Dick Malt
Printed in China
Library of Congress Cataloging-in-Publication Data
Coltart, Douglas.
  Designing and renovating larger gardens / Douglas Coltart.
      p. cm.
  Includes bibliographical references and index.
  ISBN 978-0-88192-824-2
  1. Gardening. 2. Gardens–Design. 3. Landscape gardening.
  4. Plants, Useful. I. Title.
  SB467.8.C65 2007
  635–dc22
                                    2006035351

A catalogue record for this book is also available from the British Library.

Contents

Foreword

Very little has been written about larger gardens, let alone estates, for some time. Yet, if the truth be known, it is the larger gardens of the world on which most labour is spent and design advice lavished—partly, of course, because they present more problems than small gardens do.

So a book on designing and renovating larger spaces is to be welcomed. It is out of Scotland that a new voice and practitioner of landscape and garden design has emerged. Douglas Coltart bases his new approach on earlier well-founded principles that seek not only to develop larger gardens, but also to rationalize them in the light of contemporary requirements.

For designing a larger garden is different from designing a small one. Scale, views, driveways and the general relationship to the wider landscape make it so and, very broadly, the rules are identical the world over for people, the common denominator, work in much the same way wherever they live.

The author quotes earlier design practitioners like Thomas Mawson, Jekyll and Weaver, and even Edward Kemp of 1864. There's something very reassuring about this rural revamp, which is so different from the ephemeral new urban design scene. For Coltart writes about real situations, and his words are accompanied by readily understandable plans, drawings and diagrams. His examples and case studies are applicable everywhere.

Coltart takes his reader into the philosophy of landscape, encouraging consideration and analysis of the site before moving on to develop a practical, sustainable solution to its management and maintenance. The author reflects upon our current society—user-friendly minimalism, the meadow and herbaceous perennials—and puts in a plea for a return to shrubs where climate and maintenance allows. With design theory, then, comes horticultural knowledge.

What conditions the viability of any landscape is its maintenance and management which Coltart states must be the starting point of any proposal. Yet, so often it is regarded as an afterthought—the finishing line.

Having worked all over the world and, in particular, the United States of America, I know Coltart's theories to be correct, and the nuts and bolts of how we live do not change very much wherever our gardens may be. Views may be different, trees may be taller and sites shadier, but the theory of how to cope remains the same. Climates differ of course, as does the plant material that thrives there—and although this book's main focus is design and renovation, Coltart does give a full and practical list of plant material for varying situations—plants for a purpose.

This book makes design on a larger scale understandable. Do read it.

John Brookes MBE, Hon.D.Univ., FSGD

Acknowledgements

There are many people that I must thank for their help in writing this book. Firstly, love and thanks must go to Alex, Ben and Miles for their enduring patience and support. They have suffered the intermittent bursts of tapping on my laptop and given me the space to write on consecutive holidays.

For those who gave me direct assistance, such as the designers from around the world that have provided me with photographs and case studies of their work, I am greatly in debt. They include John Brookes for Denmans, West Sussex, England and his upstate New York gardens, USA; Ian Hamilton Finlay for Little Sparta, Lanarkshire, Scotland; Douglas Hoerr Landscape Architecture for Modern Garden, Minneapolis, Minnesota, USA; Raymond Jungles for Ross-Evans Garden and Spanish Style Gardens in Florida, USA; the late Maggie Keswick and Charles Jencks for Portrack Garden, Dumfriesshire, Scotland; Niall Manning and Alistair Morton for Dun Ard, Stirlingshire, Scotland; Debbie Roberts for Nursted Barns, Hampshire, England; Debbie Roberts and Ian Smith for Perching Barn, West Sussex, England.

Thanks are also due to: Dougie at Viridarium, for help with some of the artwork; Anna and all at Timber Press for their patience and flexible deadlines; and clients such as Pat Fraser for asking why all gardening books were about small gardens and giving me the kick I needed to put pen to paper—or digit to keyboard.

Lastly, a huge thank you must go to John Brookes not just for allowing me access to some of his gardens but for being such an inspiration. Without John many designers would not be as good as they are and the profession would not be as established as it is.

Preface

I decided to write this book after a succession of clients with large gardens complained that they did not know how to tackle their outside spaces. They bemoaned the fact that bookstores were stuffed with volumes catering to those with small gardens, ignoring the particular challenges facing those with spaces of a third of an acre to say, three acres. Although the owners of larger gardens usually consider themselves privileged, the responsibility for managing this space can, at the same time, seem rather daunting.

Giving general guidelines about designing gardens large or small is ambitious, as every garden has its own very individual aspect, site conditions and size differences. Yet there are certain elements of design that hold true for almost any garden, and it is particularly important when designing larger gardens that these tenets are borne in mind from the outset. While small gardens often have a preconceived structure imposed by the very boundaries that limit their size, large spaces lack these constraints. The natural inclination of the owner might be to either consciously or subconsciously divide the garden into smaller parts whose scale they feel able to cope with. This is likely to compromise the overall potential of the garden.

Large spaces offer enormous scope for drawing on the wider landscape to produce outdoor areas with a real 'sense of place'. Though effective results are sometimes achieved by a series of happy accidents and a good instinct, having a core set of principles with which to work takes away some of the uncertainty and responsibility, and limits the potential for wasted time and resources.

The principles outlined here are rarely new, and have been described in different ways by the great twentieth-century garden designers Geoffrey Jellicoe, Sylvia Crowe, Thomas Mawson, John Brookes and others. Much of their writing is based on common sense and over time has become embedded in the work of most good garden designers and landscape architects.

My aim in writing this book has been to combine the inspirational and the practical in the way that Gertrude Jekyll and Lawrence Weaver did in *Gardens for Small Country Houses* in 1912. They used a series of case studies to illustrate the range of challenges, plans, design details and planting ideas and from these developed a framework which could be used to tackle most of the problems owners might encounter. The principles of garden design are universal and may be applied to gardens throughout the world, as the examples that follow illustrate.

During years spent in private and public practice as a landscape architect, I became disenchanted with the low level of attention to detail, as well as with the subsequent poor maintenance of landscape schemes. I found myself turning to garden design because owners of private gardens cared for their landscapes, and this allowed me to be more innovative with materials and planting styles. I discovered a natural affinity for working with larger gardens and estates, but found that not all large gardens were attached to large mansions in the country: the challenges of designing larger spaces were being encountered by a wide variety of clients, from owners of more traditional homes in towns to owners of modern bungalows in the countryside.

My book is not intended to provide a toolkit for design, but to show what makes a garden work. I hope that the tips and pointers I provide will help owners and designers improve the design of existing and proposed gardens.

Chapter 1

Finding a Garden's Character

When discussing the character of a garden with a colleague, Frederick Law Olmsted—the founder of American landscape architecture—is reported to have said: "I would not attempt to change the very pleasing natural character—I would take this present character and work it up." While some gardens have more 'natural character' than others, most will have elements that give them a certain individuality.

The house dictates

So what is it that defines the character of a garden? A garden is generally the area that surrounds a house, and in most situations it is the house that dominates and imposes its style on the surrounding space. Therefore, the first decision to take is usually whether it is desirable for the character of the house to be allowed to dictate the character of the garden. If the house is attractive, with distinctive features, it will probably be a good idea to use this to advantage in planning the style of the garden. Otherwise, gardens can be used to enhance less than attractive buildings, rectifying the work of mediocre architects by integrating the space with the surrounding landscape, maximizing the best features of a house, and screening off the worst. Ideally the garden should be much more than a dressing for a house.

Above This garden blends effortlessly into the countryside.

Opposite English red brick and flint is complemented by delicate planting.

One of the main reasons for people choosing to redesign their gardens is to make the house blend more effectively with its surroundings. The way in which a house is integrated into its setting can certainly 'make the building'. Without gardens and planting, the vast majority of homes would look like objects dropped from outer space. Carefully planned planting has the potential to frame an entrance, break up large areas of façade or even screen off neighbouring houses. The way in which the approach to a house is initially designed and laid out can instantly alter the perception of the building.

When trying to isolate the defining characteristics of a garden, owners often express the feeling that they need another pair of eyes to see it anew. Often we are too blinkered by history and daily exposure to our gardens, to get a truly objective view of them. Good design can bring out the character of a garden that lacks any discernible features or style. It is almost impossible to describe or quantify what makes the personality of a garden, but it is usually obvious when

Below A garden's shape is determined by placement of the house.

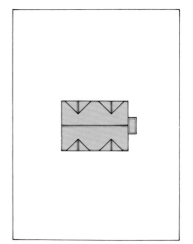 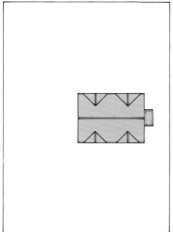 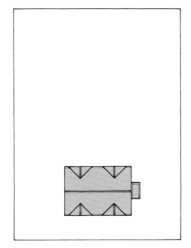

a) House sited centrally within the plot so that the garden does not appear too daunting.

b) House sited to the right-hand side of the plot, drawing attention to the large garden at the side of the property.

c) House sited to the front of the plot, creating a large garden space to the rear of the property.

A Spanish-style tropical garden in Florida where lush, bold planting anchors the house into its surroundings.

Elements of detail and enrichment, like this stainless steel gate, are used to best effect in the most frequently visited areas of the garden.

a garden lacks this character. Age often brings some character, whether or not it is character that the owner appreciates or wants to retain. What one owner will see merely as overgrown bushes, another will see as statuesque trunks to which lighting can be added to create a wonderful natural sculpture. Nature and time can re-define any garden space if they are allowed, but it might take a fresh pair of eyes to decide which features add to the existing character of a garden, and which obscure it.

Formality versus informality

When considering a garden's essential character, there will usually be some discussion of formality versus informality. Formality, in a contemporary context, does not necessarily imply straight lines of trees leading from a house, but it might imply a well-defined, year-round structure.

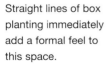

Straight lines of box planting immediately add a formal feel to this space.

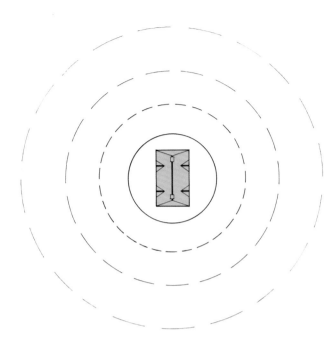

A simple demonstration of zones of input. In general terms, the closer an area is to the house, the greater the level of detail needed in the design.

One of the great benefits of a larger garden is that the owner does not necessarily have to choose between the formal and the informal, as there is likely to be room for both, and it is a shame not to experiment when the opportunity is available. My own experience has shown that if formality is to be part of a garden layout, it works best as a core framework within which informality can be introduced and contained. When designing a larger garden, a truly informal overall style is very difficult to achieve. If the garden has a large house at its heart, the straight lines of the house will often inevitably be reflected in the garden. There are not many houses that are themselves informal in design and style, probably because bricks are by nature straight, and engineering and ease of construction lead to straight lines.

Throughout the history of garden design, the more formal areas have almost always been placed close to the house. This can be seen in the gardens of the seventeenth century in Italy, the eighteenth century in France and the nineteenth century in England, and the same principle holds true today. It is natural to want the design features into which we have poured resources in terms of time and money to be placed where we are going to see them most, usually either near the house or in those areas that can be easily seen from its principal rooms. Also, it makes sense to reflect the straight lines of the house in its immediate surroundings but then to allow this formality to diminish as the distance from the building increases. If the house is in the countryside, this should also help to ensure that the garden provides a natural transition from house to wider landscape.

Care needs to be taken to ensure that distinctive styles (like the detail from an oriental-style garden shown here) are effectively placed within their surroundings.

The transition from structured to informal areas should be smooth, with no obvious junctions or tailing off of style. This natural progression from house to outlying countryside is a feature of some of the best gardens. It is this connection that truly anchors a garden into its surroundings and brings with it a 'sense of place', and while a garden should not always 'fall in line' with the underlying characteristics of the surrounding landscape, where it is possible to achieve this, it can be very effective.

Areas of contrast also have a place in the design of larger gardens, but are usually best reserved for smaller parts of the garden or individual elements within it. Then the trick becomes one of unity and balance. Balance is often achieved by mirroring, but asymmetrical balance, where two different objects sit together in harmony, can add a special mastery to a space.

Design styles within a garden can be as varied as the owner wants them to be. However, an effective overall design will depend on whether these elements suit the particular location, the house, and the needs of those who live there.

The use of oriental gardens is a case in point. Japanese and Chinese gardens can look magical in the right setting, but may look incongruous at the rear of a 1960s home. However, with careful attention to how they will be viewed, and possibly by separating them from the surrounding garden, they can be made to work. Similar careful attention has to be given to other non-native planting such as eucalyptus trees. However appealing a particular growth habit or colour of foliage, the choice of trees should be based on how well the plant will integrate with the natural colours and vegetation present in a garden.

Left Steps lead the eye and welcome the visitor to the house at Carmunnock Garden, Glasgow, Scotland.

Right A side view of a deck that functions as a ha-ha and a pleasantly elevated seating area.

Using levels

For many homeowners there is a desire to level any garden site at the initial design stage. It is obviously crucial that there are some flat areas within a garden to accommodate activities that are carried out on a patio or lawn; however, some of the most interesting gardens work with existing levels that bring with them a variety of experiences for the user, and help to visually define specific areas.

Working with the existing levels in a garden also often provides a direct link with the topography of the surrounding landscape, and the usual benefits of being 'true to a site'. Just as alien species in a garden can jar with surrounding native plants, fighting with the natural levels and aspect of a site can create similar problems. Historically, some of the largest gardens simply controlled the entire landscape to fit in with the garden adjacent to the house, but this was when labour and materials were relatively inexpensive, and would rarely be possible today. The decision to merge with or draw inspiration from the wider landscape will depend on the particular location and be driven by personal taste. It is usually difficult to fight a site's natural characteristics and make a garden blend in. In order to achieve a visual link with the surrounding landscape, the garden must echo the form of the landscape and its colours, or include some of the natural flora. If this visual link is not desired, and the owner wishes to create a style that purposely contrasts with the immediate surroundings of the garden, the approach will need to be more inward-looking and there should be a conscious effort to distance the garden from the landscape beyond.

Techniques for finding a style

When starting from scratch with a garden, it is the house and garden boundaries, combined with any views, that will dictate its character. The style of these may not even be very appealing, but the owner or designer must attempt to single out the best elements of what is there. Few gardens will be able to disguise their surroundings completely, and even if they can, this is hardly likely to achieve a unified space. The key to finding, defining or refining character is to bring the house, garden and landscape into one. Some of the most difficult gardens to design are those where the space has a complete lack of notable features and therefore represents a blank canvas. It is usually easier for a garden owner to work with or react against existing site features, especially when they have little experience of design, or have never really thought about what their ideal garden would look like. The same is true for a garden designer with an open brief from a client, and in this situation it is better for the designer to prepare initial 'loose' designs for the client to react to.

Older properties will inevitably have at least a hint of character or existing style, which is helpful as long as the owner feels comfortable with it. Sometimes this will provide an opportunity to focus on particular elements of the house or features within the garden such as brickwork or an old gnarled tree, using them

Planting in the foreground with grass in the middle distance enhances the house's air of grace and prominence.

Modern house and garden in Glencoe, Illinois (USA) where the clean lines of the house are mirrored in the simple planting and muted colours.

as a starting point for the new garden design. The inspiration might be related to colour, shape or even texture.

If an owner has lived with a garden for a long time, it can be difficult to view it objectively, and at this point the opinions of another party may help. The third party could be a designer or family member, friend or neighbour. These people could be asked what they think are the strongest features of the space. This is not simply an opportunity for them to list features they like within the garden but also to respond to the colours that define the space and perhaps to think about general questions such as whether the garden has a feel of being inward- or outward-looking; whether it relates to the house; whether it sits comfortably with neighbouring properties, and whether it has any natural features.

The colour of tiles on the house roof, or indeed any dominant element that can be seen from the garden space, can act as a trigger for the eventual design. Similarly, the shape of any existing feature can be replicated, enlarged or combined with another and used as a unifying force. The visible materials that are used in the construction of the house should be used as keys to the garden's design; either exact materials can be replicated, or their colours or textures reflected in the new design. When it comes to the objects within gardens, less is usually more. However, it should be remembered that gardens are there to be enjoyed and should mean something to their owners. No one has the definitive word on style, and a garden full of gnomes loved by their owners makes more sense than a neglected garden.

'Before' and 'after' shots of a garden that was created to maximize the surrounding views. The panoramic outlook was quickly identified as an inspiration for the design.

The bold curve of this border leads the eye on into the distant landscape which in turn provides inspiration for the colour and shape of plants used in the garden.

Below The purple colours from the roof tiles of this house were used as a starting point for the selection of plants.

Larger gardens provide the opportunity to introduce idiosyncratic elements in a gradual way, as there is space to separate and define areas, and not everything has to be seen at once. Landscape alterations or adaptations such as banks or terraces should be linked back to the house or the areas immediately surrounding the house. Man-made objects should be visually linked to the house to ensure that they are viewed as part of the overall design and do not seem incongruous.

Setting glass balls into a deck is a relatively inexpensive and low-maintenance way to catch the light and break up an expanse of decking.

The planting used to flank this path echoes the colours of the woodland to create instant unity. Simple square paving slabs, turned to become diamonds, contrast with the planting and lead the eye to the woodland beyond.

By siting a piece of sculpture within an otherwise 'wild' garden area, the space appears deliberately designed.

Whose style is it anyway?

Beauty is most definitely in the eye of the beholder, but there are boundaries and thresholds of taste that can easily be crossed, and the 'third party' can help advise on whether this might be happening. On the other hand, if the third party is a designer, the client needs to be wary of the designer's ego. Having a design totally imposed on a private garden rarely works; instead the design process should see a merging of the designer's style with the client's, and that of the existing house and garden. The process of merging these variables is seldom straightforward, so it is important for the client to remember to enjoy the journey. Irrespective of size, the idea of designing a garden can seem like a daunting task, and the related fears can be compounded as the size of the garden increases.

Some people want very little to do with their garden other than to have a pleasant space in which to relax. Some even see it as nothing more than part of the baggage that arrives with the purchase of a house. These are probably the people who can benefit most from employing a designer.

Whether owners are designing their gardens themselves, or employing a designer to do so, how do they achieve a garden that reflects their taste and style? The starting point for owners wanting to design their own gardens will be some research into existing garden designs and design styles. For those planning to use the services of a garden designer the priority will be selecting a designer with whom they can work congenially.

Choosing a designer

The internet can be an easy introduction to the world of designers, as many have websites which demonstrate their style and previous projects. If a designer has a portfolio of projects similar in size or feel to the prospective client's garden, there is already some synergy.

The client should also study as many similar gardens as possible, looking out for recurring elements to be discussed with the designer. Flower shows provide a showcase for different designers and their styles, and offer an ideal way to see the latest trends in design. However, specific designers' gardens can provide only snapshots of their styles: show gardens are just that, and so will feature elements to catch the eye or unusual materials, and can be more controversial than the designers' usual work. The important thing for the garden owner is to speak to prospective designers to get a feel for whether they would trust them and enjoy working with them. A potential designer should be encouraged to visit the garden, as design is a two-way process, and it is necessary for the designer to appreciate the garden they are to work with, not merely to see the task as another commercial project.

Once a designer is appointed, what next? It is the designer's task to take into account the individual's tastes, which should be readily apparent from objects, colours and furnishings in their home and possibly their existing garden. Designers often show clients selections of images arranged on 'mood boards' to ensure that they have captured the essence of the garden envisaged by the client. The images selected do not even have to be pictures of gardens; they can be of buildings or even pieces of furniture cut out of magazines or scanned from books. The important thing is to get an idea of how formal/informal or modern/traditional the client's taste is, in order to apply it to the garden. If a client favours images of rounded accessories and furniture, or pieces of Art Nouveau sculpture with feminine curves, this can signal a desire for similar flowing lines within the garden. Garden owners planning to design their own gardens can do this for themselves. Even those employing a designer can perform this task themselves to save time and reduce the cost. This information can be translated into overall style even down to the way in which paths are designed and how planting or spaces merge together. In addition, ideas of colour preference and types of planting can be explored through the images selected. Many clients have no idea about types of plants, and are sometimes searching for the elusive no-maintenance garden. There is, of course, no such thing, but certain steps can be taken to minimize maintenance. The initial research stages can also highlight differences in taste between partners, and employing a designer as intermediary can prove a good solution in this case!

By the time a designer is appointed, there should be a detailed list of the services that are to be provided. Sometimes the list will be a long one and sometimes minimal, depending on what the client needs. The important thing is for the garden owner to be comfortable and clear about the commitment being undertaken.

Practical techniques for visualization

It can be very useful to take photographs of a garden from the main views or entrance points—typically the garden gate, front and rear doors, windows and seating areas. The views from upstairs rooms and the kitchen window are always important too.

Tracing paper can then be taped over the photograph and the main shapes or features of the garden drawn in. An alternative to tracing over the main elements is to cut out the part of the garden that you want to keep, or the elements that have to be retained. Paste these onto a clean sheet of paper and pencil in alterations so that you can build up an impression of what could be done. Cut out shapes of plants, trees, shrubs (round blobs) or hedges (rectangles) and play about with them, trying to create an impression of what can be achieved.

It can sometimes be difficult to visualize proposed changes to a property using a conventional garden plan. Here are two alternative techniques to help you work out if a proposed treatment will work.

Photograph with overlay
In this simple technique, a digital photograph is taken of the feature under consideration, like the entranceway above, and proposed changes sketched onto an overlay (below). The success of the proposed change can then be judged and alternatives drawn on further overlays if necessary.

Photographic print and drawing
In this example, a different photographic technique was employed. First, a digital photograph was taken to show how poorly the hard paved area merges into its surroundings.

Next, the photograph was printed off and elements that needed to be changed were cut away. What remained of the photograph was then stuck down onto a clean sheet of paper and simple shapes were drawn in to represent steps, shrubs and groundcover. If necessary, multiple copies of the photograph can be made and they can be cut and drawn over until an acceptable solution is found.

Finally, using the marked photograph as a reference, a detailed drawing was made of the area with its proposed final planting scheme. The planting effectively screens the low wall and the patio seems to end less abruptly. The change of direction in the steps makes a more inviting entrance to the garden and allows people to experience a change of view.

Case study

Carmunnock Garden

The owners requested advice because they felt that their garden did not quite 'gel'. At just over three acres in size, it was a mature, well-established garden that in their opinion just didn't look as good as it should. The clients were wary of bringing in a designer because they didn't want or need wholesale change and didn't want it to end up costing them a fortune.

When dealing with attractive or imposing houses, it is important to keep the garden adjacent to them simple so their style and grandeur can be appreciated.

The garden was a classic example of one that simply needed 'polishing': there were several glaring problems that visually detracted from the garden's obvious character. Sections of fence at the front of the property had, over time, become damaged and uneven, and as a result gave an unkempt and poor impression. The existing paved patio area was clearly too small, with a table and eight chairs squeezed onto it; it was virtually impossible to walk around the table to fill guests' glasses. The patio was also visually out of proportion with the property, or at least the part of the house viewed in relation to it.

Other areas requiring work included a path adjacent to the house, which was effectively the main approach to the garden. It had a loose gravel surface with undefined edges, nearby planting was uncoordinated, and it generally looked

A highlight of Carmunnock Garden is the expansive lawn set with beautiful mature trees.

Painting the oil tank and washing line post allowed them to sink into the background vegetation.

ignored. This wrongly coloured the initial impression of the garden whose most characterful elements were some wonderful mature trees and a beautiful wide lawn.

Many of the problem elements within the garden were easily remedied. Solutions included painting the oil storage tank and clothes pole a different colour to allow them to blend in to the garden instead of fighting against it. Restoring the fence, formalizing the path and renewing plantings all improved the garden's appearance, and plans have been made to expand the patio area as well. A row of mature yew trees bisected the garden, and in their way were a wonderful feature, evoking formality and maturity. However there were so many of them that they darkened and divided the garden. Removing just one of these hundred-and-fifty-year-old giants instantly introduced light, and created an enticing means of access to another section of the garden. This is a good example of why owners should never feel obliged to retain all the planting in an existing garden just because of its maturity. At the same time it is obviously important to be sensitive

'Before and after' shots, showing how formalization of the path, renewed planting and restoration of the fence immediately improved the perception of the garden to incoming visitors.

to the value of particular plants or trees, and to be aware of any planning or local regulations which forbid their removal without prior consent. Just as regulations governing some new housing developments restrict the types of planting which can be used, there are also regulations prohibiting the removal of some plants or trees. In this case, the careful planting of specimen trees, and their use as focal points to be viewed from specific rooms of the house, proved an easy and inexpensive remedy.

Practical Recommendations

- Take photographs of the garden and study them objectively. Ask people you can trust what they think, and tell them to be frank.
- Cut out or copy images of gardens that you like prior to designing your own garden or meeting a designer, to ensure that you get a design that will meet your expectations.
- Make use of the internet, not just to select a designer, but to look at garden designers' websites generally. It gives you the chance to look at their portfolios, steal their ideas and find a style that suits your property.
- Solutions to problems within a garden do not need to be expensive, they just need an objective assessment and to be viewed within the garden's overall context.
- Consider the colour of man-made objects within a garden and ensure that they are in keeping with the garden.
- No matter how well-kept a garden is in general, make certain that there are no very noticeable elements, such as walls or gates, that require renewal or upgrading—first impressions do count!

Chapter 2

Integrating Garden and Landscape

Poignant images may evoke strong emotional responses and stir up memories of other landscapes experienced in the past.

Attempting to integrate a garden into its surroundings involves making a judgement on the character of the landscape. This is always a challenge, as the character of an area is as individual as the lines of a fingerprint. Any discussion on landscape has the potential to bring out our deepest prejudices, loves and hates—all usually coloured by our memories, particularly of the surroundings of our childhoods.

For a more objective view, there are several centuries of designers, architects and landscape gardeners from whom we can learn when endeavouring to anchor a garden into its surroundings. They have left buildings, gardens and estates that can be visited and studied for clues to what makes them successful. Designers of the past who are famous for having successfully integrated gardens into the English landscape are Lancelot 'Capability' Brown (1715–1783), Humphry Repton (1752–1818) and Thomas Mawson (1861–1933). They of course had predecessors all around the globe who were successful in the same field. Many of these well-known designers practised at a time when labour was extremely cheap, and great swathes of countryside could be moved and adapted to ensure a landscape 'fit' for any new works. It must be pointed out that they were also often working on very large areas. This grand scale of alteration and earthmoving is no longer possible for the vast majority of garden owners, and designers today usually need to

Left A classic Repton landscape in Sussex, England.

Below left This 18th-century English landscape garden at Bleinhem Palace, Oxfordshire, England, was designed by Lancelot 'Capability' Brown. It was designed at a time when manpower allowed large-scale manipulation of the landscape.

search for a more sustainable approach, working with the landscape as it exists. However, much can be learned from the general principles of these great designers of the past.

Stands of trees, avenues and vistas within a formal garden at Bramham Park, Yorkshire, England illustrate how vast plantations were used to stamp man's dominance over the landscape.

What gives a landscape its character?

Numerous influences have combined to create the landscapes that we live in. Natural landform provides an underlying framework, sculpted by glaciers, volcanoes, oceans, rivers and streams. This has then been de-forested, cultivated, or built upon by human beings over the centuries, to leave a myriad of landscape types. The nature of the soil, the brightness of the sun and the type of vegetation are among the factors that then overlay these landscape forms to further differentiate one area from another.

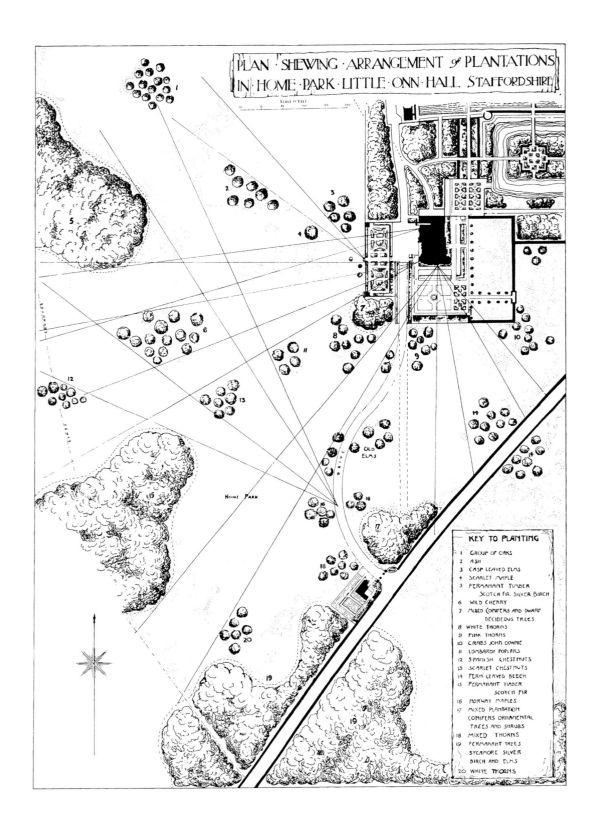

PLAN · SHEWING · ARRANGEMENT of PLANTATIONS
IN · HOME · PARK · LITTLE · ONN · HALL · STAFFORDSHIRE

SCALE OF FEET

HOME PARK

OLD ELMS

KEY TO PLANTING

1 GROUP OF OAKS
2 ASH
3 CASP LEAVED ELMS
4 SCARLET MAPLE
5 PERMANANT TIMBER
   SCOTCH FIR, SILVER BIRCH
6 WILD CHERRY
7 MIXED CONIFERS AND DWARF
   DECIDEOUS TREES
8 WHITE THORNS
9 PINK THORNS
10 CRABS JOHN DOWNIE
11 LOMBARDY POPLARS
12 SPANISH CHESTNUTS
13 SCARLET CHESTNUTS
14 FERN LEAVED BEECH
15 PERMANANT TIMBER
   SCOTCH FIR
16 NORWAY MAPLES
17 MIXED PLANTATION
   CONIFERS ORNAMENTAL
   TREES AND SHRUBS
18 MIXED THORNS
19 PERMANANT TREES
   SYCAMORE SILVER
   BIRCH AND ELMS
20 WHITE THORNS

Left This copy of a plan Thomas Mawson drew in the 1890s details the layout of a landscape in relation to a house. He has created a landscape structure by planting in the areas that are outside the main views from the house, and used trees as focal points at the end of certain views.

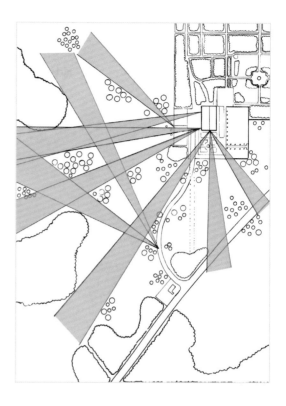

Case study

Home Park, Little Onn Hall, Staffordshire

This Mawson plan for Home Park in Staffordshire illustrates how trees have been planted to frame and block views from the house and its approaches. Designed in the 1890s, it demonstrates how to divide up a substantial area of parkland while clearly associating it with the house. This ground will have been used as grazing for animals, but the key to its success lies in the placement of trees, ensuring that it is perceived as an integral part of the house setting and essentially an extension of the formal garden. Several key locations have been identified: one on the approach to the house; three from the main rooms; and one from steps at the outer edge of the formal gardens adjacent to the house. From these points, intersecting lines radiate out, key views are left open to the boundary of the property, and in simplistic terms the other areas are planted with trees. The simple block plan shows these cones of vision. This illustrates the central part of a view where the eye would see most detail, with peripheral views on either side of it.

A contemporary reworking of the plan shows the 'cones of vision' used by Mawson to form his landscape framework and create an overall structure.

Obviously, not all areas are planted, but the majority of them have some planting. This ranges from solid blocks of trees to a small group, or individual specimens planted within the area. The solid blocks terminate the vistas, while small groups give partial screening, and specimens act as focal points themselves within the landscape. The species chosen have been carefully selected, with smaller, more ornamental trees (such as pink hawthorns) closer to the house and driveway; statuesque parkland trees (such as chestnuts) for the intermediate areas viewed as specimens or groups; and mixed plantations (including Scotch firs and silver birch) as the endpoints to views.

The garden plan shows how these principles can be utilized at any scale. The most important factor to take into account is the direction of the main views from the house, including approaches if the property is set within grounds.

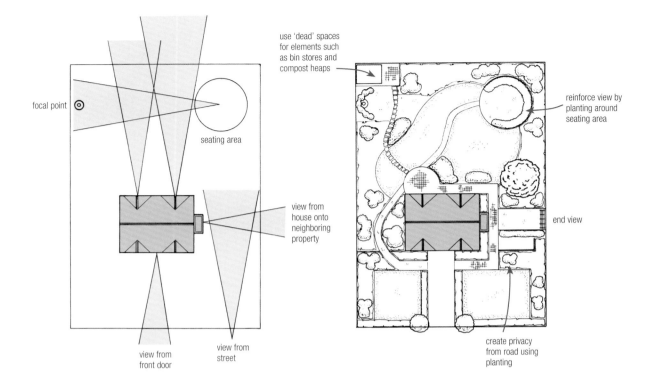

use 'dead' spaces for elements such as bin stores and compost heaps

focal point

seating area

view from house onto neighboring property

reinforce view by planting around seating area

end view

view from front door

view from street

create privacy from road using planting

These two garden plans use the 'Mawson Principle' with cones of vision from the main rooms of the house to identify the m ain views and less visible areas which can be used as secluded areas. Once the location of the seating area has been decided, a cone of vision can be used to define the best view from that too, and consequently where to create a focal point.

The sketch above shows how a rough plan of cones of vision can be evolved into a more detailed plan for a garden.

The cones of vision also indicate the areas where views are best kept open, and not planted. In these cases planting can be placed just outside the cone to further reinforce the view.

Use of plans and cones of vision

This method of creating a garden structure by using cones of vision can be applied at all scales. It is a very useful way of 'carving up' a large garden—a 'toolkit' approach to creating a unified plan which works with the house. If the views from the house have been used to help create the garden structure then the house will be anchored into an overall framework. This will work irrespective of the style of the house, providing a plan that integrates the two. Although many people find plans difficult to understand initially, it is usually true that if something works on a plan then it will work in reality. Once the house and boundaries have been drawn onto a piece of paper, it simply remains to work out where the main views from the house will be. Any trees or groups of trees outside the boundary that can be used to link the garden with other gardens or the wider landscape should be included. In addition, attractive features beyond the garden boundaries can be framed and transformed into features that seem to be part of the garden itself. It is best not to frame views that include the windows of neighbouring houses, as being overlooked is not usually desirable.

Open views to a distant church spire are seen from a seating area close to a house.

Borrowing the landscape

Whenever a garden has views to distant features within the landscape, these become obvious elements that can be framed and treated as if focusing on a piece of sculpture. This does not need to be a distant rocky outcrop or plantation of deciduous trees; it can be a church spire or row of houses.

It is slightly unfortunate, although highly understandable, that many gardens merely try to capture picture postcard landscape images; we have been conditioned into believing that they are the only landscape images worthy of bringing into our gardens. Though the remnants of the Picturesque movement still haunt us today there are, of course, a multitude of landscape types and views that can be embraced. Any attractive views from a garden should be celebrated. From cityscapes to desert, a view of the surroundings brings a sense of place, and wherever we can harness the wider landscape we should. Of course some views are downright ugly and no one would want to see them brought into their gardens, but some interest can be found in most. Even some of the worst views can be rendered interesting, and even attractive, with the correct treatment. Framing can enhance views tenfold, and with careful selection of the type of framing,

Tiers of decking diminish into the distance, leading the eye on to the wider landscape.

the unattractive parts of any view can be screened out. Large gardens are quite often blessed by views simply because of their scale and aspect and longer views within the garden are also possible. The upper rooms of a house often command views of the land of neighbouring properties and beyond and the house and garden can be designed to maximize them. These views should not be forgotten when concentrating on views that can be seen from the garden itself.

Framing with plants

Simple groupings of plants can be effectively used to frame a view in various ways: they can be grown into certain shapes to form a frame, or placed in the foreground of a scene where the natural characteristics of the plant create a frame.

The three main types of plant that can be used for framing are weeping trees; trees that grow in columnar shapes; and clear-stemmed trees. Detailed suggestions for plant choice in these categories are given in Chapter 6.

Choose trees that will grow quite large rather than the many smaller weeping trees and shrubs whose branches touch the ground. These are better used as specimens within borders of mixed plantings. The word to look out for is '*pendula*', like the English 'pendulous', meaning hanging loosely. Top-worked trees should be avoided at all costs. These are trees that have straight stems and have had a weeping tree grafted onto the trunk—rather like mutants of the plant world, they are the result of too much human intervention.

These dark, columnar trees act as a foil to the pale pink shrub, which is framed by the trees' placement on either side.

The clear stems of the trees reinforce the focal point of this garden by framing it on either side.

Viewed from the approach path to the Rijkstaad Gallery in Amsterdam, the Netherlands, the clear stems of *Fagus sylvatica* frame the view into the gallery beyond.

Columnar plants (with the suffix *fastigiata* or *columnaris*) make excellent avenues, and can also be placed on either side of an intended focal point to draw attention to it. Moreover, clear-stemmed plants can be used either as mini-avenue trees within the garden, to reinforce the directional flow of a path, or to increase the effect of a focal point.

When trying to anchor a house into a landscape it can be helpful to reflect elements of the wider landscape in the part of the garden nearest to the house, providing an obvious link between building and landscape. This might mean using some of the same types of plant, or reflecting shapes, outlines, or colours evident in the wider landscape.

The plan shows a house sited within a relatively large garden. Triangular cones of vision have been drawn showing the main views to and from the house. This will be used to determine what should be screened or framed.

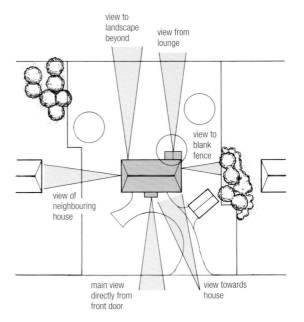

The plan developed into an overall garden layout with planting used to frame views, create privacy from neighbours, and act as a background to new focal points.

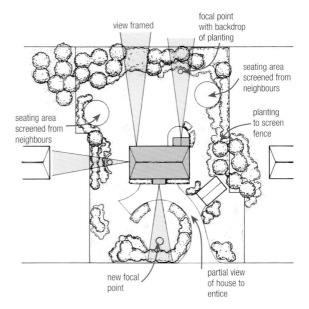

Orientation and aspect

For most property owners there is little or no prospect of buying enough land to be able to choose which orientation a house should take. However, an understanding of aspects is helpful, and, when buying a new property, it is useful to take a compass along to the viewing. It is also worth asking vendors who have lived in the house which areas receive sun and which shade, because they will be familiar with how light falls into the garden throughout the day, and how it is affected by heights of neighbouring fences, trees or buildings.

It is widely believed that none of the faces of a house should be completely visible except from higher ground. Partial obscuring of the face of a house can be achieved by placing plantings close to the viewpoints. Without illusion and surprise, over-familiarity and boredom follow. People living closely with a garden for a long period usually find that a little unpredictability adds spice to the relationship.

A formal approach to a house illustrates how shade opening out to sun intensifies the appeal of the property in upstate New York.

Shelter

Shelter within a garden is crucial, and follows logically from consideration of a garden's aspects. Where plantations of trees or even hills are to the north of a property, there will be an immediate and natural barrier against harsh winds, which can be very inhibiting in terms of plantings and garden usage. It should be remembered that plantings take time to establish and some may not have a noticeable impact for several years.

This imposing property in upstate New York illustrates the importance of a house's aspect and orientation, as the rear of the house catches the full glow of the setting sun.

Where ground slopes gently away from a house, especially to the south, it will provide an ideal opportunity to enjoy the best of any sunshine. Elevated properties have an immediate air of prominence and stability arising from their dominance over the surrounding roads and landscape. By contrast, a downhill approach to the front of a house is less than ideal. In some regions, the demand for new homes has meant that developers have tried to squeeze houses onto land that historically would have been left barren. This does not mean that prospective owners should not consider properties at the base of a slope, but that perhaps they should look for a house where the road approaches from the lower side. Where this is not possible, great attention should be paid to the views when approaching. With careful concealment of the house, and by leading to an arrival space at the same level as the house, the building can feel well situated, though a rising approach will almost certainly allow more attractive views of the garden, grounds or wider landscape.

If you have the luxury of being able to decide where a house is placed within a site, then it should maximize the potential of each aspect, with more ground to the southern and western sides. Generally, the house should also be sited about one third of the way into a site. This does not only apply to houses on great estates, but to any house in relation to the areas of managed garden surrounding it. If a house is too close to the entrance of a site it can seem mean and urban, while if it is set back from the entrance it will have an air of dignity. It is important to get the balance right, as too much land to the front of a property usually reduces the amount of private space to the rear.

A paved granite circle to the front of this house in upstate New York allows access and reduces the scale of the area in a way that a continuous surface would not.

Arrival space

Where homeowners are fortunate enough to have the option of planning the main approach to their home, this can be very beneficial, as the way people are brought to a house can have a huge impact upon their perception of the property. This includes both the direction of the approach road, and the way in which a path leads to the front door of the property from the approach road. If the main entrance to the house is not initially fully visible this will add intrigue. Where this is the case however, it is important that the main route to the house is obvious. It may seem unrealistic to alter existing access roads or approaches to a house, but if they have not been constructed to ensure maximum user-friendliness, the change can have a very positive impact. Many layouts carried out by house builders have been decided merely on cost and do not take into account what will ultimately leave the homeowner with the best usable space. Obviously, when buying a newly built property, there may be a possibility of influencing the layout of the grounds.

Ensure that
secondary routes
around properties
are markedly
narrower than the
main routes into
the house.

Left Contrast in path
widths indicates the main
route to follow.

Above The widest paths
of brick indicate the
main routes, while lighter
gravel paths indicate the
secondary routes.

Right This approach
road has been re-aligned
away from the front door
of the property, allowing
a drop-off point and
area for vehicles to park
beyond.

In a property where there might be a problem with distinguishing the main approach to the house from other routes, a hierarchy of paths can be created by varying the path widths or types of surfacing. The widest path should naturally lead to the main entrance of the property and the highest quality of surface. For instance, real stone might be used for the main paths, in which case narrower paths surfaced in block paving or gravel will be obviously secondary. There may be paths leading from the car parking area, or to the side of the property, or paths used to allow bins to be brought to the front kerb for collection.

At some properties, the main entrance to the house might not be at the 'front'. Subject to the layout of the house in relation to the sun, it may be more sensible in terms of best usable outdoor spaces to have primary access on a particular side of the house. Where homes have an existing approach road which splits on the way to the house, it is vital that paths are designed in the ways described above to make it obvious which route to take, particularly where one path leads to the front of the house and one to the back.

This property is approached from the side and had roads of a similar width going to the front and rear of the pro perty which originally caused confusion for visitors. This was overcome by narrowing one road to a pathway, thereby creating an obvious main approach road, and using planting to emphasize the front door.

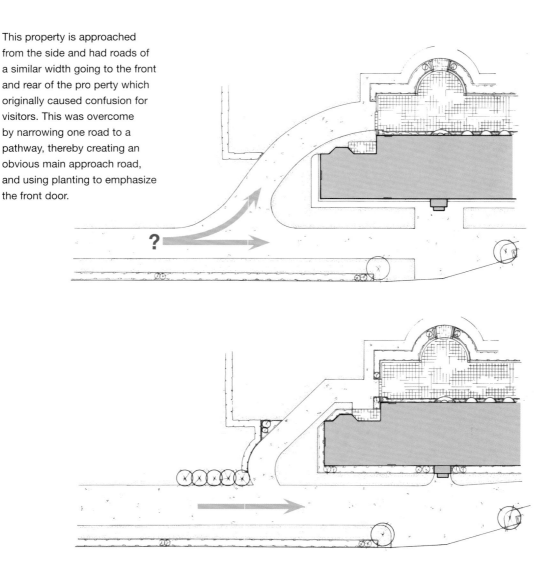

The direction of approach to the main entrance of the property can vary. It can be either a straight-on approach from the roadway; a diagonal approach; a path that curves or flows in more indirectly from the front; or a variation on one of these.

If there is scope to bring an approach from the side, or a more unusual angle, a really interesting result can be achieved. There are only two reasons for designing a path leading directly to the front door of a house: the first is when the house is very symmetrical, and a balanced formal entrance is the most visually suitable; the second is when the most natural route is straight, and users would therefore cut over an alternative path layout and ignore any design attempt to alter the approach.

A longer approach will give more flexibility for varying the route and for concealing part of the house at points along it. A curve is usually preferable to a

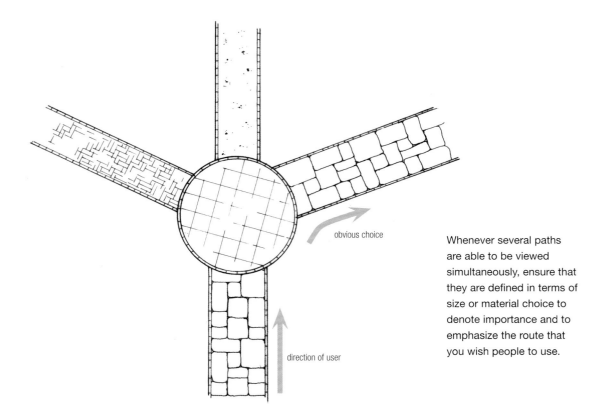

obvious choice

direction of user

Whenever several paths are able to be viewed simultaneously, ensure that they are defined in terms of size or material choice to denote importance and to emphasize the route that you wish people to use.

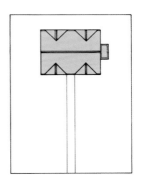 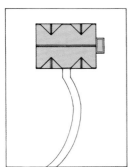 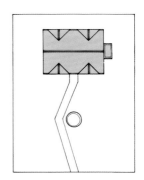 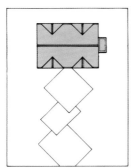

Above Four alternative layouts of paths to the front door of a property.

Right The diagram shows the shortcuts that a user might be tempted to take across a sweeping approach. Objects or planting can be used to prevent the user from taking the most direct route.

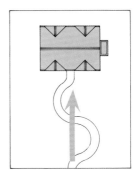 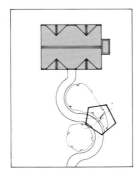

straight path if there is space; it will soften the approach and lead the eye gently towards the house.

Planting can also be used to delineate the main approach to the house. Many houses have little or no planting adjacent to them, with gravel or paving skirting their bases. As a result they appear stark, and almost as if they have been dumped in the space. It is not necessary to have masses of planting around the house, but a simple strip of grass can give the house a barrier against the harshness of monotone gravel and help to soften the angles where the house ends and the ground begins. In the same way, at the base of a tree, the trunk widens to form a buttress from which the roots spread out, visually melding the base with the ground.

As the famous Californian landscape architect Thomas Church (1902–1978), once said, "If it is not obvious where to park; if there is no room to park when you get there; if you stumble into the back door looking for the front entrance, or if the entrance is badly lighted, you have subjected your guests to annoyances that will linger long in their subconscious."

Planting and colour

Gardens that are set within the countryside will require a different treatment from those in the heart of a city. In both cases they should fit within their overall setting, and this means that the garden's dominant colours should blend with, or at least complement, its surroundings. This is especially important when

The bright colours of planting within this garden provide much-needed interest against a dull urban backdrop.

using trees and shrubs that are predominantly golden, purple or bluish green, as these are the colours most likely to fight with others. Structural plants in these colours can be planted within a contained framework of more appropriate colours that will allow them to blend them into the context of the overall landscape. The blues of eucalyptus trees will blend into the arid backdrop of the Australian landscape, but care needs to be taken when using them as external points in a city garden.

When the setting is at its most uninspiring, any colour will be a welcome addition to the landscape. Within a very colourless town setting, where the dominant shade is the dull grey of concrete, bright hues such as purples, golden yellows and blues will not only complement it, but will also bring a much needed injection of colour. If plants indigenous to the locale are used, there is likely to be a natural fit with the colours of the landscape.

Shelterbelts and woodland

Shelterbelts

Shelterbelts are often situated at the outer edges of a property and make an important contribution to the integration of the garden into the wider landscape. Typically, plants that replicate or at least complement the local flora should be chosen for a smooth transition. The creation of shelterbelts is not for the faint-hearted, and is only possible when there is an abundant supply of ground.

Shelterbelts work as bands of solid planting. A good shelterbelt should not simply become a 'green wall' that the wind bashes against, but a filter that breaks down the force of wind. It is a similar technique to the use of multiple mesh

A typical section through a simple shelterbelt structure has a mixed central band of trees, understorey planting and shrub component to edges.

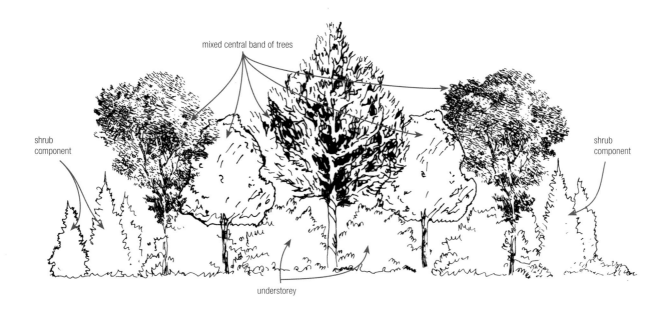

mixed central band of trees

shrub component

shrub component

understorey

This shows a
typical 20 m layout
for a shelterbelt

understorey species

dominant species

co-dominant/nurse
species

This shelterbelt is
edged with *Populus* ×
canescens to ensure its
rapid establishment.

A juvenile woodland matrix
planting has as a nurse species,
Alnus glutinosa, which has the
added benefit of tolerating the
damp ground conditions.

screens—by catching the wind it slows it down and weakens it. The result, in garden terms, is lower levels of wind that in turn means a higher temperature within the garden. Wind can be one of the most devastating forces when it comes to establishing a garden. By reducing the intensity and force of the prevailing wind, plants can be established more easily and those that are borderline in terms of hardiness can also be grown. A shelterbelt may also reduce the requirement for staking those delicate, top-heavy plants.

Essentially, a shelterbelt involves planting a matrix of plants, laid out in a grid pattern made up of a mixture of different species. This mix should include plants that will establish quickly to get some initial protection for the garden and protect other slower growing plants while they become established. The quick-to-establish plants are known as the nurse species, and are normally removed once the desired species have established. The desired or dominant species should be the species that will form the long-term core of the planting. Once the trees of the dominant species are large enough to form a windbreak, all initial plants used to 'nurse' the main plants can be removed. The key to a successful shelterbelt is in the mix of plants that are selected. It is not simply about having a stand of trees but about creating a band of planting which has a mixture of evergreen and deciduous plants. There should also be a range of plants to form a variety of layers. A shrub component will help to create this mixture and can also be also used as edge species. See Chapter 6 for further information about plant selection.

Woodland

Many owners of large gardens also have areas of existing woodland, and for some with a very large amount of space it can be invaluable for adding a different dimension to a garden. It is not necessary to own an estate before embarking upon establishing a woodland, although a large amount of space is obviously needed. There is no quick solution to their establishment and often they are viewed as a legacy for future generations. They are very similar in nature to shelterbelts and can be established in a similar manner. The main difference is that they are broader and have areas where there are open areas of canopy. A shelterbelt is a solid band of trees and shrubs, whereas a wood has open glades that let light through.

The addition of an area of woodland to any garden will undoubtedly bring wildlife into the garden. A mixed evergreen and deciduous planting with fruiting plants will encourage a huge variety of birds into a garden. A successful woodland has a range of spaces each with a different level of light providing a variety of conditions for a wide variety of plants. For some garden owners this can be a great opportunity to experiment with plants. Many bulbs and perennials now commonplace in gardens, originated from a woodland habitat and so will thrive

Bands of ivy have been planted in swathes to add interest to the shaded area beneath the canopy of the trees. Ordinarily bulbs are the best way to create interest, but the groundcover here will have year-round value.

Open areas within a woodland provide an ideal opportunity to grow vast swathes of bulbs for spring interest.

in these conditions. For other owners, the establishment of an area of woodland will minimize the maintenance load. This does not mean that a wood can be planted and abandoned, but with simple periodic tasks it can become a greatly popular and relatively manageable addition to a large garden. Whether used as a playground by children, as an area for informal walks, or as a place to enjoy shaded seating, woods can be wonderful recreational areas. When establishing areas of woodland, the normal course of action is to first establish bands of shelterbelt that will protect the woodland and speed its establishment. Typically this means shelterbelt planting five years prior to the woodland planting. More information on choosing plants for woodland can be found in Chapter 6.

Informal swathes of planting
light up these woodland
scenes in the spring, providing
an early season attraction.

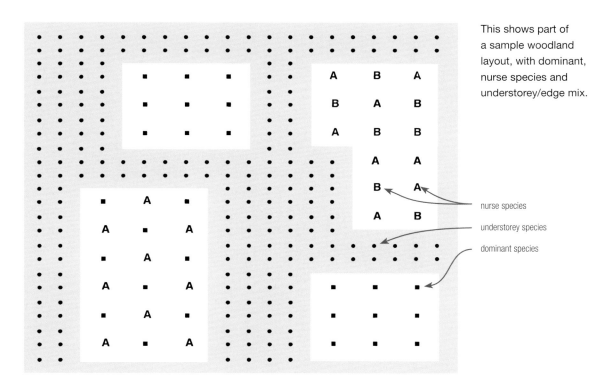

This shows part of
a sample woodland
layout, with dominant,
nurse species and
understorey/edge mix.

nurse species

understorey species

dominant species

Scrub and copse

To soften the edges of the woodland and provide a bridging element between areas of grassland and woodland, plantings known as scrub and copse can be created. These areas create another type of habitat and provide a resilient area suitable for heavy active use. The creation of informal paths, clearings, and the greater wear and tear this entails is better covered by scrubland. The species planted are similar to the edge mix for woodland, with some additions for variety. A 30 per cent canopy cover overall is the ideal, with open field layer developing in areas between. Scrubland and copses (copse is used to describe a plantation of small trees, larger than the scattered scrub tree cover) also create a more diverse visual picture across the garden.

Layout

Where scrubland is adjacent to a woodland or shelterbelt plantation, the understorey mix is simply extended out like fingers on the same grid of 1 m (3 ft.). Where it is on its own, scrubland comprises groups of 20–50 plants in single species stands (forming an overall eventual canopy cover of less than 30 per cent) at 1 m (3 ft.) spacings, or in stands of two to three single-species cells. The actual species chosen can be more decorative than those used in the shelterbelt of woodland, as they form an important link to the main plantings closer to the house.

Case study

Auchendrane House

Auchendrane House sits at the heart of a small estate. The landscape surrounding the house consists mainly of open parkland with mature plantings dating from approximately 120 years ago when the present house was re-modelled and extended. Approaching the house gave me an impression of untapped potential. The gently curving driveway, flanked by mature parkland trees, heightened the sense of anticipation as one progressed up the drive. Glimpses of open field and lawn could be seen under the weighty canopies of these giants, until the house came into sight, with its entranceway flanked by yews. The mature redwood specimens along the drive oozed grandeur but had not been looked after for many decades. As a result, even though they were very impressive, they also looked neglected.

Set within many acres, the house appeared to simply survey the surrounding landscape with no effective link. The solution was not to create great vistas that would extend from the building and tie the landscape into the garden and house, but instead to create roundels of tree planting in the adjacent fields. These round plantings would eventually become circles of mature specimen trees to reflect

An existing wall attached to one end of the house blocks access and flow around the building.

An opening created in a wall allows access around the house.

A visual link between two areas is created using a granite sett circle laid into paving.

The sweep of this drive leads vehicles away from the front door of the house to the car park, and the strip of grass and planting adjacent to the house soften the meeting of wall and gravel.

A wide pathway has been converted into a seating area.

A randomized area of paving set within grass can be used as a seating area without looking too obviously like one.

the planting that exists closer to the house. In this way, the house could be seen to stamp its authority on the landscape without being intrusive.

To the front of the house lay a large gravel area, bounded by low sandstone walls, which had effectively become a car park. There was no acknowledgement of the house, and with cars able to park right next to the front door there was little or no sense or arrival. The chosen solution was to split the large area into two, with a new yew hedge, forcing cars to park away from the main doorway. Areas of grass were also used to define the roadway and give the building space from where it could be viewed, compensating for the lack of a long driveway. This 'green skirt' not only linked the house to the garden but also provided a visual buffer, allowing the eye to focus on the building. An arrival platform was created to reinforce the sense of arrival and enhance the formality of the approach. Although the scheme was very simple, it has transformed the way that the area is viewed and used, proving that a long drive is not the only way to announce the entrance to a house. The focus of the approach in this case has become the building.

The property was originally designed as a hunting lodge and was not intended to be lived in permanently. It was also laid out at a time when sunlight was not deemed to be important in a living space, and as a result the majority of the afternoon sun hits the front of the house as opposed to the more private rear space. To put a patio at the front of the house would have detracted from the overall character, so the alternative solution was to essentially 'splatter' paving through the grass area to the side of the main door to take advantage of the sunny area. The paved space is large enough to accommodate a table and chairs, because it has not been built as one distinct area, it goes relatively unnoticed and does not detract from the house's appearance.

A further problem was that the front and rear areas of garden were divided by tall sandstone walls, and as a result the rear section beyond the walls was rarely used by the owners. To link the areas of garden, a new opening was created through an existing sandstone wall, and a circle of granite setts was laid into the ground to visually connect the two areas.

The rear garden had a very wide gravel path, effectively filling the only area of flat ground that existed. To make the area more usable, a patio was created with dimensions dictated by the overall scale of the building and its connection to the rooms outside. With the path width at either end now reduced, the eye rests upon the patio and stays within the space.

Practical Recommendations

- A garden layout should never be accepted simply because it 'has always been that way'. Ensure it has relevance for the way in which it will be used today.
- Areas within a garden can have dual functionality: at different times of day or periods during the year they can be used for a variety of purposes.
- Using similar plants in the garden and within the wider landscape will ensure a direct link. This is critical from both inside and when the garden is viewed from outside within a wider context.
- Large gardens cannot be created overnight. Many require shelterbelts or planting to screen or shelter the garden to allow the desired plants to survive. These take a few years to develop.
- It is not a good idea to plan a garden in a hurry. Get to know where the sun hits it at different times of the day so that the seating areas are in the right place for the times at which they will be used.
- Make sure that the garden is not viewed all at once. Ensure that there are elements of surprise and concealment within it.
- Take a compass into the garden and locate 'north'. Plants often die because they have been planted in the wrong place.

Chapter 3

Unifying House
and Garden

As described in the first chapter of this book, it is usually necessary to see the house as the main feature of a garden, around which all other elements must be designed. Yet while houses with existing character are an obvious starting point for good design this is not easy in the case of architecturally weak houses. The challenge for the garden owner or designer in these circumstances is to help define the garden and differentiate it from any similar gardens surrounding it. Unity of design is what differentiates a good garden from a great garden. Though it is possible for gardens to contain many disparate elements, these will require a greater degree of planning and execution. It is much easier to make a design work if an overall style is adopted, and the house is an obvious starting point for this.

These bands of brick were chosen to match the materials used for the house and to add interest and detail.

Opposite Planting is set very closely to house; this serves to anchor the house into the garden and minimize the area that requires the most labour to maintain.

Matching materials

Where homes have been built using traditional or local materials, or if they follow a distinct architectural style, there is much more to work with. By selecting the same materials as those in the building, an immediate link can be created which will ensure that the garden weathers and matures with the house. This is not to say that for a red brick home all the garden paths must be constructed using red brick, though for some of the more important paths in close proximity to the

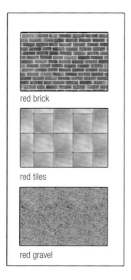

red brick

red tiles

red gravel

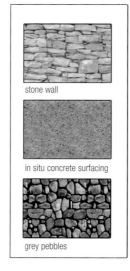

stone wall

in situ concrete surfacing

grey pebbles

cedar shingles

brick pavers

burnt ochre gravel

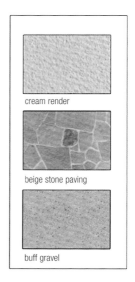

cream render

beige stone paving

buff gravel

Four vertical bands give a very simplified idea of how to co-ordinate hard landscape materials with the main colours of the house. The top row shows wall finishes; the central band shows four main paving types; and the lower band typical gravels.

house it might be a good idea. Small amounts of a similar material can be used to link with the house and then give way to different materials. If it proves difficult to source materials similar to those used in the buildings, or if the cost is prohibitive, the choice of colour becomes critical. Direct colour matching between different materials can be difficult because of the tendency of some to weather differently. It is therefore often better to co-ordinate rather than match, so that if weathering occurs there is not such a jarring of colour. Buff-coloured paving, for example, has a yellow base colour and will therefore work best placed with materials which have a yellow cast or are adjacent to yellow on the colour wheel (that is, containing shades of orange and green). When co-ordinating with red brick, the choice of colours would probably be red or have purple or orange tinges. This is a very simplistic approach, and few materials are true yellow, orange or red. If pre-cast concrete slabs are chosen to co-ordinate with the building, remember that they will alter and fade over time, and may end up quite different from the house. It can therefore be advisable to acquire samples of materials and see how they look together, wet and dry. This might seem demanding, but for most garden owners hard landscaping is a relatively infrequent and expensive activity, and therefore merits some careful attention. Catalogues should not be relied upon because the colours and textures cannot always be fully appreciated from photographs, and even if a designer is involved, it is best to ask for samples and look at them in relation to the house and garden.

The interior style of a home can often be a starting point for the garden design. Particularly for a designer, a house is an important source of information about the owner's taste in terms of desired level of detail, type of line and style as well as colour. Most owners want their gardens to be an extension of their home, and any good design should endeavour to integrate both environments. However, there is also the consideration, discussed at length in Chapter 2, of blending the garden with its wider surroundings, and there is little point in reflecting an interior style that is at odds with the inherent character of the garden or the wider landscape.

Another point of caution for designers when looking for insight in the style of a client's home, is that if interior designers have been involved in the past, it might take more searching to get to the heart of the owner's taste. It should also be remembered that as we tend to alter interiors much more frequently than exteriors, it is best to concentrate on general criteria such as continuing line and levels of simplicity or complexity because these will normally remain as constants even if the interior colours or other features change over time.

Routes around the house and garden

It is important to consider where the house lies within the garden, how the house access points are used, and which routes people use to navigate around the house and garden. The majority of houses have front as well as rear gardens; however this chapter largely deals with how the house relates to the main private space (usually the rear). This is the part of a garden where we want to be able to feel most at ease, and possibly the most important way of achieving this is to make the garden feel *linked* to the house.

How is the garden accessed from the house? It may be through a passageway at the side of the house; from doors leading from the lounge; or via a rear door from the kitchen area. The entrance has an impact as it is the initial link between garden and home. The first question to ask is whether a link is desirable. The answer is usually that it is, because this is often one of the main functions of a garden, but is a seamless transition wanted, or a feeling of entering another

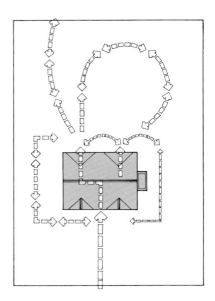

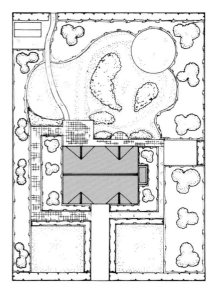

The diagrams show how identifying the potential movement through and around a house and garden (**far left**) can be used to define the hierarchy of paths and spaces within a garden (**left**).

world? There are of course levels in between these two. Inside the house some people have their entire interior decoration one colour, merging one room into another, while others prefer to have every room a contrasting colour. The garden should reflect this preference.

Aspect

Historically, when landowners planned to build a house, and could choose which direction it would face, the entrance was invariably on the northwest side. The kitchen would have been closest to the kitchen garden, with the lounge (drawing room) on the southeast or southwest, and the dining room looking north. Today, few people possess a kitchen garden, and dining rooms are not simply reserved for evening dining. Many people spend much of their 'at home' time in their kitchens, either preparing food or drinks, eating, or stacking the dishwasher. It often makes sense, therefore, for the kitchen to be situated where it receives sun and has agreeable views. This reflects how our lives have evolved and how what we require from our homes and gardens has changed.

Consideration should first be given to what the garden will be used for at different times of day. The aspect of each part of the garden will determine which part will be used for each activity. The area facing south will receive the strongest and highest intensity of sunshine, depending on what sources of shade already

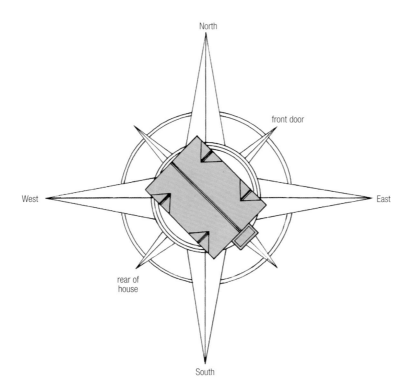

When building or re-building a house, if it is possible to achieve the optimum orientation, this will result in maximum usable space around the property.

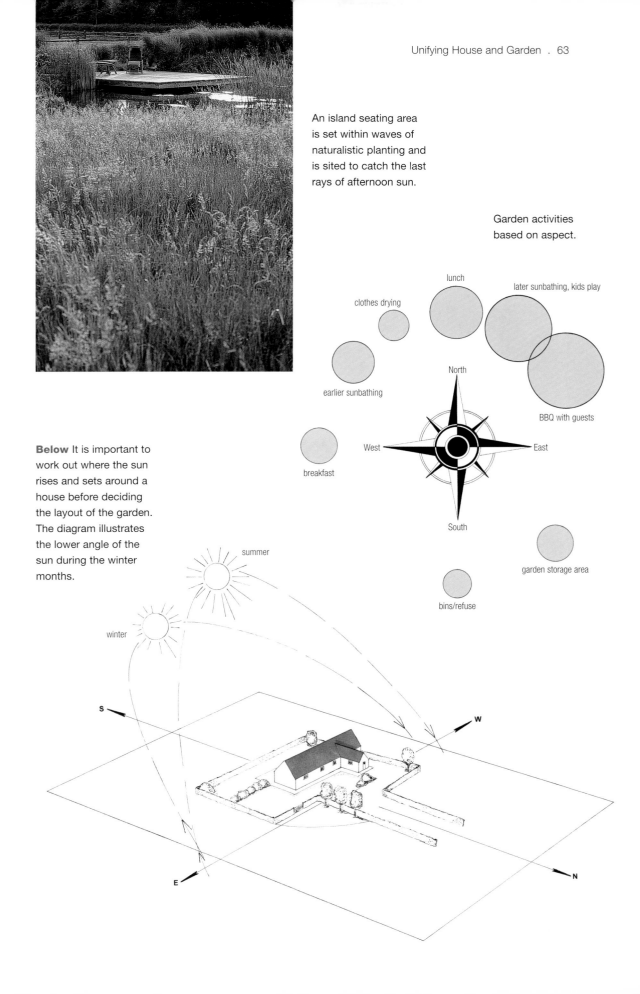

An island seating area is set within waves of naturalistic planting and is sited to catch the last rays of afternoon sun.

Garden activities based on aspect.

lunch

clothes drying

later sunbathing, kids play

earlier sunbathing

North

BBQ with guests

West — East

breakfast

South

Below It is important to work out where the sun rises and sets around a house before deciding the layout of the garden. The diagram illustrates the lower angle of the sun during the winter months.

garden storage area

bins/refuse

summer

winter

S

W

E

N

exist. This side of the house will therefore be either the area used for sunbathing, or alternatively the place where trees or shade-giving structures will be sited, depending on the owner's preferences. An area that receives early morning sun will be ideal for a small paved area that can be used for breakfasting, and the place where the last rays of sunshine hit the ground will be well suited for evening dining in the summer. If space is not an issue, multiple areas can give further flexibility of use and choice for different times of day and year. The only restriction will then be budget.

When designing areas to capture sun or provide shade, it is important to remember that although the sun rises and sets in the same place every day, the actual angle differs very slightly from day to day throughout the year. This factor is obviously more pronounced if you consider the angle of mid-winter sun against that of high summer sun.

The lower level of winter sun lessens its impact on areas that receive full sun, and they will receive it for a shorter period. This means that areas prone to frost or snow in the winter might remain in the shade as a result of the sun's low angle, and therefore will stay at a lower temperature. Paths in these areas may be prone to icing which will affect choice of hard landscaping materials and, when selecting plants, hardiness ratings will require due consideration.

Obviously function is a key aspect of garden layout, but, in terms of aspect, plant choice is critical. It is not simply that plants should be chosen to thrive in differing locations, but it is important to consider the function that they themselves are performing. Detailed planting design and varied plant combinations can make the main difference between a good and a great garden, but if the function has not been identified correctly it will never work as intended.

A seating area, sited to gain precious midday sun, acts as a central point within the garden.

A single focal point stands out because of the way in which light falls on it and the way it is set against a dark backdrop of evergreen planting.

Focal points

Focal points are very important when anchoring a house into a garden, as they can provide a way of leading the eye from one to the other, and somewhere for garden users to 'rest their gaze' when viewing the garden from the house or patio area. They can be very difficult to get right.

The importance of focal points is evident all around us. What makes us want to walk down a path or take a photograph when visiting a garden? The answer is almost undoubtedly a glimpse of something that we want to see more of. It is that urn at the end of the vista, or the dazzling autumn colour that shines out from a paperbark maple, or something that can be seen just beyond the group of trees in the mid-distance. Focal points can also physically lead us around a garden. Without something new to see just around the corner we would not be motivated to move around a garden at all.

The classical gardens of Italy and those of the French Renaissance provide great examples of the art of creating a focal point. It is probably true to say that correctly positioned focal points are the single most important key to a successful garden. It is not the quality or value of a piece of sculpture or a garden ornament that provides its impact, but how it is sited in the garden. Like a full stop in a sentence, a focal point creates an endpoint for the eye.

How many focal points does a garden need? If gardens are littered with them, they lose their impact and may become rather irritating. They should be chosen for their ability to visually link particular areas within a garden or to divert the eye where most necessary. Sometimes gardens have worthy features outside their boundaries that can provide a focal point. When there is nothing

A hanging seat acts as an intermediate focal point by drawing your eye to it and then on to the focal point beyond.

These perfectly balanced evergreen hedges lead the eye to the view beyond. As the hedges recede into the distance they diminish in size thus drawing the eye to a precise focal point.

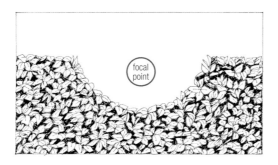

This cut-away hedge encourages the eye to rests on the arc before gazing on to the focal point.

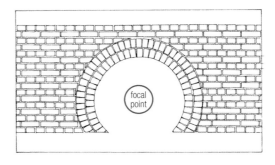

This 'moongate' pierces the brick wall and creates a window. Windows always draw the eye to them and onwards to the view of focal point.

A curving path appears to narrow as it disappears, and draws the eye into the centre of the view and onwards to the focal point or view.

These foreground trees frame and enhance the view. Choose trees that carry branches just above eye level and plant them close to key viewpoints or seating areas.

of note in the distance, or things that it is better not to draw attention to, then a focal point within the garden can prevent the eye from straying outside it. As John Brookes said, "When a site has nothing of note outside, the design must turn inwards to create its own internal point of attraction."

So what consitutes a good focal point? There is, of course, no single material or object that works to best effect. Apart from placement, it is the colour and level of detail of a focal point that will determine its degree of effectiveness.

Sculpture as focal point

A piece of sculpture is often effective when used as a focal point, particularly in a formal setting. Placing sculpture so that its qualities and detail can be properly viewed sounds obvious, but this may be enhanced by its setting or backdrop. If the object has a lot of detail, a simple backdrop will show it off to best effect. This can be anything from plain walls to simple hedging which has a flat, even surface. If the backdrop has too much interest, the intricacy of the object will be lost. Similarly, if the piece of sculpture has simple clean lines it can be set against a backdrop that has more detail. Where sculpture or objects such as pots are used to create focal points within a planting bed, the same holds true—objects with simple lines will act as a foil to detailed planting.

The use of sculpture in a garden should be considered only when it adds something definite to the scene. Different types of object should be seen in isolation, as too many together will detract from one another. Sculpture can be used as a secondary or intermediate focal point when placed in the foreground or in the middle area of a composition. Here it will allow the eye to rest, but then to drift beyond towards the final focal point of the view.

The line of vision leading to the focal point can be emphasised by planting. Trees, shrubs, and hedges, used in a balanced way on either side of the line of vision will guide the eye in the desired direction. To guide the eye in a less obvious way trees can be planted in such a way that they allow views out to other parts of the garden under the canopy. Pleached hedges (those where the branches have been intertwined) can give the same strong focusing effect, while allowing

When a sculpture is sited relatively close to the viewer, detail will hold the viewer's attention. If seen from afar, outline shape and colour will be more important.

The geometric shape of this pyramidal sculpture stands out within its setting of flowing herbaceous perennials.

Below A stone sculpture in the foreground provides an initial attraction before the colourful plants beyond draw the eye to rest.

Sculptures of sheep act as intermediate focal points in the foreground of this view.

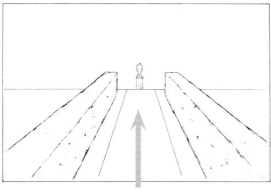
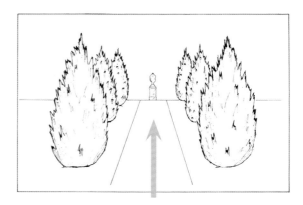
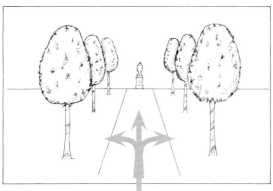
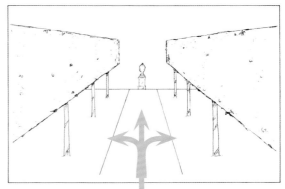

These four views all lead the eye towards a piece of sculpture at the end. The lower pair do not have such a strong directional view, as the eye is diverted by the views between the trunks of the trees. These scenarios would therefore be best used when it is desirable to have glimpses of other parts of the garden as well as the main focal point.

In this formal vista with a focal point straight ahead, there is an obvious directional pull that leads visitors through the garden.

 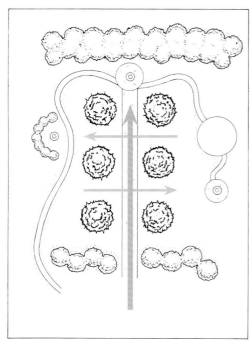

Intersecting views are usually reserved for the smaller garden, to increase the level of detail where space is limited. However in larger gardens they can also add variety. The sketch (**left**) shows a strong focused view ending with a piece of sculpture. The plan (**right**) illustrates that one can place other views across the main vista without interfering with the strong central view.

glimpses of other areas of the garden. Pleached hedges are also useful as an alternative to denser hedges for allowing light through or for enabling views to cut across one another.

Introducing a variety of views and experiences within a garden design will all add to the enjoyment it brings. Intersecting lines of sight from different areas within the garden, some to physically accessible areas, and some only to be viewed, will create interest. This technique also maximizes the apparent space, and is applicable in any size of garden.

The power of curves

When thinking of focal points and leading the eye, we often think about straight lines. However, curving lines can add a magical feel to a garden.

Illustrations in Graham Colliers' book, *Form, Space and Vision*, demonstrate how we perceive objects and create linkages between them in our minds. On first sight, the illustration (opposite) appears to show a well-balanced group of pebbles, some large and some small. As you continue to look, you find that your eye either tends to start looking from the bottom right-hand corner or from the largest shape, moving up through each pebble and creating an imaginary line. In the way that we join the dots in a colouring book, we create a string of beads out of the seemingly random picture of pebbles. The eye is always ready to be led onwards, and so will readily respond to any points of interest ahead of the line of

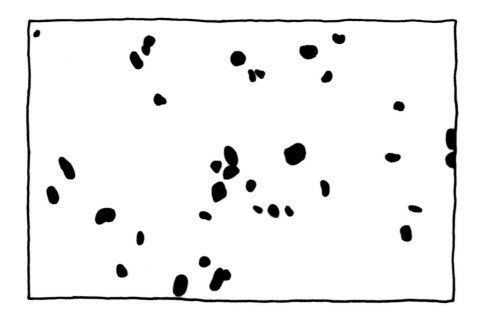

If you stare at the black dots you will probably find that your eye automatically tries to find similarities between them and connect them to create a single, unified entity. The eye naturally does this with other spaces and objects.

Plants dotted through a bed are seen as a single line of plants at this RHS Chelsea Flower Show garden.

A passageway within a student campus at Surrey University, England has a tremendous directional pull leaving no possibility to stand still. This shows just how powerful the use of curves can be.

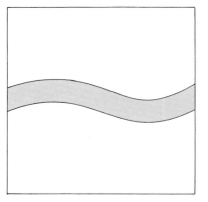

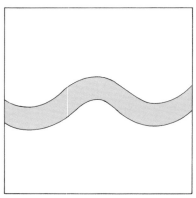

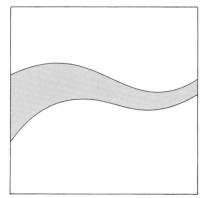

Paths with different degrees of curve

Softly flowing path: encourages users to travel slowly, looking at adjacent plants and other features. Allows everything to be viewed at once.

Meandering curve: users will speed up their journey along the path. There is potential for allowing partial glimpses of features further along the route.

The narrowing width of this path, combined with the curve, creates a strong directional flow. Users will be swept along, focused on getting to the end. There is likely to be an element of false perspective, making the path look longer than it actually is.

vision. It is this principle that we need to be aware of when designing spaces and placing objects within them. And it must be remembered that the eye will not only be attracted to plants or sculpture, but to a badly sited compost heap!

Curves can make moving around a garden feel more natural. The same distance can be travelled along straight or winding paths, but the winding route will usually feel more comfortable. Flowing lines also let the eye drift onwards and will coax the viewer into moving on. Straight lines bring an obvious formality and give gardens a sense of being man-made, with junctions feeling like deliberate pausing places. Curves can give the opposite effect: they can, of course, lead around the garden, but junctions and changes in direction are less obvious.

A caution in the use of curves and flowing lines within a design is that care should be taken to understand what they are being used for. If they become too strong they run the risk of turning what was intended as a relaxing and meandering path into a powerful directional tool, forcing the user from one area to another.

As a rule, when the curve of a path can be broken down into sections that form the arc of a quarter of a circle or more, the path becomes more directional and less flowing. Varying the width of the path in conjunction with deeper curves will pull a visitor or user through a space; this effect can be ameliorated by anchoring either end of the path into a space that is more static in nature. Stretches of deeply curving paths should be used sparingly, and work best when linking spaces also based upon parts of a circle. This should help to unify the overall design and become a bridge between areas of distinctive character. The effects of using parts of a circle are shown below.

When using gently flowing paths within a garden, care must be taken to mask the straighter routes so that people's instinct does not lead them to either consciously or unconsciously take a 'short cut'.

A combination of focal points and curves is usually a very successful. While straight lines and focal points are very formal, arcs gently lead the eye and provide a more graceful solution. Curving lines give the opportunity to place a focal point off-centre and encourage the eye to sweep over to it.

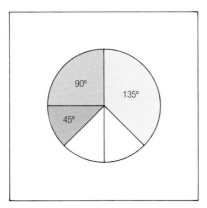

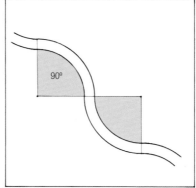

A circle is divided up into portions of 45°, 90° and 135°. By using a pair of compasses, paths can be designed using these angles and easily set out on site. Different angles create paths with different 'flows', which can be employed for various situations. By using compound curves (where there are no straight lines), and by combining a variety of angles, apparently organic curves can be created.

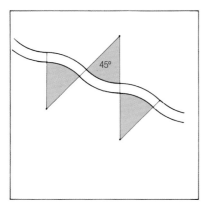

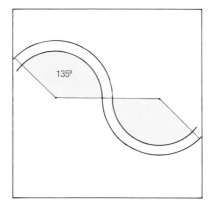

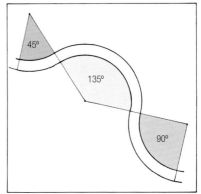

The flowing lines of landform provide an irresistible pull at Portrack Garden, Dumfriesshire, Scotland.

The bold curving outline of the body of water leads the eye to a small fountain which acts as a focal point.

Flowing lines can also be useful in directing the eye to a non-visible focal point because of the visual 'leading' properties of curves. We are naturally curious, and curves seduce us into moving on in search of an endpoint just out of reach around the next bend. The use of flowing lines in garden design is of course not new. One of the greatest exponents of the curve, 19th-century American landscape architect Frederick Law Olmsted, wrote: "We should recommend the general adoption... of gracefully curved lines, generous spaces and the absence

The curving path leads the eye to the distance where it rests on the clock tower.

A focal point at the end of a straight path.

A focal point at the end of a sweeping path.

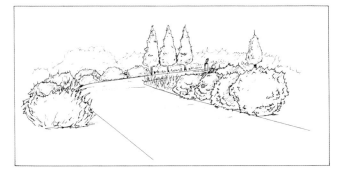

of sharp corners, the idea being to suggest and imply leisure, contemplativeness and happy tranquillity."

The benefits of curves are widely appreciated; when briefing designers, garden owners often request that curves be used to create relaxing spaces. The only circumstance in which a designer might advise caution with this option is if the house design is very heavily based on straight lines. In this case it might be better to reflect these lines in the immediate proximity of the house and allow them to give way to curving lines further into the garden.

Case Study

Hazeltonhead Garden

The clients in this case did not like their front garden. A white picket fence surrounded a poor quality lawn with an assortment of shrubs and conifers strung out around its periphery. The owners had never used the front garden and simply looked across it to the distant views on the horizon. It is common for garden owners to concentrate on certain areas to the detriment of others, and the front garden is often the area that is not maximized in terms of use or effect.

The inspiration for the design for Hazeltonhead Garden came from the curving stone walls that twisted over the undulations of the local fields. A series of three circular dry stone walls evolved from this, acting not only to define the space but also to provide some shelter. In building the walls, a new area with a different microclimate was created, and it was found that more tender plants could be grown here.

The strongly sweeping edges to this path draw the visitor to the patio area at its end.

The focal point of this view is the house itself. The paths narrows as it nears the house and effectively draws the eye straight to the house.

As the front garden had been under-used there was an obvious opportunity to create a seating area with a view. The owners were extremely fortunate to have a view out over rolling countryside, so it made sense to make a focal point of the vista. In this case a circular space was also designed adjacent to the seating area, which will eventually become a small pond. With young children at home this is currently a sand pit, but it is always worth remembering that children grow up very quickly; once the children go, parents are often not keen to quickly clear away the signs, and many gardens sport a large trampoline, even when the former users are away at college!

Because the clients in this case liked the informality of curves, flowing lines were used to effectively draw them into the garden space. In addition to the curvilinear path, there is also a narrowing which creates a dynamic line, drawing the eye down to the seating area. Inside the stone walls, herbaceous perennials have been used to create drifts of colour that skirt the edge of the lawn. The garden lacks any structural planting or plants for year-round interest; instead this is unashamedly a summer garden that will recede into the background for the rest of the year.

Use of colour

Colour preference in the garden is as personal as it is inside the house. It is an absolute truth that no two people are alike, and consequently their tastes will be as individual as they are. Colour has the power to induce moods and feelings that can influence the entire experience of a garden and along with other elements it is a vital factor in the underlying structure and design. It can be a transient element in a garden, or it can be the factor that consistently lifts the garden to a higher level. Colours can be used to relax or excite, and to bring instant feelings of warmth or coolness to a garden as to an interior. The use of colour in a garden must therefore be fully considered.

Green will almost always be the predominant colour in a garden. If colour is not given due consideration, then green will certainly prevail and some seasonal colour will occur naturally too.

 Penelope Hobhouse once commented: "Colours are never perceived in isolation, but are always influenced by others that are present in the picture." With this in mind, owners of larger gardens should rejoice as they have the advantage of a variety of spaces where different colour themes can be experimented with without impinging on each other. In the same way, a large house with many rooms can use a different colour scheme in each room, while an open-plan apartment or barn conversion will require that all the decoration works together.

It is not only size that has an effect on colour. The location of a garden and the amount of sunlight it receives will have a direct impact upon the colours

Bright orange dahlias contrast with the blue flowers of *Nepeta mussinii*.

Below
The light green foliage and white plumes of *Aruncus dioicus* contrast with the blue flowers of *Darmera peltata*.

Below right
The small silver leaves of *Helichrysum petiolare* scramble among the deep red flowers of *Hydrangea macrophylla* 'Hamburg'.

The late flowers of *Nerine bowdenii*, which typically appear in early autumn, can add an injection of colour at a point when most other flowers are fading.

Far left The bright flowers of *Hemerocallis* 'Stafford'.

Left Delicate pink flowers of *Astrantia major* 'Rubra'.

that work within it. Pastel colours often work best in gardens that are shrouded in dull cloud, as the differences between muted colours are more obvious when they are not blasted by sunshine. It therefore follows that in sunny locations we can use far brighter and stronger colours in gardens. On the other hand, what looks most effective in a sunny climate runs the risk of appearing gaudy and overly bright in a damp and rainy location. In California, bright, fiery oranges will seem appropriate, whereas in northern climes they can be out of place and overpower the rest of the garden.

When using plants as a source of colour, different plants will obviously have different effects. Trees and shrubs come in a variety of colours and will offer seasonal changes, but their main benefits will be those of structure and form. Herbaceous perennials and bulbs are the real instruments of colour in a garden. Careful planning can control and manipulate their effects to create interest and colour throughout the seasons, not only in spring and summer. By careful selection their season can be extended at both ends. Some early-flowering perennials can be effective as soon as the snows of winter disappear, and others start later but go on flowering until late October. At the height of winter, the garden will rely for colour on its evergreen shrubs and trees, but also on dead flower-heads

The bleached white stems of the *Betula utilis* var. *jacquemontii* provide striking winter and spring interest.

Above Pinks and reds harmonize, while they contrast with the green from the opposite side of the spectrum.

Above right Pink heads of *Sedum telephium* 'Matrona' add impact among *Phormium tenax* 'Atropurpureum' and the seedheads of *Stipa tenuissima*.

Right Muted harmonious colours ensure that the border is viewed as an entity.

and standing grasses, which can paint beautiful frosted pictures—albeit mono-chrome ones. Annuals can be used to create periodic accents of colour within any scheme, but they are the most labour-intensive of plants for achieving this. With careful planning, bulbs can fill the remaining seasonal gaps.

When introducing accents of strong colour it is best to use them in isolation from other colours so that they stand out against their background. The best effects are achieved by selecting colours from opposite sides of the colour wheel. Therefore, if an accent is required in front of a green hedge, the most effective colour would be red. If a purple beech hedge is surrounding the garden then a yellow or golden plant will often work best.

Another key decision when using accent plants is how long you want this focus to last. If it is to be permanent, then evergreen trees and shrubs will be most effective, whereas if it is only for a very short period, bulbs or annuals could be used. If the colour accent is to last for just a season, the foliage on a deciduous shrub may be suitable. Colourful pieces of sculpture can fulfil the role of colour accents all year round and are certainly the most constant. The size of the space available for such a feature will affect the choice of where, with what, and how it should be created.

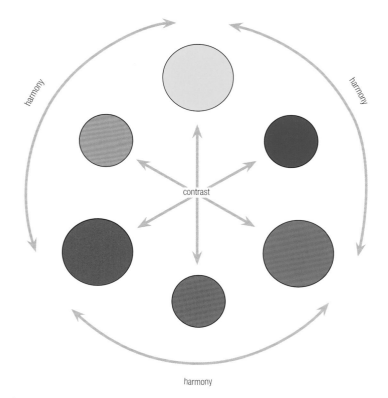

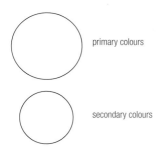

A colour wheel shows the three primary colours—yellow, blue and red—and the secondary colours—orange, purple and green—which are made by combining the two adjacent primary colours. Contrasting colours can be found at opposite sides of the wheel, and harmonious colours are those adjacent to each other on the wheel.

primary
colours

secondary
colours

contrasting colours
fight each other

complementary
colours harmonize

Blue and green are adjacent in the colour spectrum, but the very dark hue of the background *Taxus baccata* lets the pale blue-flowered Himalayan poppies stand out.

Situated at the opposite end of the colour spectrum, red is the colour that will stand out the most against a green background.

Colour guidelines

In general terms, limiting the colours chosen for a particular area of a garden (or of a room in a house) to one section of the colour wheel will promote harmony and restfulness. This does not necessarily mean shades of pink and pale blue; it can just as easily mean vibrant oranges and reds. By minimizing the number of colours, a visual jumble will be avoided, and a calmer space achieved. The logical progression from this is to ensure that when specific ranges of colour are used in different areas of the garden they are viewed separately. This will necessitate the creation of discrete areas, or at least a manipulation of views and experiences. The only alternative to this is to ensure that the colours are kept apart by season or flowering period. Using plants with a range of flower colour within one area, visually separated by their flowering period, will create a dynamic space that is constantly changing. This requires a great deal of planning, and a detailed understanding of the plants' characteristics and growth habits. As a general rule, when trying to keep colours apart, white can be used for its 'breaking' effect—it helps prevent colours from 'fighting' with each other.

Certain basic, timeless rules are relevant to any situation: generally, plants with lighter foliage are good for brightening up darker areas within a garden, while in lighter areas bright colour and contrasts are more appropriate. The silvery foliage of lavender, for example, is naturally suited to sunnier, well-drained areas, whereas plants with golden foliage can be effectively used to brighten up dull, damp corners of a garden. Detailed suggestions for plants that can be used as a feature due to their striking colour or habit, are given in Chapter 6.

Photographing your garden

It can be helpful to photograph the different areas of your garden for comparison. This is useful when considering any aspect of the garden whether related to colour or structure. Black-and-white images are very useful for showing the relative intensity of colour and indicating the relative colour weight of the elements. It is not necessary to use black-and-white film; instead simply photocopy colour prints in black-and-white. This will highlight the overall composition of the garden without the distraction of colour variety. When creating a formal view it can ensure the balance of a view in terms of strength of colour, and when creating an informal look it will ensure that elements camouflaged by colour do not interfere with the composition. It can be quite a surprise when looking at a black-and-white image of a garden to find which plants and colours are the strongest.

It is again worth remembering the words of Penelope Hobhouse: "You can plan colour but not always control it." Perhaps if we are too controlled with our use of colour we will never make any mistakes, and mistakes are often a route to invention. Nature is constantly making combinations that delight and surprise us—so perhaps any colour strategy should serve as a guide, rather than a rule.

Boundary treatment

The boundaries of gardens are not simply for delineation of space and ownership but form an integral part of the garden. The trees and shrubs that grow on garden boundaries become the backdrops to everything within them and, as such, their importance should not be underestimated. The colour and shape of the planting have an important impact on the rest of the garden. If the planting is evergreen it will remain as a constant, whereas deciduous plantings will change with the seasons and have a cyclical impact. Evergreen plants can be relied upon to act as foils to decorative plants, but can be at odds with the wider landscape. Care must be taken to ensure that where views extend outside the garden boundary, the planting blends in.

Screening

When screening out ugly landmarks or neighbouring houses, it is worth bearing in mind that placing the screening element closer to where the view is taken from will allow the use of a smaller screen.

Whether the elements to be screened are inside or outside the garden, the initial step is to work out from where they are most visible. The unwanted element might be anything from an ugly landmark in the distance, to a neighbour's first-floor windows or the unsightly compost heap in the corner of the garden itself. Within a garden, using plants to screen off offending objects is usually the simplest and cheapest solution, though it will not be instant. Solid screens of fencing and walls are obviously more expensive and require careful integrating into the overall design of the garden. Plants can reach heights that walls and fences cannot; conversely it can be difficult to stop plants from growing once they have produced the desired result and blanked out the offending object.

Most gardens, especially in relatively new properties, are effectively boxed in by the boundary walls or fences. It is these walls that dominate the views from the house and garden. In large gardens, these boundary fences and walls are much less dominating, and with longer views, objects outside the garden can have much more of an impact.

Being overlooked by adjacent properties is a common complaint and is typically what drives people to seek out some sort of screening. Neighbouring windows that overlook the garden can be very intrusive and difficult to blank out. It is normally unrealistic to try to screen an entire garden from prying eyes, but important to make sure that key areas, such as sunbathing spots and eating areas, are screened.

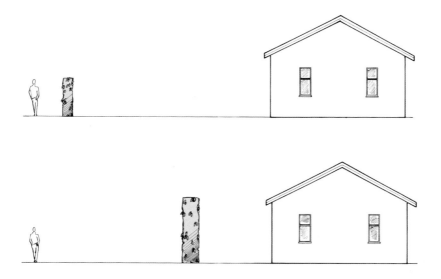

When attempting to screen an object, a relatively small screening element can be used if it is placed close to where the offending object is to be viewed from. If the screen is to be placed further away from the viewpoint, it will need to be bigger.

Aspect can be the most infuriating thing when it comes to screening and, for some unlucky owners, screening may mean losing light and sunshine from their gardens. The advantage of a large garden is that there is the luxury of enough space to be able to sacrifice some in order to gain privacy. Those with small gardens have very limited options in this respect, and it may come down to a choice between privacy and sunshine!

Screening with plants

When screening with plants, selection is critical. Most people want a fast solution to their problem, and consequently choose plants that will rapidly screen the offending object, but the potential problem of plants not knowing when to stop growing has already been mentioned. The solution to this is to double-plant—creating an initial screen with a fast-growing species while the desired screen has time to grow and establish, and then removing the first plants.

The maintenance requirements of the plants used must also be considered prior to planting. Too often, a hedge is used as a screening device without taking into account the long-term implications of controlling its height and width. Deciduous plants can make very effective screens, if the obvious seasonal

A quick-growing hedge species can be used to accelerate the creation of a screen. When slower-growing trees have matured sufficiently to block the view, the hedge can be removed.

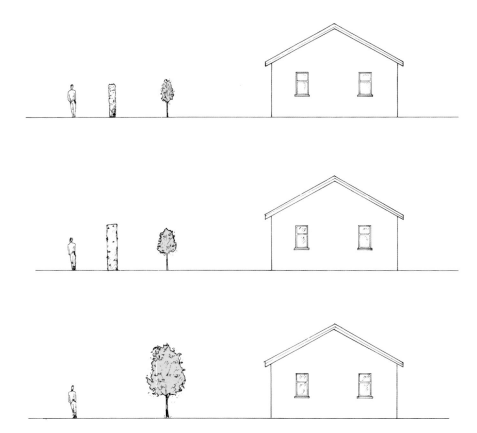

changes are appropriate. If the peak period of garden usage coincides with the optimum effect of the deciduous screen, which will often be the case, the seasonal restrictions will not pose a problem.

Plants for screening

Plants within this grouping are listed in Chapter 6 according to the type of screen that they can provide, and also the approximate speed at which they can become effective. They are divided into groups of plants that will form solid screens and those which will act as 'filters', allowing partial views through. It may seem an unusual concept to have screening elements that will not entirely screen an object or area, but these are useful for defining spaces without entirely restricting views, or for allowing partial glimpses of something which entices the visitor onwards. In addition several groups or mixes of plants are listed that can either be left as a mixed grouping or have a successional element to them: some are

Bamboo can act as a screen if planted densely, or as a filter to allow views through if planted more sparingly.

Above The gently waving flowers of *Verbena bonariensis* act as a very fine filter and take some of the formality away from the crisp geometric paving and planting beyond.

there to provide initial screening, while the slower-growing trees have time to establish and eventually become the main plants within the group. Each plant has its own characteristics and will create a slightly different type of screen, from completely evergreen, through semi-evergreen, to deciduous.

Evergreen plants are in some ways ideal for screening as they remain in leaf throughout the entire year, and thus provide an effective screen all year round. It is worth noting, however, that continual evergreen often (although not always) comes at the expense of any discernible flower or seasonal interest.

Semi-evergreen plants are similar to the evergreen varieties but in colder climatic zones they will adopt deciduous tendencies. They can offer more interest than true evergreens and can successfully be used as barriers in areas of the garden that are mainly used during the summer months of the year. It may not be so critical in certain areas to have a complete screen, and only when those areas of the garden area in use.

Deciduous plants will shed all their leaves at some point of the year, usually the autumn, but also sometimes in periods of stress. Some change colour prior

The flying ducks at Chaumont-sur-Loire Garden Festival illustrate the dramatic and complete screening that grasses can provide at the peak of their yearly growing cycle.

The bright purple autumnal foliage of the deciduous *Acer palmatum* 'Atropurpureum' serves as a design feature.

to shedding, which can provide seasonal interest and be used as a feature within a garden design. Care should be taken that this coloured focal point is desirable within the overall design of the garden. Mixed plantings can produce a multi-coloured autumnal background, which can help the garden to blend into the surrounding landscape.

Plants that can be used as 'green walls' are listed in Chapter 6 as two distinct groups: those that form informal edges to a garden, and those that are best grown as formal hedges. Where no height has been given for these plants it is because they can be trimmed and kept to desired heights.

'Floating' steps form a link through a water body, but more importantly act as a sculptural element in their own right.

Linkages

All gardens need to have their areas linked. Unless you are dealing with a range of discrete rooms that you do not want to relate to each other—and that would be highly unusual—most gardens work as a whole because the individual areas are joined by some sort of common thread. Like a Meccano model, all the areas need to be joined with nuts and bolts before the garden can pivot and work. Quite often it is easiest to visualize and create these linkages on a plan.

The initial link must be from the garden entrance to the house, and this could be on any side of the house. It is effectively the first point from which you will experience the garden. If the house has been built in isolation, or without any consideration for the garden, then a starting point must be created.

This starting point could be a part circle of paving that surrounds the exit from the house, or a distinct feature that is set away from the house but is visually

Paths link spaces and
act as a unifying force
within a garden.

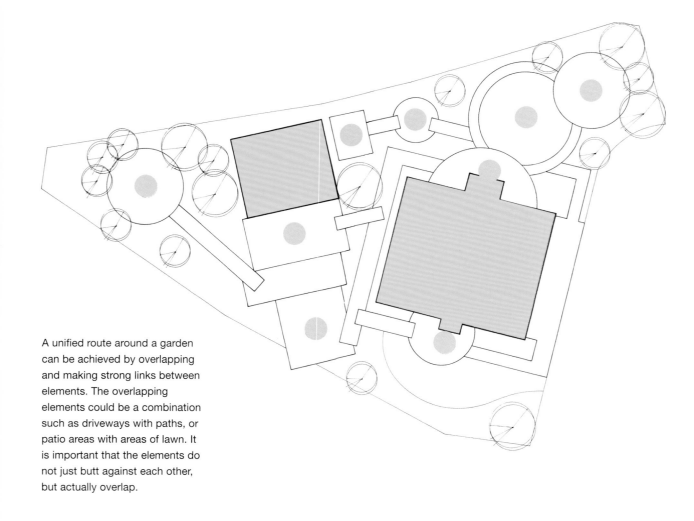

A unified route around a garden
can be achieved by overlapping
and making strong links between
elements. The overlapping
elements could be a combination
such as driveways with paths, or
patio areas with areas of lawn. It
is important that the elements do
not just butt against each other,
but actually overlap.

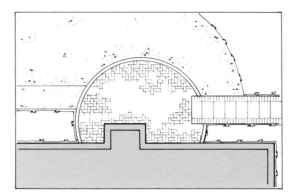

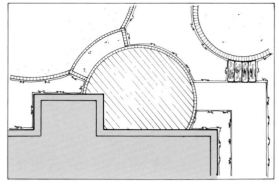

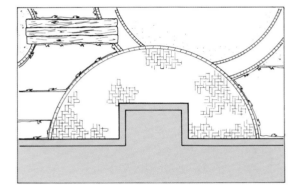

The use of paved areas
adjacent to the entrance or
exit from a house can help
to link the house into a wider
garden layout.

A pathway overlaps an area
of gravel to provide a strong
link between the two areas.

an obvious starting point into the garden. It just depends upon how the house
has been built within the site. Within many new housing developments, the
houses bear little or no relation to the site, or indeed have been built in a way
that is at odds with the site and aspect.

Techniques can also be used to alter the existing linkages of space to make
more use of the site or bring in features that are currently being ignored as a
result of the layout.

In a large garden, space allows the use of plants and trees to link areas in a
way that is simply not possible in small-scale gardens. As focal points draw the
garden visitor through various spaces, the lines of the garden also achieve this.
If you consider the massive avenues of formal trees that radiate from the Palace
of Versailles in France, the focal point is initially nowhere to be seen. The lines

Above A pergola is used to link two distinct areas of a garden. The treatment on either side of the semi-enclosed path is very simple, allowing detail to be used at either end.

Right Giant stepping-stones form a wide flowing path through the garden. Using individual stones ensures the path does not dominate, and becomes secondary to the planting.

Above A band of crushed stone creates an informal bed which also allows access if required.

Right A wild garden appears to be 'managed' by the simple introduction of a mown pathway.

of trees guide us through the garden from one linked area to another, or even draw us out into the wider landscape. On a less grand scale, paths, whether they are defined by edges or blended into adjacent plantings, are probably the most obvious linking tool that we possess. A garden linked solely by paths might not seem that interesting however. Variety is the key to creating interesting spaces and a valuable garden experience.

Walks

One of the great benefits of owning a larger garden is the opportunity to be able to walk through it. Larger gardens, both formal and informal, will usually benefit from a network of paths running through them, allowing the garden to be fully experienced and opening up different views of the house and garden. The paths themselves need not be formal in character, and indeed some variety in type and make-up is usually an advantage. They do not even need to be constructed, but could simply be mown paths through an area of grass to provide an ephemeral but nonetheless intriguing feature.

Most gardens, even smaller ones, can also benefit from non-essential paths. Whether bark woven through existing belts of trees, or stepping-stones through a shrub border, there is normally scope for some form of secondary paths.

Levels

When planning the relationship between a house and garden it is often very beneficial to have areas that cannot be viewed in their entirety at one glance, and gardens with changes in level can be some of the most interesting examples of this. Although they can require extra thought and resources, they can also make some of the most exciting gardens.

Levels can also create opportunities for patios and seating areas to be set at vantage points commanding views both inside and beyond the garden. This can add a dimension that owners with gardens on the flat can only dream of. Changes in level also provide a variation in the physical journey within the garden: steps can increase the sense of anticipation, intriguing the user with the knowledge that they must lead to somewhere or something of interest.

Hillside gardens can be a problem when they are difficult to access. There can be unusable areas of the garden that are too steep to plant and too dangerous to mow. For these reasons, as well as offering an opportunity to garden owners, establishing usable levels is one of the main reasons for employing the services of a garden designer. Occasionally it proves impossible to make the slopes workable and on these occasions the alternative is to create terraces. This usually involves moving considerable amounts of earth and engaging with the inherent challenges of retaining walls and drainage solutions.

Two seats maximize garden views from the edge of a raised decked area.

Practical ways of dealing with extreme slopes and gradients within a garden are discussed in Chapter 4.

Steps

When selecting material for steps it is crucial to consider how often they are to be used, and in what conditions. First, the location within the garden is significant. Are the steps very near to the house and leading into the garden, or at the end of the garden perhaps leading to less structured areas? If the steps link a house to a patio or other seating area, it can be assumed that they will be heavily used. If, in a large garden, they lead to an area that will be less visited, then a low usage can be assumed. Stone and brick are the most robust materials, and will cope with greater punishment. By contrast, steps made with timber risers and bark infill will have a shorter lifespan and be less appropriate for heavy use.

The dimension of the riser (height of step) in relation to the dimension of the tread (depth of step) will alter the way the steps feel to walk upon. If the riser is too steep or too shallow, the steps can feel awkward to use. In addition, if the tread is too short or too long it can also be uncomfortable to walk on depending upon the user's length of stride. There is no suggestion that steps can be designed to magically fit everyone, but there are relatively standard dimensions

Ratio for good step proportions is:
riser × 2 + tread = between 550 and 700 mm.
650 mm is ideal.
In this example: 150 × 2 + 350 = 650

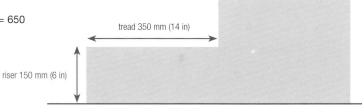

tread 350 mm (14 in)

riser 150 mm (6 in)

The angular shapes of this garden echo the shape of the building where a triangular section of wall projects from the house. The garden 'falls' into the landscape beyond through a series of terraces.

Below The colour of the brick wall is reflected in the material used in the steps to provide a unifying effect.

Features such as steps must be designed in relation to the scale of space, not simply the demands of usage. These steps are at a scale that would not be out of place within a public park, and yet relate to the scale of the house and provide a wide relaxed flow out onto a lower section of the garden.

that work for most people. As well as the functioning aspect of steps, dimensions can be altered to add to the garden experience. Steep, narrow steps leading from one area of a garden to another can add to a sense of anticipation. Deep, shallow steps immediately enforce a slower, more relaxed pace of walking. These considerations are another way of influencing the users' perception and experience of the garden. They become another important way of manipulating not only the space, but the journey through the garden.

Case Study:

East Fife Garden

A new house was built in a grassed, two-acre, walled garden. The owner of the property had made great progress in creating the garden from scratch, but felt that not all the elements worked well together and substantial areas remained unused and did not relate to the house. Initially an oak fence was erected which effectively chopped the lower end of the garden off, with the intention of creating a wildflower meadow. Psychologically this was a good idea for the owners as it immediately created two distinct areas that could be treated differently in terms of maintenance. The garden was dominated by lovely but imposing stone walls, which required integration. In addition, the garden had neither a logical starting point, nor a natural entrance, and therefore didn't feel connected to the house, which was a bit like a spaceship that had landed on a grass field. There were many attractive individual elements but little cohesion.

These beautiful but imposing stone walls need to be broken up visually by planting to prevent them from dominating the space.

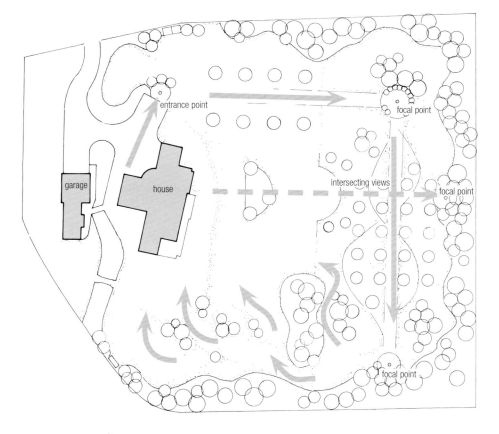

Plan of East Fife Garden. The stone walls provide a boundary to this garden. An entrance point was created which then leads on to a series of focal points and avenues which have been designed to maximize usage of the entire garden area.

At East Fife Garden, the primary aim was to unify the external space and was achieved through the use of focal points. The starting point was to make a natural entrance. This was created directly ahead of the front door of the house and in line with a gate in the fence to the lower end of the garden. It is important to get a sense of where it feels natural to enter a house; for some homes the rear door would be the most logical starting point, depending upon the layout of the building and how it has been sited within the grounds.

An avenue of trees was planted to strengthen the line to and from this entrance, and a focal point created to entice the visitor down into the garden. The focal point in this case was a broken circle of scented azaleas. First a complete circle was planted centrally at the end of the avenue of trees. The selected plants were removed at the points in the circle where people enter and exit. The circle acts rather like a hub. It operates in the same way as the starting point for the garden in that it brings in people from one direction, holds them in that space, and then sends them out in another direction.

An orchard was planted in the lower area of the property, and paths were mown to allow access and provide visual interest when viewed from above through the top windows of the house. Although orchards are quite popular with people who have large gardens, few actually want the volume of apples that will invariably be produced. Most like to plant a wide variety of apple trees so that the period of apples ripening is spread over a longer period. This also allows for a mix of culinary and dessert apples, as well as some that store and others that need to be eaten immediately. A nice feature of the orchard, although not strictly related to focal points, is that a pattern is formed by the flowering habits of the matrix of trees selected.

This is evident when viewed from above and the owners in this case will be able to see a sequential pattern of flowering trees from their bedroom window. Also, when looking down the central path towards the focal point, the view is balanced with the trees on either side of the avenue effectively being a mirror image of the other. The central avenue through the orchard has a sculpture as a focal point, reinforced by an arc of planting behind it. Once the visitor has reached the sculpture, the way back up to the house is less defined. It does not need to be as structured as the rest of the garden journey because the house is clearly visible, and any visitor logically knows to head back in that direction. It is a pleasant experience to drift back in the general direction of the house past a variety of borders and beds. Distinct from the overall landscape structure is a small arbour placed in a direct sightline from the house, and forming a specific focal point to be viewed from the kitchen window. On the periphery of the garden, swathes of structural planting have been undertaken to partly screen off sections of the wall and leave others open for visual variety. The planting acts as a backdrop for the rest of the garden, lessening the impact of the surrounding walls and gently linking them into the overall scheme.

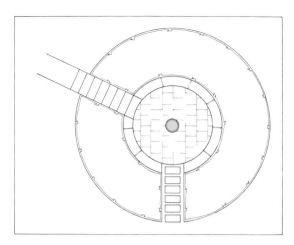

Four plans show how the directional pull of a garden's entrance point can be differently enhanced by adding a variety of plantings.

Left This relies upon the central feature to draw the visitor into the orientation point and to then send them off into the garden.

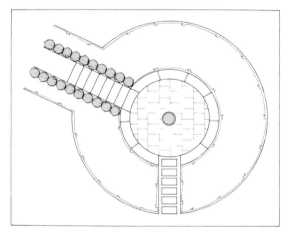

Right The view of the central feature is reinforced by planting to either side of the approach pathway.

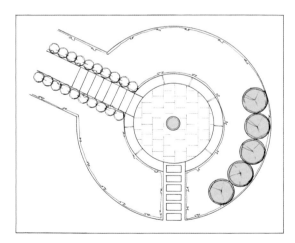

Left This view has a backdrop of planting to the rear of the feature: its impact could be increased by the use of contrasting colour.

Right This exhibits the most in terms of maximizing the appearance of the central feature. A tree has been added to each side of the path, serving to frame the feature.

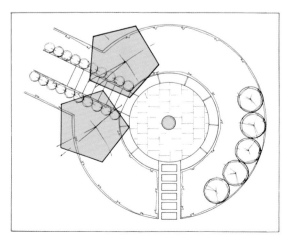

A sculpture acts as a focal point, reinforced by balanced planting to its rear. The view shows how to emphasize a piece of sculpture without necessarily leading the onlooker up to it.

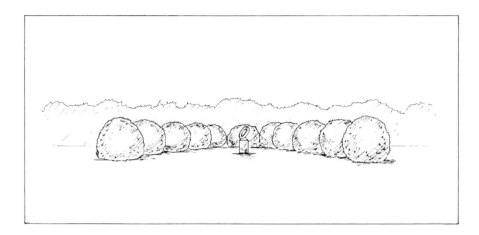

Balanced hedge planting on either side frames the focal point and provides a strong directional pull, ensuring that the onlooker is led right up to the piece of sculpture.

Fagus sylvatica (beech) hedges have been used to define this enclosure and will draw onlookers to the piece of sculpture and into the central space.

Practical Recommendations

- Make the most of all areas of your garden.
- Do not design or designate an area of a garden specifically for children. Spaces should be designed to be flexible and have the potential to be adapted over time.
- When part of a garden is distanced or perceived as detached from the rest of it, strong design tactics should be used to link it with the house and the rest of the garden.
- Even when a garden has attractive existing features such as stone walls, ensure that their effect is maximized but that they are not allowed to dominate.
- A slopes within a garden should be viewed as an opportunity, not a problem. Changes in height bring interest and vantage points to a garden; steps draw the eye onwards; and slopes allow the eye to glide from one level to another.
- If an area does not link into a garden, create a new entrance point to make sure that it does.
- Create 'nodes' or 'joints' in a garden to link the various areas and ensure that users experience the entire garden.

Chapter 4

Managing the Larger Garden

The small-scale materials used in this patio ensure that the space will feel comfortable and not dwarf its users.

When a garden feels private and human in scale it will almost certainly be appealing. Whatever the size of the garden, we must feel comfortable in its space, and aware of being enclosed. We are returning to the much discussed concept of the 'garden room', an idea based on the fact that the walls that surround us, whether decorated in wallpaper or made from tightly clipped yew, act as a buffer against the elements, prying eyes, and the outside world in general.

In our minds we apply our human-scale associations to every space and landscape we see. We only know how immense the Grand Canyon is by measuring it in relation to ourselves or to things with which we are familiar, such as another person standing admiring it, a helicopter flying through it, or an electric pylon that stands to the side of it. Standing on the edge of the Grand Canyon will probably not feel all that comfortable, but we will feel comfortable in the fenced-off enclosure that delineates the public viewing area. Gardens are no different—we can have magnificent vistas, but to feel at home most of us need spaces that put us at our ease.

Larger gardens give the opportunity for open expanses, but we will feel most comfortable viewing them from the comfort of a patio or seating area, so that we feel secure. We all seek sanctuary, and this is one of the primary functions of a garden. When briefing a garden designer, most clients will have some degree of privacy as an initial requirement. Whether relaxing with a drink at the end of the day, or putting out the rubbish in the morning wearing only a dressing gown, most people would rather be unobserved.

In a larger garden, the temptation to break down every space into small, intimate areas should be resisted. Owning a large area of land allows the luxury of treating different areas of the garden in different ways. While some areas can be private and enclosed, others can be unapologetically spacious.

There are no hard and fast rules governing what makes a space work in terms

Opposite The concept of the 'outdoor room' is taken to the extreme. These walls would feel very dominating and uncomfortable for anyone sitting on the bench for a long period of time.

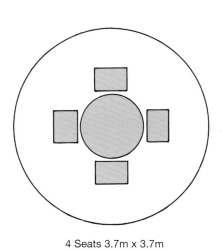

4 Seats 3.7m x 3.7m

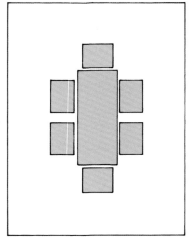

6 Seats 4.5m x 3.25m

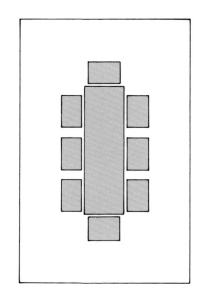

8 Seats 5.0m x 3.25m

The three diagrams give a guide to basic minimum sizes for a patio. For aesthetic reasons a larger area may be required in order for it to be in scale with the house and the surrounding space. In general terms a patio should allow for people to be seated and have sufficient space behind them for someone to walk around and fill up their glasses!

of its size; this is very personal and subjective. However, there are general guidelines which can be useful when planning and managing a larger garden.

How to achieve proportion

"Does the garden have an architectural system of its own or is it part of the landscape?" (Aben and De Wit 2001). De Wit explains that when creating a garden room, if the surrounding 'walls' are below three metres high, too much of the surroundings will intrude into the space and it will not feel contained. If, on the other hand, they are over six metres high, the user will feel no relationship to the walls and the feeling can be threatening, as if standing in a well. These guidelines are a useful starting point but they are affected by the size of the space, the distance from which the user is able to view the walls, and the slope of the ground.

De Wit uses another rule of thumb to define the area of a patio, suggesting a minimum space of 4 × 4 m (12 × 12 ft). She believes that we should be able to see the bottom outer edges of the space within our normal cone of vision.

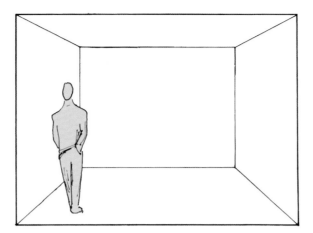

Rectangular spaces which are 1.5 times the height of their users are relaxing, human-scale spaces.

Proportion A figure is shown standing within spaces of differing sizes. This can act as a guide when determining the size or proportion fo spaces within a garden. There is no right or wrong—each produces a different effect. When determining the scale of spaces or the heights of the walls and plants that surround them, it can be useful to visualize walking through or sitting in them to get a sense of how the space will make its users feel.

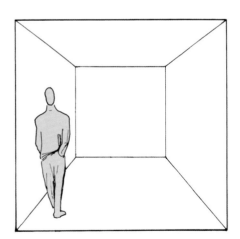

Square spaces normally make users comfortable, though they tend to feel 'formal'.

Tall spaces dwarf users and do not feel restful for any long period of time.

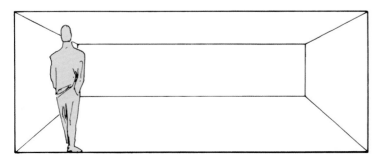

Wide, low spaces can make people feel exposed and vulnerable.

Left The central cone of vision should be borne in mind when siting focal points or key areas of planting in relation to areas from which they will be viewed.

Right When deciding how to either define or divide spaces, the use of shrubs and hedges at varying heights will produce different results.

Below right Palladio's "seven sets of the most beautiful and harmonious proportions to be used in the construction of rooms".

The average relative dimensions of the kind of rooms we are likely to feel comfortable with in the twenty-first century were first experimented with in the Renaissance period. Designers of the time aimed for a feeling of space, yet took care not to overpower the individual or lose the feeling of containment that a room should ideally provide. The important thing to do when designing a space is to draw a cross-section through it and place a person in it—either the potential user of the space, with their precise height and eye level, or an average person 1.7 m (5 ft. 6 in.) tall with an eye-level of 1.5 m (5 ft.).

The diagrams opposite show how the garden must relate to those using it. They illustrate how high elements need to be to divide space, create a barrier or screen elements. In the Renaissance it was the Italian architect, Palladio, who took the rules of harmonic proportion to their apparent limit. But can these rules of proportion be used in our gardens? If we think of gardens as outdoor rooms, is there a magic formula for successfully dividing them that, not only makes the garden work as a single entity, but also creates a natural flow between house and garden? In *The Four Books of Architecture*, published in 1570, Palladio outlined what he thought were, "seven sets of the most beautiful and harmonious proportions to be used in the construction of rooms."

There is no reason why these rules of proportion should not also be used as a guide to designing the sizes of different areas of a garden. It seems logical that these proportions should also be used when creating a balanced patio area or deciding the exact dimensions of an area of lawn. Many designers and some

A knee-high hedge or solid barrier acts simply as a visual definition.

A shoulder-high hedge or solid barrier acts as a physical, but not a visual barrier.

Above eye level, a hedge or solid barrier is both physical and visual.

Waist-high shrub plantings, closely planted, will provide a physical but non-visual barrier.

Above eye-level specimen shrubs will act as a physical and visual barrier.

Above eye-level trees will act as a visual definition of space but not be a physical barrier.

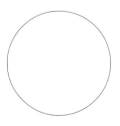

circle

square
1 : 1

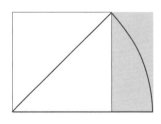

diagonal of the square
1 : 1.414

square plus one third
3 : 4

square plus a half
2 : 3

square plus two thirds
3 : 5

double square
1 : 2

non-professionals wanting to design their own gardens, have an intuitive sense of scale, but for those who don't these guidelines can be ideal starting points when faced with a blank space.

Scale is, of course, just one element of effective large garden design. In the words of Thomas Mawson:

> In the first place a garden should always impress us as being a place for flowers rather than shrubs. Secondly, the flowers should have a cared-for appearance, for a slovenly, ill-kept garden is as bad, if not worse than none at all. The arrangement should be, as one writer very properly expresses it, a series of outdoor apartments rather than a panorama that can be grasped in one view. Thirdly, that, whilst a garden is to proclaim itself as a thing that has been made, it is for the accommodation and enjoyment of nature's bountiful supplies. Further that a garden has to serve the double purpose of foreground to the landscape when seen from the house, and as base or setting to the house when viewed from the surrounding country; in short, that it is the link which connects the house and landscape.

A table and chairs nestle under a tree, providing a secluded link between house and surrounding countryside.

Maintenance

Increased maintenance is the over-riding concern that many owners have when getting larger gardens designed or redesigned. The need for low maintenance forms an integral part of almost every initial project brief. Unfortunately, the low-maintenance garden does not exist! All gardens require some maintenance. There are some elements that can be designed to minimize work, but gardens, by their very nature, require a fair amount of work.

This hebe gives a well-tended appearance to a border without the need for a twice-yearly trim that box requires.

This highly manicured lawn at Skeldon in Ayrshire looks so perfect that it deters people from walking on it and is certainly not for families who play football.

Lawns, trees and borders

The three main areas of a garden that will require maintenance are lawns, trees and borders. Lawns can seem the most demanding, simply because they require weekly work in summer in order to keep them looking neat. As grass grows, so does our obsession with keeping it under control. Good design can help in a variety of ways, including a well-planned layout of the lawn itself so that it may be cut by a ride-on lawnmower. Some lawns can be designed to suit the width of a mower, but there are very few gardens capable of being cut by ride-on mowers alone—virtually all will have areas that need a smaller mower as well. Areas around trees or adjacent to walls, and edges to borders, are further places where a larger machine will be ineffective. Removing the most extreme

Bands of ivy are used to create beds of planting that visually break up the areas of grass and also limit the maintenance requirements.

Mowing at different heights can create interest within a larger open area of grass at different times of the year.

Below This brick-edged border reduces the area that needs more maintenance while anchoring the house into the garden. The grass edge can easily be kept neat with a strimmer.

The simple use of *Prunus laurocerasus* and *Hedera helix* ensure that this border requires minimal maintenance and yet it will still appear crisp and well tended.

gradients in lawns by terracing, and cutting edges into longer sweeps, will help make cutting easier. Edging with edging shears or a strimmer is a notoriously unpopular pastime. There are two ways in which we can minimize the edging time: by laying a mowing strip or by using a proprietary edging. These methods do restrict growth; simply by not allowing the grass to spread, they will reduce its expansion sideways. The lawn will still require some attention, but in the form of trimming rather than having to get out the edging iron and cut back the edges regularly. A brick or stone margin set just below the cut level will prevent the owner or gardener from having to edge the grass. There will be an initial cost but in the long term this will cut the maintenance burden significantly.

Lawns like bowling greens can easily become an obsession, and although a beautifully kept lawn can be very appealing, lack of time or money make it unachievable for most garden owners and we should not be too perfectionist.

Trees and shrubs can be classed as permanent plantings, and as such they fill a lot of area and require a relatively low level of maintenance. If planted over areas of gravel, paving, or low-growing groundcover, they can be the most effective way to achieve a garden that looks maintained without continual input. Nonetheless even gravel and paving require periodic attention. Gravel may require raking, and both will need removal of leaf debris and weeds at certain times of the year. The use of trees and shrubs will cut down maintenance levels over the medium- to long-term although there will still be a certain level of input until they are established. When planting shrubs and trees, the impact is not usually realized for at least three years following planting. Of course when dealing with trees and their intended structural impact, the eventual desired effect may take fifteen to twenty years to be realized.

In areas that are particularly difficult to maintain for specific reasons, such as slopes, groundcover plants may also be used to reduce the overall burden.

Slopes and gradients

There are many degrees of slope, each of which has its own implications for usage and maintenance. It is usually only when one attempts to walk up a slope that the degree of its surface angle becomes apparent. In terms of angles, anything beyond 45 degrees is normally too steep to walk upon and therefore a problem to maintain. If the slope is a grass area it can mean an uneasy balancing act to keep it short, and if the sloping area is larger than a few feet it becomes a circus act with a lawnmower swinging on the end of a rope. This should never be recommended as a way to maintain a lawn, and alternative types of planting should be used to avoid the problem. The choice then is to find which are aesthetically pleasing and function the best.

In general terms the lower-growing, ground-hugging plants are better at retaining the soil. The way in which the plant spreads and propagates itself will determine how well it can hold the soil on a slope. The key is in selecting plants that will quickly knit together and stop soil from being washed downhill by rainwater. However, beware of plants knitting together so quickly that it becomes difficult to prevent them from spreading beyond the problem area.

In terms of using materials other than plants on slopes, it goes without saying that certain materials work better on certain gradients. There will be angles where gravel will migrate downwards, bark will slide off, and soil will become washed easily downhill. For each degree of slope there will be an optimum material, and common sense should prevail. It is obvious that loose materials such as gravel and bark will slide down a slope once it gets to a certain angle. If a particular material must be used for design reasons, then the steepness of the slope will have to be lessened. When using gravels on slopes, avoid smooth or rounded stones and always try to select a type that has angular pieces to lock them together and minimize the potential slippage. The depth of gravel can also have an effect—if it has been laid too deeply then it will be prone to movement when walked upon and accentuate the effects of the gradient.

Terracing

In hillside gardens, flat areas are, of course, at a premium. Almost everyone finds a need for some flat space whether for a table and chairs, the barbecue, or playing ball games and in small hillside gardens terracing may be a necessity. In larger gardens, it is more usual to see a combination of flat and sloping areas, and large garden owners should remember to celebrate the joys of slopes. They can provide an opportunity to display plants to good effect, and can also act as natural places for running water, which always brings interest to a garden.

If areas do have to be flattened, this will obviously require earth moving. Thereafter, there is naturally a requirement to retain the slope by holding the earth back in some way. There can be no doubt that any work in the garden

Below *Bergenia* × *hybrida* 'Silberlicht' used as groundcover.

Hedera helix is used to retain this gentle slope adjacent to a sweeping set of steps.

Hosta sieboldiana var. *elegans* will thrive in areas of partial shade, and certain cultivars will lighten up dark spaces.

Right *Parthenocissus henryana* used as groundcover to retain a slope.

will have a financial implication, but retaining walls, at least over a certain size, require the services of a structural engineer, which can be expensive. There are no official requirements for an engineer to be consulted. It is a personal decision that will be influenced by the existing soil conditions and the required height of wall. If there is a need for earth retention on any slopes adjacent to a property, it is always best to have an assessment from a structural engineer to ensure that there is no chance of slippage onto the house. Even if the owner is not concerned about this possibility, the condition of the slope may influence future purchasers of the property. Beyond the area closest to the house, an engineer should also be consulted when walls over 500 mm (20 in.) are needed.

The type of soil within a garden has a large effect upon the potential stability of any retaining wall. Heavy clay soils will naturally hold themselves together in contrast to fine sandy soils, which will collapse instantly. By digging a small hole and leaving it exposed to the weather conditions the soil type will become apparent. No soil type will make it impossible to have retaining walls but on some deeper foundations will be required, and on sandy soils the walls might be more difficult to construct.

If there is any doubt at all about heights or stability, professional advice should always be sought. Where any wall is used to retain soil there will be an inevitable build-up of water behind it. Usually this is solved by 'weep' holes, which are essentially holes through the base of a wall. For aesthetic and safety reasons, a drainage pipe usually needs to be laid behind a wall to collect the water, and then linked into a drainage system.

The appearance of any wall within a garden should be considered carefully. Where possible the material used should reflect the colours or materials of the house, helping to visually link house and garden. Common materials used to build retaining walls are brick or lengths of heavy-duty timber. Concrete blocks are typically used to provide structural stability when higher walls are required.

Managing the changing effects of shade

As trees grow, their impact on a garden changes. Any growth will undeniably extend the area of shade thereby altering the growing conditions of all plants in close proximity. This has quite a bearing upon the initial choice of plants, and without foresight some plants will die or struggle, as overstorey plants cast shade. This is where a long-term view is essential; it should always be remembered that gardens evolve over time. When putting shrubs and trees into schemes remember that they will form the core planting, and so will be the ones that outlive many of the others. This means that it is important to decide on certain key plants that you like and which have interest over a period of time, while initial plants can be sacrificed as the others mature and grow.

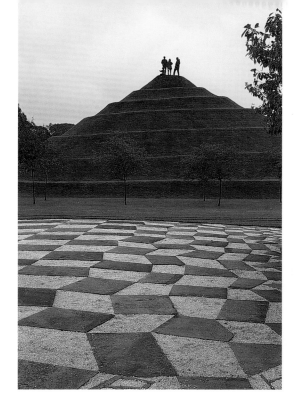

The scale of a grass mound can be worked out by relating it to the group of people standing at its summit.

Cohesion is brought to this long strip of terrace through the use of colour. The contrasting surface materials in toning colours help break up the area into comfortable spaces without losing the sense of unity.

Managing scale

Opening up an attractive view of the wider landscape beyond a garden can provide a very effective way of diminishing the garden's apparent size. There will be just as much lawn to cut, but when you look at it, it might not seem so daunting! The best idea is to frame a portion of the view, select the best part, and treat it as a focal point. Care should be taken if the garden is not large enough to take this treatment as it could look dwarfed by the larger landscape.

Colour can be also be manipulated to give the illusion of more or less space. Areas of colour contrast, such as large areas of block paving to the front of a house, seen in relation to small strips of planting, will give a visual reduction in size. The converse technique can also be employed, using materials of similar colour to make an area seem larger, and by creating linkages in colour to give the illusion of a single unified space. Although it may be rare for spaces in a larger gardens to be visually enlarged, they may need some manipulation and colour can often bring greater cohesion. For example, colour can pull together uneven boundaries and make the house sit better within the overall plot.

Visual enlargements

Even when designing larger gardens, there is sometimes the need to enlarge the appearance of a part of the garden to ensure that there is an overall balance around the property. One of the easiest ways to achieve this is to bring the wider landscape into the garden.

The curving lines of paving lead the eye into the garden and landscape beyond.

Integrating the immediate surroundings

In many large gardens and estates there are areas, such as fields, which will never be maintained to the same standard as the lawns surrounding the house. The key is to make these areas look as if they are an integral part of the garden. Ways to achieve this are by introducing wildflower meadows, plantings, or prairies with cut paths. These will dramatically reduce levels of maintenance, as well as adding a new dimension to the property in terms of both size and style.

Many larger houses have areas of farmland within the property that need to be incorporated into the estate. One possible solution is to introduce roundels or planted circles of trees to evoke a sense of management and to turn pastures into grazed parkland. Another solution is to create a focal point on the boundary of the property, for example, that can be seen from the house. Sculpture in the distance can join the landscape with the house and gives the perception of a deliberately designed space. The sculpture itself need not be an expensively commissioned piece, but something as simple as a monolith or standing stone. It could also be a piece of distinctly ornamental planting which stands out from a backdrop of more general woodland. The key factor is that it looks as if it has been deliberately sited.

The classical landscapes of the famous landscape gardeners William Kent (1716–1783) and Lancelot (Capability) Brown (1685–1748) used sculpture in this way by placing follies in the landscape as the end point to a vista. They demarcate the boundaries of land or views and ensure that the entire landscape is brought firmly into the garden.

Gardens with natural slopes, especially where there are views are from the higher ground, are ideal when it comes to having a seamless integration with

A section through a typical ha-ha. Ground has been excavated to form a ditch which acts as a field boundary and allows uninterrupted views from the garden.

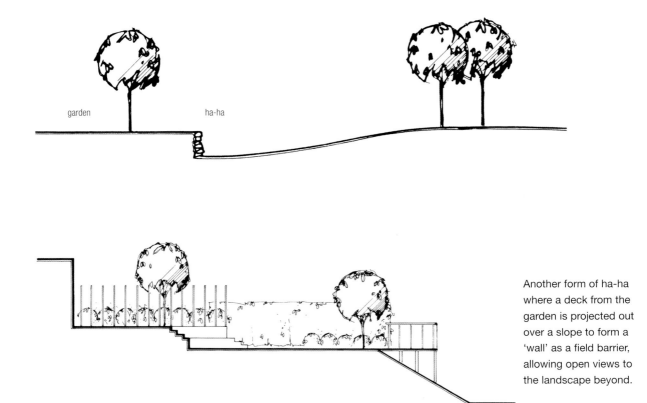

garden   ha-ha

Another form of ha-ha where a deck from the garden is projected out over a slope to form a 'wall' as a field barrier, allowing open views to the landscape beyond.

the landscape. Historically the ha-ha—a ditch to prevent cattle getting into the garden from adjacent land—also provided a means of allowing uninterrupted views.

A fence or defined boundary can ruin the view and cut the space in two, so if no boundary is required, there is an instant bonding between garden and landscape. In the scheme shown above, the slope has been used to great effect and the garden effectively drops off. 'Infinity pools'—pools of water with no visible outer edge—work in the same way in gardens adjacent to the sea, making them look as though they are continuous with it.

Levels

Levels within a garden naturally divide spaces. Steps can be used to either formalize the obvious difference in levels or to link two areas. By extending the steps into both the higher and the lower areas, a strong link can be created. As already discussed in detail in Chapter 3, it is important to employ the same material used for the steps to make the extension in order to ensure that visually the steps form an entire object.

Larger properties demand larger features—these steps are designed to be in scale with the house.

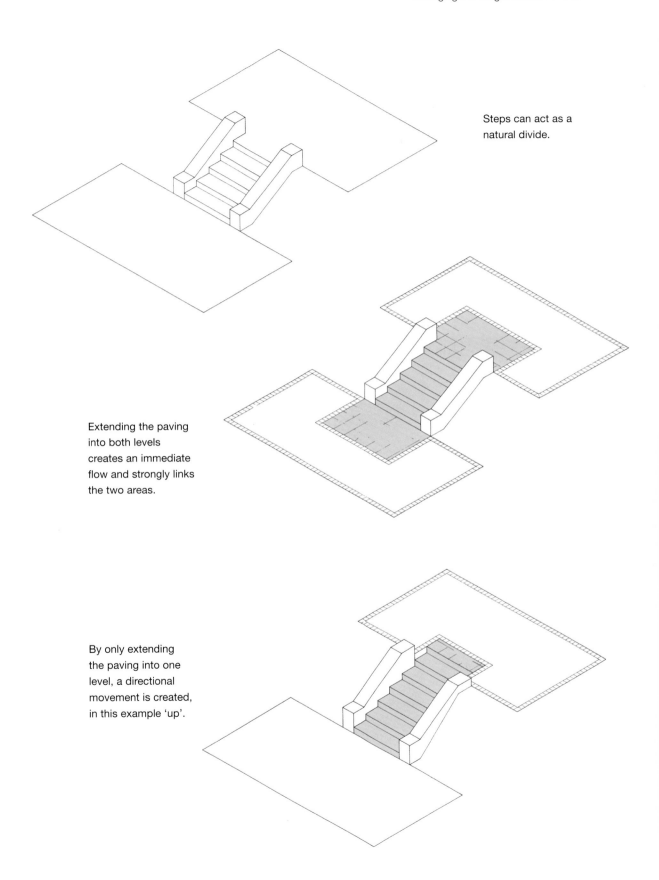

Steps can act as a natural divide.

Extending the paving into both levels creates an immediate flow and strongly links the two areas.

By only extending the paving into one level, a directional movement is created, in this example 'up'.

Quirky objects and *trompe l'oeil*

Other elements for managing the proportions of a garden involve surprise and change. While it is always good to have an element of flexibility in a garden, where it is not only the planting that alters with the seasons but also the placement of sculpture or other unusual objects, quirky elements and effects should not be relied upon. Gardens that strive to be different just for the sake of it are unlikely to survive the test of time. When using *trompe l'oeil* (trick of the eye techniques) or mirrors, the same caution applies. Used well, they can add something special to a garden, but should not be integral to the overall design and layout.

Since the apparent size of a garden is increased by having a close-mown lawn, the converse will also be the case: by leaving areas of grass, rough areas will seem smaller. When shadows and openings appear at either side of a garden, it increases the perceived size of the garden. Having smooth walls or fences

A water feature provides a focal point within a garden at Hampton Court Flower Show, Surrey, England.

Below The golden head of Apollo is a focal point and its effect is accentuated by the naturalistic style of the garden at Little Sparta, Lanarkshire, Scotland.

Balanced gateposts capped with giant replica hand-grenades frame the entrance to a themed section of the garden.

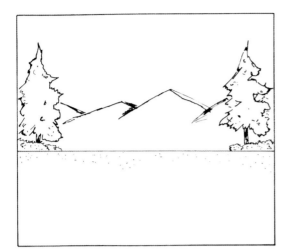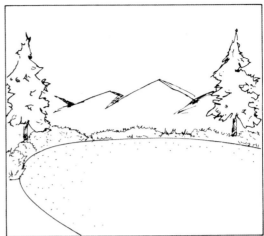

at either side of a garden will make the shape seem longer and again, 'rough' boundary treatments will visually shorten it. Visually reducing the size of your garden may help to make it seem more intimate, but remember that it will still require the same amount of maintenance!

Tricks of the eye can be useful when either trying to either disguise the size of a garden or to change its appearance. However, the use of mirrors or painted scenes should be approached with caution. As with most rules of design and aesthetics, it is important that techniques for tricking the eye are deliberate and not an apparent design error! In the same way, if symmetry is intended, accuracy should be the aim, as if one element is slightly 'out' it will ruin the whole effect.

When a border is viewed with a landscape backdrop, giving it a curving edge will make it blend more easily into the wider landscape.

Practical Recommendations

- Remember, where possible, to bring spaces down to a human scale.
- Concentrate areas of impact close to the house and where the garden is most used.
- Before trying to decide how large your patio area should be, measure your kitchen or dining-room table, see how many people can sit around it comfortably and then allow enough room for someone to walk around it.
- If any views exist from the garden, make the most of them. They may not be classically beautiful, but by carefully framing or leading the eye their effect can be maximized.
- Be very deliberate about paths and linkages within the garden. It is easy to under-design gardens. Ensure that any frequently used routes are appropriately defined and surfaced.
- Aim to have a series of walks or routes through the garden, each offering a different experience of the property.

Chapter 5

Gardens for Today

Reflections of society

Today, there is an undeniable trend towards gardens that are as low-maintenance as possible. This seems to be largely due to changes in the nature of family life over the past half-century or so. Now, it is common for all the adults in a household to be out at work for most of the day, meaning that time at home can be limited, and in some ways, more precious. The role of the garden in people's lives has changed as a result of this, and while there will always be some keen gardeners, many people will want the time they spend in their gardens to be more recreational and not always involving routine chores and maintenance.

We are used to cleaning our homes on a regular basis, but gardens need more than sweeping and dusting. They are living, growing entities that require nurturing and treating with a certain degree of skill. It is anxiety about a lack of that skill that makes some people a little fearful of their gardens. In reality, gardening can be as complicated or as easy as the individual makes it. Keen gardeners will know exactly how fruit trees should be pruned or how to treat any number of plant diseases, but this is not a prerequisite for owning a garden.

Anyone can enjoy apple trees in their garden and it matters little if they do not look as pretty or yield as much fruit as those that have been pruned by a professional gardener. Gardens can and should be designed to fit with the skills and desired level of input of the people who own them. A good designer will never saddle clients with levels of maintenance that are unsustainable in terms of their skills or available time.

Another consequence of changing work patterns is that gardens are used at different times. There is a need to extend the period over which the garden can be used both on a daily basis and over the seasons. People often want to be able to use their gardens at night, or at least early evening, from early spring to late

Apple trees bring welcome flower and fruit to any garden without demanding much time or effort. The blossoms are shown off to great effect when trained against a wall.

Opposite The crisp lines of the pool are carried through to simple blocks of planting which combine to create a serene, minimalist scene.

Lighting this tree
has turned it
into a night-time
'sculpture'.

autumn. They also require areas that are close to, and easily accessible from, their houses, which can be used for dining or sitting out. In northern temperate climates, many people like to make the most of every drop of sun as soon as it appears. Thus, when designing gardens, we place patios and seating areas to chase the sun around the house until it vanishes. Similarly, in very hot climates, gardens are planned to make the most of shade as it moves around the property.

The need to fit our gardens around our working lives has made the introduction of lighting a necessity. It can be used in many ways and create striking effects. Focal points during the day can remain focal points at night with the help of uplighters and spotlights set on trees or sculpture. Lighting can also be used to create a mood within a garden. Therefore, though some clients at first connect the idea of exterior lighting with images of Las Vegas, when subtly used they might be surprised at the way it can transform their gardens. Lighting is not only about aesthetics; it is also functional and can be helpful in achieving safety at night, ensuring that steps and changes in level are clearly visible.

The main issue facing owners of larger gardens is how to achieve a minimal maintenance burden. This burden can be significant—many owners of large gardens spend one day per week during the summer cutting grass—so the subject needs careful consideration. This is not to say that garden owners necessarily resent time spent in this way, because many of them will have bought larger gardens expecting to spend a lot of time caring for them. The majority of owners would, however, choose to reduce the time taken up with carrying out routine work, so that more time can be spent on more enjoyable tasks. Many people only learn the joy of caring for a garden later in life when other responsibilities have lessened. Once the bug has been caught they can become obsessional in the amount of time and effort they are willing to devote to their gardens.

Large-scale trends

There are several prevalent movements within garden and landscape design at present. Prominently displayed at flower shows, such trends are becoming increasingly popular with owners of large-scale spaces seeking to re-create the effects in their own gardens.

Trends within garden design are not dissimilar to trends within any other sphere of design. They are, however, slower to surface and relatively slow to enter the mainstream consciousness of the public. Fashions in garden design are influenced not simply by issues of style, but also by wider issues such as sustainability. This much-flaunted word means a great deal to some and not much to many. Gardeners are likely to be more in tune with nature and aware of the consequences of their actions. For many gardeners sustainability means not creating waste, and being as self-sufficient as possible. That may involve turning all garden waste into compost and re-using it within the garden rather than sending it to a landfill site. Others may choose to have gardens that do not require irrigation or watering but are designed to thrive within their local site conditions. Both of these preferences are becoming more prevalent. The decision may involve not conforming to what is expected, such as having a lush lawn that relies on banks of sprinklers dousing it with imported water. These

This show garden is interesting for its limited use of colour, simple areas of paving, and structural tree planting combined with herbaceous perennials.

decisions should not ultimately mean that huge areas of the populated world are returned to sandy barren desert, just that other forms of design and planting will need to be used to create the desired effect. As with other aspects of life, we cannot have everything. If clients request grass because they play golf then it may be inevitable, but it should be at the back of everyone's minds to at least consider the options and not instantly opt for the most obvious one. Within this chapter I have singled out three trends which are increasingly visible within the design of gardens. They are: minimalism, new styles of planting and the impact of gardens at flower shows. These are by no means the only major current influences on gardens, but they are having an impact that cannot be ignored.

Minimalism

The art of minimalism is not just about removing all the clutter from a garden. It is about paring the garden down to leave the core elements with a much greater scope for the impact of line and style. However simplicity in itself does not constitute minimalism. A minimalist garden is one which is simplistic in design but rich in line and form, and which will promote a sense of calm.

The sense of calm will be engendered not only by the lack of clutter, but also by the lack of objects that can divert the brain, leaving it freer to think about other things, and giving the garden the potential to be a contemplative retreat. Minimalism has, of course, been around for centuries in some of the simplistic garden spaces created by the Japanese and Chinese through to the Moorish gardens of Spain. With the architecture of Le Corbusier in the 1930s came the advent of what could be classed as minimalist architecture. It is probably true to say that minimalism never quite took off in garden design in the same way. Architecture at the time was seen as the preserve of the rich, and never quite made it into the mainstream. This was even more the case with gardens. There was more incentive to design minimal gardens in arid or semi-arid areas where plant choice was more restricted, but in climates that can support a wide range of plants there was less of a reason to pare down the palette.

The trend for minimalism in design generally demonstrates a need to 'come up with something different'. This is not to cast judgement on the merits or integrity of the designers using this style, but it shows that they are wondering what will mark out the late twentieth and early twenty-first centuries from earlier periods in terms of garden design. The recent taste for a huge variety of styles within gardens will mean that this period will be not be famous for a single, over-riding style.

Within the current 'melting pot' of garden design the resurrection of minimalism can be largely attributed to the English garden designer Christopher Bradley-Hole. There are examples of minimalist gardens being created throughout the

Simple rectangular shapes combine to create a minimalist paradise at this Chelsea Flower Show garden.

The clean lines of the boardwalk act as a foil to the swaying bands of herbaceous perennials.

Lush green planting accentuates the colour and line of the white pergola and paving in this modern tropical garden.

Above right Bold, wild-looking planting is restrained by the clean lines of the swimming pool.

world, but the show gardens and writings of Bradley-Hole bring these disparate icons of style together to form a worldwide style movement. It seems that minimalism is a style that will always be with us, more prominent in some periods than others, each time slightly changed to reflect current beliefs and thinking.

The minimalist garden could be seen as the ultimate artistic experience— a work of art that can be walked through, surrounding those experiencing it. Of course a huge number of gardens and spaces could be viewed as works of art, using plants, timber and stone instead of canvas and oils. Perhaps because shape and form is such a vital part of minimalist gardens, visitors experience a heightened awareness of the space around them.

How to design a minimalist garden

Simplicity of line in the structure of the garden is reinforced by using a limited range of plants, encouraging the onlooker to focus on the form of the plants themselves. Instead of a bed of irises composed of a variety of colours and shapes, the minimalist garden designer would use fewer varieties to emphasize their colour and form. Minimalist designers also use plants as specimens, as if they are exhibits in an art gallery.

The minimalist design must have a very strong concept. Integration with the house will usually be key, and the building itself is likely to have a strongly modern feel. Many successful minimalist gardens are closely associated with homes

When the planting and shapes used within a garden are simple and uncluttered, colour can be introduced to built structures with dramatic effect.

that have been designed using clean lines, limited materials and strong colours. This does not mean that thatched cottages or ordinary suburban houses cannot have minimalist gardens, but in these cases extra care would be needed in managing the relationship of the garden and the house.

Care should be taken that these gardens do not become too clinical. Clean lines can be complemented by planting, water or lighting which introduce elements of change and variety. A garden does not want to feel like a stone or concrete epitaph.

The walls that are a common feature of minimalist gardens become excellent tools when screening is required. As dividing and framing elements they give a rigid framework to the garden and clearly define the spaces. Water is an element that adds to any garden, but in a minimalist garden its effect is multiplied.

Minimalist gardens tend to have an inward focus and are naturally suited to courtyard gardens. They are historically reminiscent of courtyard sanctuaries which hid from the outside world and the heat of foreign climes.

They can encourage peace and tranquillity through restraint in colour and line. It is difficult to find a design recipe for peace, but simplicity seems to work. Space between elements can be as important as the walls that enclose the space or the plants that divide it. Use of light is crucial in minimalist gardens, whether reflecting off shining planes of stone or in the shadow cast by a specimen tree. In sun-drenched regions of the world shadow can be used to maximum effect. In the greyer north of Scotland, walls may have to be lighter and shapes stronger to

The Yves St Laurent garden in Marrakesh is a classic example of the enclosed Moorish courtyard.

gain such contrasts. The effects of light and shade in minimalist gardens can be used equally dramatically at night.

Minimalist guidelines:
- Aim for clean, uncluttered walls
- Obey the rules of proportion (see Chapter 4)
- Focus on the form of the plant either as a specimen, as a group of one species or a matrix planting, usually of grasses, linking to the wider landscape.
- Use water as a focal point, either as flat reflective planes or a very simple gently flowing feature.
- Be bold when designing in a space with few existing characteristics. When the site has existing beautiful views or natural features, use restraint.
- Keep materials simple.
- Do not attempt to integrate the garden into the natural landscape: clean lines and bold shapes will give an asymmetrical balance with nature.

A traditional border of summer herbaceous perennials in a classic Scottish garden.

New styles of planting

Naturalistic and prairie planting

Renowned plantsman, Piet Oudolf, has been very influential in a re-awakening of interest in herbaceous perennials. Typically associated with English cottage gardens, and recently often regarded as old-fashioned, herbaceous plants are now being given a new lease on life, and through their careful breeding and use, a new style of garden design has emerged. Following in the footsteps of the German designer Karl Foerster (1874–1970), a key figure in the selective breeding of herbaceous plants, Oudolf has brought forward new cultivars whose parents would have been recognized in our grandmothers' gardens. Foerster systematically preserved some herbaceous plants that would otherwise have been lost to us. He believed, like Oudolf, that the garden plants we have become used to garden plants that have disproportionately large flowers for the size of plant. By using plant cultivars (cultivated varieties), which are closer to their native ancestors, the effect is a much more natural one. As a result of selective breeding, these cultivars are much more robust and self-supporting so the need for stak-

A simple band of *Perovskia* 'Blue Spire' is used to dramatic effect here against a background of dark brown timber.

This up-to-date version of the traditional herbaceous perennial border includes a much more limited palette of plants with their number increased to bold effect.

ing and propping top-heavy plants is dramatically reduced. Oudolf undertook extensive field growing of traditional favourites, which allowed him to carefully select the best of the traditional plants. In addition, new and exciting colours and shapes of flower have also been cultivated and can be combined with plants selected for their longer flowering periods.

These techniques have enabled Oudolf to experiment with a new style of design using herbaceous perennials which has come to be called 'naturalistic planting', 'prairie planting' or 'wave planting'. This concentrates more on the overall look of a planting scheme rather than the individual plants within it, focusing first on the shapes of flowers and seedheads, then on leaf shape and texture, and only finally on the colour of the flowers and foliage. This is quite a leap from the traditional way of selection primarily by the colour of flowers and foliage. Experts such as Oudolf have also made a point of reviving some of the species and varieties that have lost gardeners' favour over the decades. By studying plants in their natural environment, and focusing on the way in which shapes and colours combine in nature, they have been able to replicate a more natural planting style with herbaceous plants within gardens.

Oudolf suggests some useful recipes for combining plants. The effect of the plant lasts, he stresses, "from when it first emerges from the ground in spring to when its rain-lashed and frost-scoured remains collapse sometime over the winter." It is this over-arching view of a plant's form and attributes throughout the seasons that promotes a proper understanding of it. Only with a truly in-depth knowledge of plant characteristics and growth can the naturalistic planting schemes be created. Schemes have been designed around plant groupings based on the shape of the flowers or flower-heads of species that complement each other if they flower together, or upon flower, seedhead and plant shapes that combine well.

Oudolf divides herbaceous perennials into five groups of flowers or seed-heads. These are:

1. **Spires:** imagine a church spire, upward-pointing with flowers packed onto a stem such as *Digitalis* (foxglove) species.
2. **Buttons and globes:** pretty self-explanatory, balls on stems such as *Echinops* species.
3. **Plumes:** imagine feathers, loose flowery heads that can be used with stronger shaped plants such as *Filipendula* species.
4. **Umbels:** short flower stalks emerging from a common point, like umbrella ribs such as like *Daucus carota* (wild carrot).
5. **Daisies:** or daisy-like heads such as *Echinacea*.

These five shapes are combined with a variety of screen, curtain and filler plants to form the basis for a scheme, obviously taking into account the colour and texture of the plants as well. Such planting schemes can appear complicated to create but there is quite a lot of repetition throughout any herbaceous border. The plants identified as fillers and screens are good for backdrops and to link groups of plants which have quite distinctive features.

The circular brick feature is set within swathes of screen and curtain plants. It acts as a 'hinge' within the garden, serving as a temporary stopping point before leading on to another path.

Bold swathes of herbaceous perennials adjacent to the house complement the period feel of the property while the overall sweep of the planting brings a bold, modern style to the garden.

The seedheads of *Phlomis* have an important sculptural presence during the autumn and winter.

In very simplistic terms, the starting point is to select groups of two or three plants that seem to work together in terms of colour and shape, and then arrange them into groups by height. The tallest of these groups should be planted at the rear of the bed, the shortest towards the front. Approximately ten plants now form a section of flowerbed. This can then be repeated with a grouping of plants of a different size. These groups are repeated alternately along the length of the bed with linking plants between. The linking plants should obviously be of a similar size to the plants adjacent to them, but also provide a contrast.

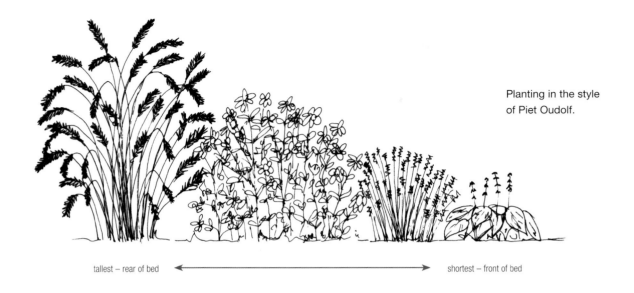

Planting in the style
of Piet Oudolf.

tallest – rear of bed ⟷ shortest – front of bed

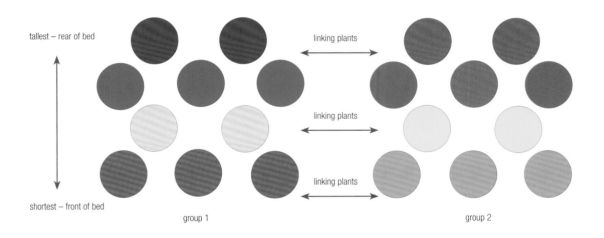

tallest – rear of bed

linking plants

shortest – front of bed

linking plants

linking plants

group 1

group 2

The style of planting shown in Piet Oudolf's plan is not just about a short burst of colour in the height of summer. By focusing on the form of the flowerhead, he has created aspirational images of herbaceous plantings during the autumn and right through winter. At these times some traditional herbaceous borders could be barren of interest, but within his schemes, seedheads and grasses combine to form beautiful frosted images. A word of caution for those with gardens in very damp areas is that many plants will tend to rot in the winter, requiring more careful selection of plant cultivars to allow seedheads to remain intact for any length of time.

Planting design is very subjective and personal, and it is important that while following the guidelines of the experts, the garden owner experiments with his or her own blend of plants. It is also important to remember that while experts

A great swathe of lavenders provides periodic dramatic colour but allows the eye to be drawn to the wonderful stone and brick walls at other periods of the year.

such as Piet Oudolf will suggest lists of possible plants for certain climates, they are unlikely to be global templates, and plant choice will need to vary from country to country.

The current trend for using herbaceous perennials within gardens has one major drawback: where a garden relies on the beauty of these plants alone, they are obviously very susceptible to the changes of growth and time. Looking back through history, the gardens of the great plantspeople have not endured, while the more formal Classical gardens of Italy, France and even England, still persist centuries later due to their structure and use of plants, not the plants themselves. When it comes to gardens filled with beautiful perennials, the effect will be very short-lived if maintenance is not carefully observed. It is not solely a case of weeding but also involves regular dividing and re-planting, every three to five years.

Many experts have a very ruthless attitude toward plants, systematically weeding out all those that do not perform as successfully as they could. It is an attitude we can all learn from. Too often we accept plants that are either there before we buy a garden, or plants that have sentimental value. By returning to the wild relatives of the garden cultivars, there is a natural affinity with the landscape beyond. Planting schemes can evoke a real sense of emotion in the onlooker. They are capable of transporting the visitor to a different dimension and giving gardens a real 'spirit of place'.

The structural capabilities of plants have become a focus of Piet Oudolf's plant breeding and that is what has guided the plant selection process. As well as herbaceous plants, Oudolf also likes to use more architectural features in the garden. Whether it is the well-defined path network, the clipped hedges that divide spaces, or the brick walls that form the boundaries, they can all act as wonderful foils for this loose and naturalistic style of planting.

And what about shrubs? Many people, much as they may like herbaceous perennials, could never live with a garden barren of woody shrubs. Shrubs can of course be combined with herbaceous perennials—the important thing to consider alongside aesthetics is the extent to which they will be in competition with each other for space and water.

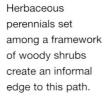

Herbaceous perennials set among a framework of woody shrubs create an informal edge to this path.

The impact of show gardens

Show gardens have a major impact upon what garden owners, as well as garden designers, expect from a garden. Whether the Bundesgartenshau in Germany, the Canadian Festival in Quebec, Chaumont Garden Festival in France or the famous Chelsea Flower Show in London, the impact that these 'fashion show-cases' have upon the gardening world cannot be underestimated. They are the catwalk equivalents of the garden world and the ideas and trends that are first displayed at these events are destined to influence our back gardens. Although rarely slavishly copied as designer fashions are, they have a big impact upon the types of planting and styles of design that become part of many gardeners' 'wish lists'.

Some clients do ask designers for an exact copy of a show garden to be some-how transposed onto their own plot, but a good designer will warn that every

This garden displays the level of 'polish' and attention to detail that has come to be expected by owners accustomed to seeing show gardens.

The radial patterns within this garden have been reflected in the shape of the bold curving water body. This ensures that the garden is unified with each element leading into the next.

site is different, and the plants may not suit the site conditions. It should also be pointed out that show gardens are designed to be temporary with no consideration of the longer term. However, the designer should be able to find out what elements of the show garden a client particularly admired and adapt these ideas for the different location and aspect.

The appearance of instant gardens like those at the flower shows does present a challenge to the garden designer, as some clients will ask for elements, if not the whole thing, to be replicated. It is of course possible to plant a mature specimen and achieve an instant appearance of age, but how can growth then be frozen in time? Gardens mature slowly, and their appearance changes constantly.

It is difficult to achieve a static look unless a garden is very minimal in terms of planting and unless those plants are slow-growing with little variation.

The combined influence of show gardens, along with the current obsession for 'garden makeover' television programmes, does encourage people to think that a quick fix is possible for their gardens. These are usually owners with little experience of gardening—anyone who spends time tending a garden soon finds that nothing is permanent, or unchanging. The show garden phenomenon is not new—they have been in evidence for as long as growers have wanted to showcase plants, or architects set their design statements in context. It must be realized, however, that although they seem like giant sweetshops, they can sell only ideas and inspiration. Display gardens are merely objects of desire.

Materials and garden furniture are the elements of show gardens that are, to some extent, easy to copy. Tasteful examples of garden furniture seen at flower shows turn up at the local DIY store within a matter of months, and manipulation of aspects of the hard landscaping of our gardens is possible and can create new effects. Show garden designers are constantly searching for new ways to inspire and amaze. We see metal gabion baskets, normally retaining slopes at the side of motorways, transformed into architectural pieces of sculpture with rows of blue glass bottles replacing grey stone chips. Clusters of optical fibres turn them into seats for night-time. It is when we see the ordinary transformed into the extraordinary that our minds race as we attempt to see how they could be used in our own spaces. To some extent, they usually can. Since it is unlikely that many new materials will appear and be used extensively within gardens, it is the designer's challenge to re-invent the old. Timber, stone and plants are there waiting for a new twist to be applied to them. We see plastics, metal, glass and concrete come and go, but natural materials are perennially popular and practical.

Water is another enduring element of show gardens. It never fails to add an additional dimension to any garden. The value of its sound, either when cascading or trickling, cannot be underestimated. It has the power to mesmerize and bewilder onlookers. Even a still, reflective pool captures the sun and clouds racing across the sky, or pulls the eye across it to a focal point beyond. Water is constantly being used to new effect. Two of its inherent qualities—the ability to cling to smooth surfaces, and that of combining with air to create a white foamy mass—mean that the possible effects are endless.

One of the great things about show gardens is the meticulous level of detail that is employed. It is not just that every battered or bruised leaf has been removed in an effort to win over the judges' approval, but the demonstration of a systematic and thorough approach to looking at every element within the garden. It is that attention to detail that can prolong the enjoyment of any garden.

Extra points of interest obviously provide more to hold the visitor's attention for longer. These don't have to be formal points of interest such as pieces of sculpture, but features such as brick paths laid in an interesting pattern. To a

This dramatic garden centres on a waterfall which is guaranteed to add an extra dimension to any garden and is particularly effective in a show gardens as it attracts onlookers.

The simple ornament and muted gravel ensure that attention is directed towards the colourful, wide-ranging planting.

degree, this effect is also more to do with creative input than money spent. Like interiors, gardens that reflect the personalities of their owners always have a special charm. While there are not so many obvious ways of doing this in a garden—it is not as easy to display family photographs in a courtyard—there will nevertheless be ways that the owner's personality can be seen outside. The style of ornament and colour schemes employed are obvious ways. Injecting elements of humour and things that are personal will give the garden an individuality that will set it apart from others.

Successful show gardens usually have a strong concept or theme underlying their design. This will not always be appropriate for a private garden, but taking elements of an existing or proposed style, and repeating them throughout, will help to unify the space. This can be done through colour, materials, or other elements in the garden. Of course if there is a strong desire for a certain overall style, such as a Mediterranean feel, this can be reinforced by building upon any features that are sympathetic to the theme.

The treatment of plants in show gardens can turn out to be fairly unrealistic when applied to real gardens. In show gardens they are arranged for instant effect and in a real garden, growing at different rates, their spacing would almost certainly not work. Show garden plants will be chosen to be flowering at the same time and to look their best for a very short period. In a real garden some all-year-round colour is usually the aim rather than a mass of colour at one time. And the maintenance challenges that afflict any gardener are not an issue in a show garden where there are no children or pets to make dirty footprints on white-painted concrete walls, where grass cuttings have not fallen into the beautifully crafted stainless steel rill, and frost has not cracked the ornate terracotta urns. There are lots of questions that we should ask before wishing a show garden into our back yard.

Practical Recommendations

- When it comes to plants like apple trees, do not worry about precision pruning. Unless you are planning on trying to get the largest crop just enjoy them for their aesthetic appeal.
- Simplicity in the garden is easy to achieve and can lead to calming, serene spaces.
- You can afford to be bold when designing in a space with few existing characteristics but when a site has either beautiful views or natural features restraint is called for.
- When selecting plants for a garden focus on the overall shape and long-term appeal of the plant, not just the instant and short-lived effect of when it is in flower.
- A garden does not have to be made from expensive materials to be interesting it is often more about how materials are used than the materials themselves that makes a garden interesting.
- Concentrate detail within a garden at the points where users will spend time. Pay special attention to spaces around seating areas and try to add interest to views that you wish users to spend more time enjoying.

Chapter 6

Useful Plants for Design Purposes

The plants listed here are grouped according to the function they are most successfully used to fulfil. The list is by no means exhaustive—it is merely intended as a preliminary list that illustrates the way certain characteristics of plants can be used to perform a design function. The plants selected here are generally very robust and will grow throughout Europe and in much of the United States but there are, of course, hundreds of alternatives that may be equally effective and better suited to very specific site aspects and conditions. The key is to understand what characteristic of the plant makes it suitable for a particular purpose.

Plants for Framing and Focal Points

The following list identifies plants that stand out as suitable specimens for framing and use as focal points because of their distinctive shape, colour or other characteristics.

Weeping plants

Betula pendula 'Youngii' (Young's weeping birch), 4.5–7.5 m (15–25 ft.) Dome-shaped, weeping tree whose branches will reach the ground. Good autumn colour with nicely fissured trunk on the mature specimens. A good weeping specimen whose autumn foliage will act as a focal point.

Cedrus atlantica 'Glauca Pendula' (weeping blue Atlas cedar), 15–16 m (50–55 ft.). A slow-growing tree that looks at home in very large gardens. Its attractive foliage is silver-blue to grey-blue. Best for framing parts of the wider landscape.

Opposite Weeping trees can be used to draw the eye down their pendulous foliage and through to views beyond.

Ilex vomitoria 'Pendula' (weeping Yaupon holly), 3–4.5 m (10–15 ft.) The light-coloured, smooth bark on this specimen provides a lovely contrast with the dark green leaves. It has outstanding translucent red berries and is a useful plant to frame views or objects within a garden, given its relatively small size.

Prunus × *subhirtella* 'Pendula' (weeping Higan cherry), 3–6 m (10–20 ft.) A dramatic specimen that catches the eye particularly when flowering in early spring.

Salix purpurea 'Pendula' (purple osier, American weeping willow), 3.5–4.5 m (12–15 ft.) A graceful, narrow specimen with long, sinuous wands tinted purple and covered with long, slender, glaucous leaves. The beautiful tinges of purple make this tree a subtle focal point within a garden.

Columnar plants

Carpinus betulus 'Columnaris' (common hornbeam, European hornbeam), 7.5–12 m (25–40 ft.) This deciduous tree has oval, dark green leaves and it forms a dense solid mass of foliage. A lovely tree that looks its best in a well manicured setting, so is well suited to formal areas close to the house. It works well as a focal point or to line either side of a driveway where it can frame the property and accentuate the sense of arrival.

Ginkgo biloba (maidenhair tree, ginkgo), 9–14 m (30–45 ft.) One of the brightest, yellow-leaved trees for autumn. The unusual, fan-shaped leaves make this an interesting tree to have in any garden. While its autumn colour is dazzling, take care when siting this tree that it does not over-dominate.

Juniperus chinensis 'Robust Green', 4.5–6 m (15–20 ft.) A handsome, upright, mid-green, columnar tree. Works well in conjunction with a focal point but equally can be used *en masse* as a dense screen. Suits a large garden setting.

Prunus 'Amanogawa' (ornamental cherry, Lombardy poplar cherry), 4.5–6 m (15–20 ft.) Tightly formed upright tree that has clusters of small pink flowers in April and May. These pink pillars can dazzle in springtime and against a purple backdrop will create a strong focal point. Like other columnar plants, it can be planted on either side of a feature to frame it.

Robinia pseudoacacia 'Pyramidalis' (false acacia locust, black locust), 12–15 m (40–50 ft.) An upright form of this attractively leaved tree that has lovely pendulous flowers. In some locations it is considered a weed but good specimens are very attractive. They can be great plants for use in the garden as focal points or for naturalizing into the landscape beyond and linking with specimens in the garden.

Taxus baccata 'Fastigiata' (Irish yew), 1.2–1.8 m (4–6 ft.) Deep green evergreen foliage grows faster than is commonly perceived. Excellent as individual specimens although care should be taken to not plant too many as their foliage may darken the overall appearance of the garden. Yew's classic shape makes it very good for flanking a focal point. Immediately lends a formal look to a garden.

Tilia cordata 'Greenspire' (small-leaved lime, little leaf linden), 9–12 m (30–40 ft.) Mid-green leaves on this attractive tree cast quite dense shade, which can be useful in the right location. The upright and rapid growth habit of this specimen makes it a good choice to flank either side of a garden feature or view.

Other upright trees which also make strong focal points are:
Crataegus monogyna 'Stricta' (hawthorn)
Chamaecyparis lawsoniana 'Stewartii' (Stewart golden cypress)
Fagus sylvatica 'Dawyck' (beech)
Populus nigra 'Italica' (Lombardy poplar)
Quercus robur f. *fastigiata* (English oak)
Sorbus aucuparia 'Fastigiata' (rowan, mountain ash)
Thuja plicata (Western red cedar)
Tilia platyphyllos 'Fastigiata' (lime, linden)

Clear-stemmed plants

The following trees all have a visible lower section of trunk which is very useful in defining spaces without impeding views. They are extremely valuable in areas where a canopy of shade is required and as a result make ideal trees to place seating under. Their clear stems can also be valuable in terms of providing a vertical framing element.

Acer rubrum 'October Glory' (scarlet maple), 13 m (40 ft.) Tall, round-headed tree that is among the last to change colour in autumn but when it does the dazzling red colour makes it stand out as a focal point.

Betula utilis var. *jacquemontii* (Himalayan birch), 6–9 m (20–30 ft.) Mid-green, toothed leaves on a slightly narrow, open tree famed for its stunning white bark that is particularly evident in winter. The white verticals of the trunks make it ideal to frame either side of an object.

Gleditsia triacanthos 'Sunburst' (honey locust), 5–6.5 m (18–22 ft.) Medium-sized tree that looks similar to *Robinia*. Yellow foliage can look at bit sickly on its own so ensure that it is with mid-green plants or has them as a backdrop.

Liriodendron tulipifera (tulip tree), 18–24 m (60–80 ft.) A big tree that has lovely mid-green leaves and flowers like tulip blooms that unfortunately do not appear until the tree is at least ten years old and by that time they can be pretty high up.

Quercus palustris (pin oak), 15–20 m (50–60 ft.) Quick-growing tree, ideal for planting in large expanse of lawn. Lower branches are slightly pendulous and nice to look under towards a feature or view beyond.

Tilia americana 'Nova' (American lime, American linden), 12–18 m (40–60 ft.) Great for glossy green foliage, but not suited to areas prone to drought. Sweetly scented cup-shaped yellow flowers in midsummer on a tree that casts deep shade.

Other trees with clear stems:
  Acer platanoides (Norway maple)
  Betula papyrifera (paper bark birch, canoe birch)
  Liquidambar styraciflua (sweet gum)
  Catalpa bignonioides (catalpa, Indian bean tree)
  Crataegus viridis 'Winter King' (green hawthorn)
  Fagus sylvatica Atropurpurea Group (purple beech)
  Platanus × *hispanica* (London plane tree)
  Prunus cerasifera (cherry plum)
  Quercus coccinea (scarlet oak)
  Quercus rubra (red oak)
  Robinia pseudoacacia (false acacia, black locust)
  Salix caprea (goat willow, pussy willow)
  Zelkova serrata (Japanese zelkova, swaleaf zelkova)

Plants for Woodland and Shelterbelts

Plant materials and methods of planting

Plants used to create woodland and shelterbelts can of course be any size, but when sites are windy and prone to extremes of weather, small is best. Small plants will establish and grow more quickly than larger plants that often 'stagnate' for several years before they start growing. A further reason is that woodlands and shelterbelts tend to be large, and anything other than small plants would make the planting overly expensive. Typically, two-year-old plants will work best as they can be bought cheaply and planted easily.

The planting of any large area within a garden is typically carried out in autumn or spring to ensure that the plants can be bought bare-rooted ensuring a further cost saving. A bare-rooted plant is field-grown and dug up by the nursery and then replanted by the purchaser while it is still dormant. Only deciduous species may be treated this way. Interestingly, once a plant is containerized, its price rises dramatically.

Barerooted plants do not need a big hole dug for them. Simply cut a slot into the ground and insert the roots of the two-year-old plants with a measure of slow-release fertilizer. Once the tree has been firmed in, a layer of mulch should be placed around each plant to restrict nearby weeds from competing with the newly planted trees. It is advisable to have previously sprayed the entire area of the shelterbelt or woodland with weedkiller to limit initial competition and allow the plants to establish more rapidly. When planting, any side shoots should be removed to encourage vertical growth and minimize water loss through the leaves. Often, protective fencing will be required around the perimeter of the shelterbelt to stop rodents getting into the planting. This fence should also typically be at a distance of 2 m (6–7 ft.) away from the planting, to prevent deer or other larger animals from reaching over and eating the young plants.

Shelterbelt Guidelines

- Shelterbelts should be a minimum width of 20 m (60 ft.) to work properly as a windbreak and visual barrier. Typically they are planted using a grid system. This makes planting, tree removal and maintenance much easier.
- Nurse and dominant tree species should be planted on a 2 m (6 ft.) grid, with the understorey species on a 1 m (3 ft.) grid. This will ensure that the trees are not too close together, and that not too much will have to be removed once the trees start growing. It becomes a balancing act between initial impact and follow-up maintenance.
- The blocks that form the main part of the shelterbelt are made up from two main groupings. The first are known as the co-dominants and these plants

will form the main part of the structure of the shelterbelt. They are typically a mix of two species that will rapidly and easily grow in the specific conditions of the garden. The second group is a mixture between nurse and dominant species: the nurse species will provide rapid growth and shelter the dominant species until they are established.

- Groups of co-dominant species and nurse/dominant mixes are normally planted in two-species blocks to make thinning and felling operations easier, with at least 10 plants in each block.
- By planting a band of the understorey plants on the edge of the belt, a more efficient vertical edge will be created and this will perform two functions. It will produce a larger area for the wind to hit, and also discourage people from entering the belt while it is establishing. Understorey species should be planted in single species blocks of at least 10 plants (preferably 20–50) to make an impact.
- Shelterbelts are usually on the edges of a garden and not next to the major areas of use. Consequently they can be planted in large blocks. The planting is for a purpose and is not merely aesthetic.
- The width of shelterbelts, size of groups and width of understorey bands are all flexible to suit specific site requirements. The wider it is, the more impact it will have.

Shelterbelt planting mixes

In general within shelterbelts, 90 per cent of the planting should be trees, with the remaining 10 per cent being understorey planting. That 90 per cent of trees can be further sub-divided into 72 per cent of dominant/nurse group species and 18 per cent co-dominant species.

Two planting mixes have been given here. The key when planting your own shelterbelt is not to rigidly copy the actual species chosen but to understand why they have been chosen and replicate the types of planting using species that will thrive in your region. The mixes have a combination of fast-growing and evergreen species, and these will give rise to the eventual main shelterbelt planting which in these cases is *Fraxinus excelsior* (ash, European ash). This dominant planting should reflect the types of planting within the wider landscape of the garden and could be anything from *Sassafras albidum* (common sassafras) to *Abies lasiocarpa* (subalpine fir, Rocky Mountain fir).

Wet or badly drained sites

		%
Nurse:	*Betula pubescens* (common white birch)	5
	Larix kaempferi (Japanese larch)	15
	Picea sitchensis (sitka spruce)	15
	Salix caprea (goat willow, pussy willow)	5
Co-dominants:	*Alnus glutinosa* (black alder)	10
	Populus nigra (black poplar)	10
Dominant:	*Fraxinus excelsior* (ash, European ash)	40
Total tree component:		100
Understorey:	*Cornus alba* (red-barked dogwood, Tatarian dogwood)	25
	Crataegus monogyna (common hawthorn)	15
	Prunus padus (bird cherry, mayday tree)	10
	Rosa canina (dog rose)	10
	Sambucus nigra (common elder, elderberry)	25
	Viburnum opulus (Guelder rose, European cranberry bush)	15
Total understorey component:		100

General to dry sites

		%
Nurse:	*Betula pendula* (silver birch)	10
	Larix kaempferi (Japanese larch)	15
	Picea sitchensis (sitka spruce)	15
Co-Dominants:	*Alnus incana* (grey alder)	10
	Populus trichocarpa (black cottonwood)	10
Dominant:	*Fraxinus excelsior* (ash, European ash)	40
Total tree component:		100
Understorey:	*Corylus avellana* (cobnut, European filbert)	15
	Crataegus monogyna (common hawthorn)	25
	Prunus padus (bird cherry, mayday tree)	10
	Rosa rugosa (Ramanas rose, sea tomato)	10
	Sambucus nigra (common elder, elderberry)	15
	Symphoricarpos albus (snowberry, common snowberry)	15
	Viburnum opulus (Guelder rose, European cranberry bush)	10
Total understorey component:		100

Woodland Guidelines

- The same matrix principles should be applied as for shelterbelts, for example, 2 m (6 ft.) spacing for canopy trees, 1 m (3 ft.) for understorey and edge shrubs and trees.
- Differentiate between light-demanding and shade-tolerant understorey (as the wider woodland plantations need this differentiation more than the relatively narrow shelterbelts).
- Tree blocks should be single-species or two-species (50/50 mixes) with a minimum of 20 plants per cell.
- Understorey should be planted in bands between and around the tree cells (with light-demandin g species to edges, and shade-tolerant within the plantations) in single-species groups of a minimum of 20.
- The blocks are less regular than those in shelterbelts and the understorey structure does not form an even grid pattern across the plantation. Planting should be flexible to suit specific site requirements. Light-demanding understorey species can be used to edge cells.
- Nurse species can be planted together as co-dominants in a block, singly, or with the dominant (most frequently).

Woodland Planting mixes

In general within woodland, 80 per cent of the planting should be trees, with the remaining 20 per cent being understorey planting. Two typical planting mixes are shown. The key when planting your own woodland is not to rigidly copy the actual species chosen but to understand why they have been chosen and replicate the types of planting using species that will thrive in your region. These examples show *Fagus sylvatica* (beech, European beech) as the dominant and desired main planting. However the ground conditions may not at first be suitable to allow these plants to grow. Where this is the case an alternative plant can be used initially and after 10 years or so, during thinning operations, the beech can be introduced to the planting. At this point the woodland will have established enough to afford protection to, or the ground may have dried out enough to provide more favourable growing conditions for, the dominant species.

The creation of a productive area of woodland can also bring with it aesthetic benefits, as shown by the magnificent autumnal colours of this *Fagus sylvatica* (beech).

Wet or badly drained sites

		%
Nurse or co-dominant:	*Betula pubescens* (common white birch)	15
	Salix matsudana (Hankow willow)	15
	Alnus glutinosa (black alder)	15
	Populus nigra (black poplar)	15
Dominant:	*Fagus sylvatica* (beech, European beech)	40
Total tree component:		100
Understorey: (Shade)	*Ligustrum vulgare* (privet, common privet)	15
	Prunus padus (bird cherry, mayday tree)	15
	Salix gracilistyla (rose gold pussy willow)	10
	Viburnum opulus (Guelder rose, European cranberry bush)	10
(Edge mix)	*Cornus alba* (red-barked dogwood, Tatarian dogwood)	10
	Crataegus monogyna (common hawthorn)	10
	Rosa canina (dog rose)	15
	Sambucus nigra (common elder, elderberry)	15
Total understorey component:		100

Normal to dry sites

		%
Nurse or co-dominant:	*Alnus incana* (grey alder)	15
	Betula pendula (silver birch, European silver birch)	15
	Populus trichocarpa (black cottonwood)	15
	Prunus avium (bird cherry, mayday tree)	15
Dominant:	*Fagus sylvatica* (beech, European beech)	40
Total tree component:		100
Understorey: (Shade)	*Corylus avellana* (cobnut, European filbert)	15
	Rosa multiflora	15
Note: these categories overlap	*Symphoricarpos albus* (snowberry, common snowberry)	15
	Viburnum opulus (Guelder rose, European cranberry rose)	10
(Edge mix)	*Crataegus monogyna* (common hawthorn)	20
	Prunus spinosa (blackthorn, sloe)	15
	Sambucus nigra (common elder, elderberry)	10
Total understorey component:		100

Plants for Use as Accents

Accent plants may be defined as those that have an attractive feature or useful characteristic which may not be obvious at first glance. They often have bark or flowers that can provide a wonderful point of interest within a garden at certain times of the year or a growth habit which is either unusual or useful.

Deciduous

Acer saccharinum (silver maple), 9–12 m (30–40 ft.) Tall tree with a broad crown, it can be slightly brittle branched so avoid planting in windswept locations. The best feature of this tree is its rapid growth, which provides early impact, but this quick growth is at the price of it being quite weak so arrange for it to be be succeeded by more robust specimens later on.

Aesculus hippocastanum (common horse chestnut), 7.5–9 m, (25–30 ft.) This heavy tree with a large spread is the stereotypical tree for parkland. Spectacular 'candles' of flowers in the spring and early summer. The roots can be quite disruptive so it is best suited to being planted in wide open spaces. This big tree does need water throughout the summer to thrive.

Betula papyrifera (paper-bark birch, canoe birch), 9–12 m (30–40 ft.) Smooth white bark that peels off in layers. Fairly large, irregularly toothed leaves turn yellow in autumn. It comes into its own as an accent plant in winter when its stunning white bark shines out, especially against a dark backdrop.

Catalpa bignonioides (catalpa or Indian bean tree), 6–9 m (20–30 ft.) Large upright flowers can be seen above late-breaking, large, heart-shaped, light green leaves. The flowers turn into runner-bean-like seedpods in the autumn.

Liquidambar styraciflua (American sweet gum), 6–12 m (30–40 ft.) Beautiful trees with maple-like leaves that colour brilliantly in autumn to crimson and other colours. If it is important to your garden scheme that all the leaves are the same colour you will have to buy either named varieties or select the perfect specimen from the nursery when the leaves are turning their autumn colour.

Metasequoia glyptostroboides (dawn redwood), 8–12 m (30–40 ft.) Rapid-growing, upright, deciduous conifer with an overall conical shape. In addition to its strong shape the feathery foliage attracts attention because it goes from bright green to bronze and then to bright yellow over the course of a year.

The spring-to-late-summer, light-coloured foliage of *Acer pseudoplatanus* 'Leopoldii' not only brightens up this otherwise sombre border but also acts as a strong focal point for over half of the year.

Other plants can also be used as accent:

Acer platanoides (Norway maple); fast growing
Acer pseudoplatanus 'Leopoldii' (sycamore); light-coloured foliage
Betula pendula (European white birch); white stem
Carpinus betulus (European hornbeam); easily grown
Carpinus betulus 'Fastigiata' (erect European hornbeam); columnar form
Fagus sylvatica (beech); parkland specimen tree
Fagus sylvatica Atropurpurea Group (purple beech); foliage colour
Fraxinus americana (white ash); fast-growing shade tree
Liriodendron tulipifera (tulip tree); unusual leaf shape
Quercus robur (English oak); parkland tree
Quercus rubra (red oak); autumn colour
Robinia pseudoacacia (false acacia, locust tree); attractive leaves
Rubus cockburnianus (white-stemmed bramble); pale chalky stems in winter
Sophora japonica (Japanese pagoda tree); creamy-white flowers
Tilia americana (American lime, American linden); large leaves
Tilia cordata 'Greenspire' (little-leaf linden); fragrant flowers

Rubus cockburnianus illustrates the dramatic effect that some plants can have at certain times of the year. In spring and against a dark backdrop its stems shine out from borders but when it comes into leaf it disappears and blends into the background planting.

Evergreen

Abies concolor (white fir), 24–30 m (80–100 ft.) Bluish green tree that makes a lovely specimen with cones growing like candles on the branches. Often used as a Christmas tree but if you have the space this tree does not deserve to be cut down.

Araucaria araucana (monkey puzzle tree), 21–27 m (70–90 ft.) Originating in Chile, this unique-looking tree has become a standard in older gardens. It works well either as a focal point or within mixed scale boundary plantings. They confer a sense of cultivation on distant edge-of-property plantings. The base of the trunk on older specimens resembles an elephant's foot!

Cedrus atlantica (Atlas cedar), 16–21 m (50–70 ft.) These statuesque conifers look at home in any parkland setting. As they get older the lower branches gracefully arch downwards. 'Glauca' is the blue version of this tree but be warned, like most blue plants they need careful co-ordination with their surroundings to fit in correctly.

Juniperus × pfitzeriana 'Pfitzeriana Aurea' (golden pfitzer juniper), 1.5–1.8 m (5–6 ft.) This plant is mid-green in colour with a golden tinge on its extremities. It provides an irregular solid focal point that can be used to lighten any view or vista.

Picea pungens 'Glauca group' (Colorado blue spruce), 21–30 m (70–100 ft.) Large, silvery-blue, broadly conical conifer that is often planted in gardens that cannot cope with a dominant tree of this scale and colour. Use sparingly as a feature and for smaller areas look for scaled-down cultivars.

Pinus strobus (Weymouth pine, Eastern white pine), 18–24 m (60–80 ft.) One of the most attractive pines as its light, airy nature makes it look quite graceful when set on a lawn. Ensure that it is not too exposed as the needles of this blue-green conifer can burn in strong winds.

Additional evergreen accent plants:
    Cedrus deodara (deodar cedar); graceful parkland tree
    Picea abies (Norway spruce); fast growing
    Pinus nigra (Austrian pine, European black pine); wind break
    Taxus baccata (common yew, English yew); very dark foliage

The peeling bark of *Acer griseum* continues to make this a valuable tree in the garden long after its leaves have fallen for the winter.

Specimen Trees for Borders or beside Decks

Trees that are ideally suited to be sited near decks include those that have attractive bark or other characteristics at eye level. They may also have light foliage that can be looked through or thicker foliage that casts valuable shade onto the seating area.

Acer griseum (paper-bark maple), 6–7.5 m (20–25 ft.) The leaves appear insignificant until autumn when they turn magnificent shades of red. The bark is a wonderful reddish brown and it peels away in paper-thin sheets. This is a good border tree for naturalizing a garden into the wider landscape.

Crataegus phaenopyrum (Washington thorn), 7.5 m (25 ft.) The most graceful and delicate of the hawthorns with leaves that go from green through orange to red in the autumn. The shiny red fruits hang on well into the winter and can provide an attraction for birds. When sited adjacent to a deck area the winter feeding birds provide some welcome garden activity when viewed from indoors.

Gleditsia triacanthos 'Sunburst' (honey locust), 5–6.5 m (18–22 ft.) This is a relatively large tree for siting close to a deck but it provides a wonderful degree of light shade. New growth takes the form of fine, bright leaves that turn to green in the summer and yellowish in the autumn.

Koelreuteria bipinnata (Chinese flame tree), 9–12 m (30–40 ft.) Late summer interest with bright yellow flower panicles that turn to bright, rose-coloured fruits in autumn. Casts nice dappled shade onto decks and patios.

This bamboo at the late Christopher Lloyd's garden, Great Dixter, England, provides a wonderful sense of division while still affording views through to other areas of the garden. This effect could also be achieved with the sparing use of grasses.

Pistacia chinensis (Chinese pistache), 9–12 m (30–40 ft.) Good red autumn foliage over grey, slightly furrowed bark. These trees can look slightly awkward and uneven in habit when young but once mature, their dense crowns will cast a deep shade making them useful near a deck.

Prunus cerasifera 'Pissardii' (purple-leaved plum), 10 m (30 ft.) Few fruit are ever borne on these trees but they do bear striking purplish red leaves. These provide contrast in a border and will either stand out against green or golden backdrops or act as a purple backdrop to plants with light coloured foliage.

Other trees for borders or beside decks:
    Amelanchier × grandiflora 'Princess Diana' (snowy mespilus, service-berry) Large border shrub with profusion of white summer flowers. Very hardy with red-orange leaf colour in the autumn.
    Ulmus parvifolia (Chinese elm); medium-sized tree, good deck shade.

Plants for Screening

Screening plants are required in almost every garden irrespective of scale. They can be quite bulky and so are normally easier to use within a large garden setting. They are generally used to either to screen offending objects or views, or to sub-divide areas within gardens.

Evergreen

When it comes to screening offending objects or views, evergreen trees and shrubs will provide complete cover throughout the year. These permanent visual barriers form ideal core plants within a garden. It is worth remembering when using plants to screen that their usage is dependent upon where the offending object is viewed from. This may mean that plants are planted individually or as a group depending on the scale of the problem.

Filter

Juniperus chinensis 'Kaizuka' (Chinese juniper, Hollywood juniper), 2.5–4 m (8–12 ft.) A rich green conifer with an irregular habit. As the branches grow, in what seems like a random manner, gaps emerge which allow light and wind to pass through.

Viburnum rhytidophyllum (leatherleaf viburnum), 2.5–4 m (8–12 ft.) An excellent plant to ease the transition between garden and surrounding countryside. Its upright, irregular form allows it to blend from garden to wider landscape. Large, oval-shaped leaves combined with clusters of red berries make this decorative shrub especially useful for screening.

Weigela florida (weigela), 1.8–3 m (6–10 ft.) This is a low-maintenance shrub that flowers in April to May to great effect. Due to its star quality when flowering it will become something of a focal point but its loose habit will allow views to lead on from it.

Solid

× *Cupressocyparis leylandii* (leyland cypress), 15–18 m (50–60 ft.) Despite its notoriety, in the right hands this can form an effective dense dark green boundary. Unfortunately, it is often used as a quick hedging solution (it can grow over 1 m [3 ft.] per year) and problems occur when it is not maintained properly, particularly in urban situations.

Ligustrum lucidum (waxleaf privet), 4.5–6 m (15–20 ft.) Large, informal, boundary or screening shrub. A low-maintenance option, as long as you are prepared for the eventual height of this plant. White panicles of flowers show up in the summer against the oval-shaped, glossy, mid-green leaves.

Ilex aquifolium (English holly), Reaches up to 9 m (30 ft.) Dark evergreen screen that can be cut to form an effective screen or hedge at most heights. Useful as an understorey plant within woodland and to make the link between garden and woodland. Other notable forms such as 'Aurea Marginata', which has yellow margins, can be used when a lighter overall appearance is required.

Ilex opaca (American holly), 3–6 m (10–20 ft.) Dark green, broadly pyramidal shape can provide an excellent link to the more informal wider landscape. It is best when viewed against greenery its shape is too dominant against the sky unless it is part of a formal layout.

Pinus nigra var. *austriaca* (Austrian pine), 18 m+ (60 ft.+). Plant 1.8 m (6 ft.) apart to form an effective but wide screen when using as a large barrier screen. Its dark green colour can form a very useful dark backdrop to specimen plants within a garden.

Taxus baccata (yew), 9 m+ (30 ft.+) It can be left loose and informal or clipped into a formal shape. As a result, height and density can be controlled to suit most locations and its use can be tailored for use as a variety of backdrops. Wrongly perceived to be slow growing!

Ternstroemia gymnanthera, 2.5–3 m (8–10 ft.) Good deep green colour that bridges the gap between dark and mid-green plants. A useful plant that can be used at woodland edges as it will tolerate shade or partial shade.

Semi-evergreen

In colder regions semi-evergreen plants will adopt deciduous tendencies. Nonetheless, many offer more interest than true evergreens and are ideally suited for use as barriers in areas of the garden that are mainly used during the summer. They may also be worth considering for situations in which it is not critical to have a complete screen.

Filter

Phyllostachys aureosulcata (yellow or golden groove bamboo). Up to 9 m (30 ft.), this is a wonderful, very hardy screening plant that may need containment because of its vigorous spreading growth. This treasure is a definite gem for those with large gardens and the space to enjoy it. Bamboos are some of the best plants for screening and can be used as a filter when contained into narrow depth or complete screen when grown as a wide band. The soft green colour of its leaves will lighten up darker areas within a garden.

Phyllostachys nigra (black bamboo), up to 7.5 m (25 ft.) Commonly used in the design of Japanese gardens and noted for the blackish stems which can be found on mature specimens. Its vigorous, spreading growth makes it a valuable screening plant.

Solid

Escallonia 'Donard Star', up to 1.5 m (5 ft.) Compact upright habit with dark glossy green leaves and small rose-pink flowers. This plant forms a dense barrier and is happy in coastal locations as well as inland. It may become semi-evergreen in colder zones.

Deciduous

These plants will all shed their leaves at some point during the year, usually in the autumn, but also as a response to stress. Typically, deciduous leaves show a variety of colours, some spectacular, before they fall and these can be used as a feature within a design. Care must be taken, however, to ensure that they do not create distinctive focal points that distract from the overall design. Mixed plantings can produce a multicoloured autumnal background, which can help the garden to blend into the surrounding landscape.

Filter

Buddleja davidii (butterfly bush), up to 3–3.5 m (8–12 ft.) Open and rounded, this bush can provide a loose screen. It is noticeable for its lilac flowers and as the name suggests its ability to attract butterflies. It has a long flowering period and can be useful to naturalize gardens into landscape backdrops. The alba variety provides, as its name suggests, a white-flowered alternative to the parent plant.

Hippophae rhamnoides (sea buckthorn), 3–4.5 m (10–15 ft.) Willow-like leaves are carried on this shrub which has a very loose habit. It has insignificant white flowers and a mass of small orange fruits are borne on the stems of the plant. Excellent at breaking the force of the wind.

Tamarix ramosissima (salt cedar), 3.25–3.5 m (10–12 ft.) Excellent for naturalizing, this plant has light to medium leaves joined by delicate pink flowers in the summer. It is open and airy and its upright, irregular habit produces a loose but varied screen. Good for allowing partial views to other areas of the garden.

Miscanthus sinensis 'Gracillimus', Height 1.2–1.8 m (4–6 ft.) Very versatile grass which is useful for its green summer foliage followed by creamy feathery plumes in autumn. The foliage will remain through all but the most severe of winters and provides attractive standing foliage. Suitable as a filter if planted thinly as a narrow hedge. *Miscanthus sinensis* 'Variegatus' has creamy white stripes along the length of its leaves.

Plants for Hedges

Hedging plants are normally shrubs that can be planted together to form a division either within a garden or as a boundary demarcation. Informal hedges tend to be wider and looser in form whereas formal hedges tend to be used in more manicured areas of the garden and require regular cutting to maintain their shape.

Informal hedges

Informal hedges can be classified as those where the plants are allowed to grow as they would normally as individual specimens. They will respond to some minor pruning to keep their overall form but are not as onerous in terms of maintenance. For those with large gardens where space is not an issue they can reduce the level of input that would be required to maintain a formal section of hedge.

Deciduous

Euonymus alatus 'Compactus' (winged spindle, winged euonymus), 1.5–1.8 m (5–6 ft.) Dense, mounding shrub suitable for larger properties where an informal boundary can blend into surrounding plantings. Dark green leaves turn brilliant red in the autumn.

Hibiscus syriacus (mallow, althea, rose of Sharon), 2.5–3 m (8–10 ft.) Blooms in August and September with normally pink flowers shining from the mid-green foliage. Its upright and loose habit forms a barrier without appearing too solid.

Spiraea nipponica 'Snowmound' (snowmound spiraea), 1.2–2 m (4–6 ft.) A plant that looks best *en masse*. It is a loose but generally rounded shrub with small dark leaves. The stems are covered in a mass of small white flowers in May or June.

Evergreen

Juniperus pfitzeriana (Pfitzer juniper), 1.5–1.8 m (5–6 ft.) This plant is mid-green with a hint of grey and is useful for its understated qualities. It provides an irregular solid backdrop or low screen that is insignificant but very effective. 'Aurea' is the golden variety of this stalwart.

Prunus lusitanica (laurel, Portuguese laurel), 1.8 m (6 ft.) A good, medium-sized shrub with glossy, rich green leaves and hawthorn-scented, creamy flowers in June. Good informal 'green wall' but take care if planting them under larger trees as they can easily become 'leggy' and spindly in shade.

Tsuga canadensis (Eastern hemlock, Canadian hemlock), 1.5–2.1 m (5–7 ft.) when used as a hedge. A large tree that can become a beautiful specimen, although its feathery foliage responds extremely well to being cut into a loose hedge.

Viburnum tinus (laurustinus), 1.8–3 m (6–10 ft.) Dark green leaves that bear white/pink heads of flowers in late winter/early spring. It will respond to trimming but is best left relatively informal.

Formal hedging

This type of hedging is generally the most labour intensive, where plants require pruning on a cyclical basis. They can bring a formality and rigidity to a garden and will give the impression that the garden is well maintained. They can be used sparingly to give this impression in any garden and their used should be focused on areas of key usage. Heights are generally not appropriate when considering plants for use in areas of formal hedging as they can be pruned and cut to the required size.

Deciduous

Carpinus betulus (hornbeam) Dark green leaves turn yellow in the autumn. A dense, tight hedge can be formed using this plant. Excellent plant that works best in a manicured setting.

Fagus sylvatica (beech) Useful plant whose attractive bright green leaves turn orange in the autumn. Although deciduous, the dead leaves will remain on the plant through most winters, continuing to provide a solid hedge.

Clipped box balls instantly lend borders a maintained appearance even if the majority of the bed requires little attention. This same effect can be created in borders by planting tightly growing specimens among plants with 'looser' habits.

Above right The tightly abutting leaves of *Parthenocissus tricuspidata* create a green wall as the plant ascends the building.

Evergreen

Buxus sempervirens (common box, English boxwood) This has become the classic material for close hedging in formal gardens. It is often kept as a low hedge beneath knee height but it can reach 5 m (15 ft.) when given free rein. The small leaves mid-green leaves make it ideally suited to being clipped into any desired shape.

Parthenocissus tricuspidata (Boston ivy) Excellent plant for effectively transforming a brick wall or timber fence into a 'green wall'. This dark green vine with three-lobed leaves will climb anything and can form a green wall in the tightest of spaces. The crimson leaves in autumn are to die for.

Taxus baccata (common yew, English yew), 1.2–1.8 m (4–6 ft.) Deep green foliage that grows faster than is commonly perceived to form a tight crisp hedge of the desired height.

Thuja occidentalis 'Holmstrup' (white cedar, Holmstrup eastern arbor-vitae), 2.5–3.5 m (8–12 ft.) Dark green, scale-like leaves hang in sprays, can form a close tight hedge when tightly clipped.

Thuja plicata 'Fastigiata' (Western red cedar, Hogan cedar), 3–3.5 m (10–12 ft.) Excellent for tall, narrow, dense screens. It has dark green scale-like leaves that hang in flat sprays and respond well to trimming. It may need some shade to avoid summer burn in the warmest conditions.

Plants for Groundcover

Groundcover plants are normally planted in areas where weed growth is to be suppressed or in areas where routine maintenance would prove too awkward. These difficult areas to maintain tend to be either sloping pieces of ground or areas that are relatively inaccessible making normal degrees of maintenance impossible. The degree of shade on to the ground will provide a limiting factor in the growth-rate of any plants selected, as groundcover is normally planted under trees and shrubs.

Evergreen

Most available groundcovers tend to be evergreen in nature, and that is simply because their weed suppression or slope stabilization qualities are required all year round.

Arctostaphylos uva-ursi (bearberry, red bearberry) This spreading groundcover carpets slopes liberating them from routine maintenance. It has bright green glossy leaves and small pink/white flowers. Although slow to get established, once it takes hold it can form a great mat.

Cotoneaster × suecicus **'Coral Beauty'** (cotoneaster), 1 m (3 ft.) Nice groundcover for partial shade or sun. Small arching stems bear pale mid green leaves with pale pink flowers and fruit. Good contrast when used in schemes with ivy and coniferous groundcovers.

Hedera helix (English ivy) This is perhaps the most commonly used ivy with heart-shaped mid green leaves and can seem slightly unimaginative. Other cultivars do exist however and they have a variety of shades and sizes of leaf which can be combined to great effect. Ivy this can seem a bit boring with its only virtue being that it is green but it is excellent at retaining slopes and for growing under trees where many others would fail. Can be a great home for slugs and rodents though.

Juniperus rigida subsp. *conferta* (shore juniper), 15 cm (6 ft.) Soft bright green needles of this groundcover will tolerate seashore exposure. If you want a denser, bluer and more heat-tolerant form go for 'Blue Pacific'.

Liriope spicata (lilyturf, creeping lilyturf), 20–25 cm (8–9 in.) Dense grass-like plant with narrow green leaves and pale lilac to white flowers in summer. Great for shaded or semi-shaded areas. Mow or strim once per year in early spring to see plant look its best.

Pachysandra terminalis (Japanese spurge), 15–30 cm (6–10 in.) Good plant for those hard-to-reach shade areas. Mid-green florets of leaves with insignificant white flowers in the summer. The variation in height of this groundcover is dependent upon light levels so in deeper shade it will reach the maximum given height but in sun, the minimum.

The following are good groundcovers with their notable feature highlighted:
Ajuga reptans (bugle, carpet bugle); purple foliage with blue flower spikes.
Cotoneaster salicifolius 'Repens' (dwarf willowleaf, cotoneaster); red fruits.
Juniperus horizontalis (juniper); green coniferous carpet, loose in character.
Juniperus horizontalis 'Wiltonii' (blue rug juniper, blue carpet juniper); glaucous blue.
Rosa pimpinellifolia (Scotch rose, burnet rose); suckering shrub with spines!
Vinca major (greater periwinkle); good for banks.
Vinca minor (lesser periwinkle, dwarf periwinkle); blue flowers, smaller-leaved version of previous.

Deciduous

Deciduous groundcovers bring seasonal interest with them as opposed to evergreen ones, which vary little throughout the year.

Epimedium versicolor (barrenwort), 30–35 cm (10–12 in.) Mid-green, heart-shaped leaves on slender stalks with insignificant white flowers in spring. Outstanding groundcover especially for naturalizing under woodland trees and for use in rock gardens.

Hosta sieboldiana (Siebold plantain lily), 60–90 cm (2–3 ft.) Blue-green leaves 30–35 cm (10–15 in.) arch from the centre of this plant. Pale lilac flowers are present in the summer but it is the distinctly veined, heart-shaped leaves that are the stars. A favourite of slugs. When planted together form a dense shade under their leaves.

Rubus tricolor (bramble, blackberry), 20–30 cm (8–10 in.) Furry red bristles and glossy foliage are carried on long prostrate shoots. They root on contact with the soil and quickly form an impenetrable low mass. Use in areas that you want to ignore because although little maintenance is required it is not that decorative *en masse*.

Further Reading

Aben, R., and S. De Wit. 2001. *The Enclosed Garden*. 2nd ed. Rotterdam, the Netherlands: 010 Publishers.

Beveridge, C. E., and P. Rocheleau. 1995. *Frederick Law Olmsted: Designing the American Landscape*. New York: Rizzoli.

Boyd-Brent, J. 2005. 'Harmony and Proportion'. About Scotland Art Pages. www.aboutscotland.com.

Bradley-Hole, C. 1999. *The Minimalist Garden*. London: Mitchell Beazley.

Brookes, J. 1969. *Room Outside*. London: Thames and Hudson.

——— 1984. *A Place in the Country*. London: Thames and Hudson.

Church, T. 1955. *Gardens are for People*. New York: Reinhold Publishing Company,

Downing, A. J. 1850. *Treatise on the Theory and Practice of Landscape Gardening, adapted to North America, with a View to the Improvement of Country Residences*. 4th ed. New York: Putnam.

Collier, G. 1963. *Form, Space and Vision: Discovering Design Through Drawing*. Prentice-Hall. Upper Saddle River, NJ, USA: Prentice-Hall.

Crowe, S. 1958. *Garden Design*. West Sussex, UK: Packard Publishing Limited.

Hobhouse, P. 1985. *Colour in Your Garden*. London: Frances Lincoln.

Jekyll, G., and L. Weaver. 1920. *Gardens for Small Country Houses*. 4th ed. London: Country Life.

Jellicoe, J. 1996. *The Collected Works of Jeffrey Jellicoe: Studies in Landscape Design*. vol. 3. Woodbridge, UK: Garden Art Press.

Jellicoe, J. & S., et al. 1986. *The Oxford Companion to Gardens*. Oxford: Oxford University Press.

Jensen, J. 1939. *Siftings: The Major Portion of The Clearing, and Collected Writings*. USA: R. F. Seymour.

Kemp, E. 1864. *How To Lay Out A Garden*. 3d ed. London: Bradbury and Evans.

Palladio, A. 1965. *The Four Books of Architecture*. New York: Dover Publications Inc.

Mawson, T. H. 1900. *The Art and Craft of Garden Making*. London: B.T. Batsford.

Mackellar Goulty, S. 1993. *Heritage Gardens: Care, Conservation and Management*. London: Routledge.

Nichols, F. D., and R. E. Griswold. 1978. *Thomas Jefferson, Landscape Architect.* Charlottesville, VA, USA: University Press of Virginia.

Oudolf, P. 1999. *Designing with Plants.* London: Conran Octopus Limited.

Repton, H. 1907. *The Art of Landscape Gardening.* London: Archibald Constable & Co., Ltd.

Tunnard, C. 1938. *Gardens of a Modern Landscape.* London: The Architectural Press.

Turner, T. 2005. *Garden History: Philosophy and Design 2000 BC – 2000 AD.* New York: Spon Press.

Useful Organizations

Society of Garden Designers, Katepwa House, Ashfield Park Avenue, Ross-on-Wye, Herefordshire, HR9 5AX, www.sgd.org.uk

Landscape Institute, 33 Great Portland Street, London W1W 8QG, www.l-i.org.uk

Association of Professional Landscape Designers, 4305 North Sixth Street Suite A, Harrisburg, PA 17110, www.apld.com

American Society of Landscape Architects, 636 Eye Street, NW Washington, DC 20001-3736, www.asla.org

Contents

Contents by Project Type

Note: Most projects in this book include, by their nature, more than one function. A few guidelines to categories below:

Mixed-Use Developments: reserved for those with substantial mix of uses within buildings (beyond accessory parking or retail included in buildings listed as office, residential, etc.).

Communities: wide mix of uses, typically on cleared land, with new buildings and infrastructure.

Urban Redevelopment: large in scope, including existing construction and infrastructure.

Remodeling/Re-use: including specifics on re-use of individual buildings.

Other project types: largely devoted to listed type (not listing, for instance, inclusion of recreation in residential projects, plazas with office buildings, or street improvements in urban redevelopment).

Introduction

The key characteristics of good urban development can be distilled from a review of current projects.

In their various ways, the projects presented in this book revitalize the public realm that has been sapped for decades by dispersed development, dominance of the automobile, and misguided planning and zoning policies. As I've examined all of these 150-plus projects, certain of the most promising qualities of urban development for this new century have come to the fore.

One widely accepted goal of urban projects is to achieve a mix of functions that will generate round-the-clock activity. Attendant benefits include the opportunity to walk, not drive, from home to work or shopping and the reduction in total resources devoted to parking – with many of the spaces serving residents at night and workers and shoppers by day. Mixed use also establishes a day-and-evening economic basis for a richer variety of retail and dining facilities. There are rarely good restaurants, at any price point, in districts occupied only by day workers.

Mixing pedestrians and vehicles on the same right of way, reversing decades of planning dogma, has now become a criterion for good urban development – or even good shopping center remodeling. Few people, it turns out, enjoy vast parking lots or garages, but we must not forget that vehicles do little to enhance the pedestrian experience, so the setting shared by pedestrians and vehicles demands subtle design. And some pedestrian-only precincts, which are found in admired historical cities, are still desirable.

A well-designed urban complex projects a strong sense of place. It has memorable architectural elements and/or spatial compositions of its own, and it effectively incorporates – at best capitalizes on – local attributes of climate, topography, and traditions.

Many projects are able to benefit from the reuse of existing structures. The best incorporate them without papering over their design peculiarities, their accumulated scars, or the dissonant juxtapositions that often come with adaptation to new circumstance. No theme-park restorations, please.

Good community or urban redevelopment plans make effective connections with the surrounding community, including but not limited to knitting their streets into existing networks. The kinds of uses accommodated should complement the surrounding area, without undermining existing activities and without creating jarring social shifts at project boundaries. Admittedly, real-world pressures often make such ideal relationships hard to achieve.

Where a project is one element of a larger revitalization process, there is no question that it must be designed to support that larger set of goals, at best exceeding the requirements of the plans they contribute to.

Good urban projects support public transportation. Density and mix of uses are keys to aggregating enough riders to support a bus or rail line. Clustering higher-density residential around stops or stations also supports adjoining commerce, which in some notable cases makes the transportation node a destination in itself.

Promotion of economic and social integration is an objective of many of our finest urban developments. The separation of people by economic strata, while not totally avoidable, can be reduced in many creative ways. Many of the new communities and neighborhoods presented in this book encourage an economic mix by offering a wide variety of residential units within a small area – studio apartments, lofts, "granny" units over garages – in a fine-grained mix with more lavish residences. It has been proven over and over that, given a sensitively designed environment, affluent residents will happily opt to live among people with a wide range of resources and lifestyles.

Sustainability has become something of a buzz word lately, but there is no question that it is the obligation of all designers – all people – to conserve resources and reduce waste. While one of the proven ways is to encourage walking instead of driving – or even taking the train – there are many other architectural and planning strategies. Much of the savings of energy and material resources are the province of mechanical engineers and product designers, but architects can do much to reduce the demand for artificial lighting, air conditioning, and heating, while choosing building components wisely. Planners and landscape architects can make valuable contributions to minimizing traffic and pollution, promoting natural ventilation, directing rainwater runoff, and providing for natural shade.

Somewhat sadly, many of our most creative urban efforts involve mitigating the effects of earlier public work by adapting thoroughfares built to please traffic engineers to make them appealing to pedestrians, by making freeways more compatible with surrounding neighborhoods, by dividing monumental vacant plazas into places of human scale and activity, and by carving attractive open spaces out of massive building clusters. As the following pages indicate, we are mending our past urban ways at the same time we are creating new environments that foster real public places – environments where people enjoy the company of strangers.

John Morris Dixon, FAIA

Preface

Richard M. Rosan,
FAIA
President,
Urban Land Institute

Creating competitive, attractive cities that are cherished for generations is the goal of many cities, developers, planners, and urban designers today. Anyone who works in any aspect of the land use profession affects where and how people live, work, and play. And, while there is much left to be accomplished, people around the world are rediscovering the power of cities to connect people, to give them a sense of pride and belonging.

It is becoming increasingly obvious that as our world becomes more urbanized, cities are struggling with many of the same issues: managing growth, responding to demographic changes, building enough affordable housing, providing adequate transportation options and parking, and in general, finding the best way to rebuild, restore, and renew our urban areas.

The impact of urbanization is evident in countries around the world. People are moving to cities and urban regions as never before. By 2025, the United Nations projects that urban population growth will make up about 90 percent of the world's population growth. It estimates that in 20 years, 85 percent of the population in the United States will live in urban areas; in Europe, 83 percent; in Asia, 55 percent; and Africa, 54 percent.

Even at a 55 percent urbanization rate, Asia's population is so huge that an enormous number of people—well over 1 billion—will be living in urban areas. Currently, China, with 1.3 billion people; and India, with close to 1.1 billion, house more than one-third of the world's population. The U.S. ranks a distant third, with 295 million; followed by Indonesia with 241 million; and Brazil, with 186 million.

We can expect mega cities—a term coined by the UN to describe cities with at least 10 million inhabitants—to become increasingly commonplace. The United Nations projects that in just 10 years more than 20 cities will have more than 10 million people. Of these, only two—New York and Los Angeles—will be in North America. Six cities—four in Asia, two in Latin America--will have populations exceeding 20 million.

Clearly, it's not a matter of whether growth will occur. It's how and where growth will occur. To be sure, growth brings economic and social benefits, but if growth is mismanaged, it also can mean greater poverty, inadequate infrastructure, land scarcity, and a deteriorating environment.

Building competitive cities means building more than just places to live and work. It's about creating places that inspire, places with character, places that draw people through a powerful sense of identity. In cities around the world, changing demographics and changing household formations are having a profound effect on what is built and where it is built.

While every city has its own personality, there seem to be common characteristics behind every successful urban regeneration: strong political leadership; the creation of an environment for intellectual stimulation and creativity—to be a "brain-gain" city rather than a "brain-drain" city; tolerance of diversity; a commitment to provide housing to people with a variety of incomes; a solid track record in creating long-lasting public-private partnerships; a commitment to transit-oriented development and transportation infrastructure; and a dedication by the local officials to aggressively preserve land for parks and open space.

The cities that are able to offer a high quality of life—in the form of efficient transportation, recreational and cultural amenities, diverse neighborhoods, and a safe, clean, lively environment—will be the winners. This applies to both high-growth cities, which are scrambling to keep up with population increases, as well as low-growth cities, which are scrambling to retain and attract residents.

Creating places that give wonderful memories should be the ultimate purpose of urban regeneration. As community builders and place makers, all of us have a tremendous responsibility in shaping both the private and public space in which people carry out their lives.

180° Design Studio

1656 Washington
Suite 270
Kansas City, MO 64108
816.531.9695
816.531.9695 (Fax)
Kklinkenberg@180deg.com
www.180deg.com

180° Design Studio

180° Design Studio

New Town Theater District
St. Charles, Missouri

The distinctive crescent shape of the two-city-block site called for an appropriately formal design response for this mixed-use development. The symmetrical pair of curved buildings, each with about 28,400 square feet, will house residential units over street-level retail, civic, and office spaces. At the far ends will be matched loft buildings of about 10,800 square feet each. The central pair of pavilions will be linked by an over-the-street bridge to form one office building of about 27,400 square feet. Delicate canopies along the curved buildings are patterned after colonnades from the Old Market in Omaha. Smaller two-story "carriage house" residential structures behind the formally laid out buildings will make a scale transition to adjoining neighborhoods. The Classical design of the complex will create "an instant landmark," in the words of planner Andres Duany.

Opposite, top: Overall view of crescent around public plaza.

Opposite, bottom: Portion of crescent with steel canopies of historical character.

Above left: Central pavilions linked by bridge over street.

Left: Elevation of one central pavilion.

Rendering: Arnold Imaging.

180° Design Studio

New Longview
Lee's Summit, Missouri

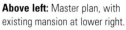

The site of this 260-acre planned community is Longview Farm, the 90-year-old country estate of a lumber baron, which is listed on the Historic Register. The design preserves 14 of the 17 farm structures and integrates them into a walkable environment. Numerous previous proposals for the property had been turned down by the community. A multi-day public design charrette conducted with the community achieved almost unanimous support for this master plan. Months of work were spent with city staff on the details of the rezoning. The mixed-use development will include 1,100 residential units, 250,000 square feet of retail, and 250,000 square feet of offices, plus space for civic structures and public open spaces totaling 70 acres. A regional arterial road that was planned to bifurcate the site was redesigned as a multilane boulevard that accommodates the traffic while enhancing the community.

Above left: Master plan, with existing mansion at lower right.

Left: Park land around mansion.

Clockwise from photo above: completed houses; residential neighborhood; civic center reusing farm buildings; multifamily crescent; variety of building types along boulevard; theater; houses and neighborhood retail.

13

180° Design Studio

Crescent Creek
Raytown, Missouri

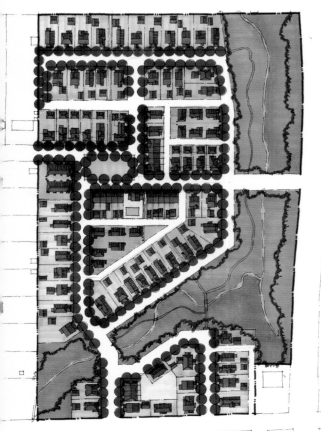

For a 22-acre site adjoining an existing Post-World-War-II neighborhood, planning and architectural design were carried out for 130 residential units. It was essential to make the development attractive yet very affordable. Rezoning for a planned residential district required establishment of strict design regulations. The six types of dwellings include townhouses and single-family houses, ranging in size from 1,100 to 2,600 square feet and in price from $150,000 to $275,000. A pool and clubhouse are included in the project. Existing streets were extended through the new development but "tamed" to reduce speed and discourage through traffic.

Above: Typical street and houses.

Left: Master plan.

Below left: Central green.

Bottom left and below: Typical houses nearing completion.

180° Design Studio

Ottawa University Master Plan
Ottawa, Kansas

This campus master plan features a new student learning center and upgraded residential and athletic facilities. The objective was to create a stronger campus feeling, with a true center and a series of "outdoor rooms." Parking is dispersed around the perimeter of the site. An axial green at the main entrance offers numerous parking spaces integrated into a formally landscaped setting. Residential buildings line another axial green. A tower marking the center of the campus rises above a circular plaza at its front and aligns on the far side with the 50-yard-line of the athletic field. New buildings are to vary in character from relatively large-scaled and symmetrical for focal buildings to more intimate and irregular for the residential structures, all of them clad in traditional materials.

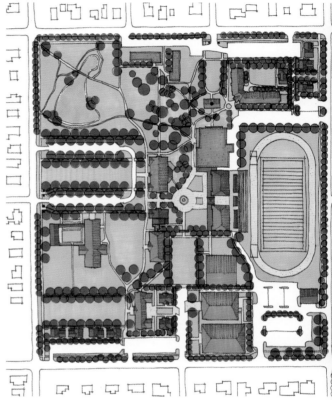

Top: Circular plaza and signature tower at campus center.

Above: Residential green, with small-scaled student housing at right.

Above right: Master plan.

Right: Axial entrance green.

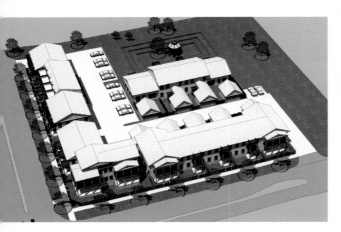

Top and above left: Elevation and digital model of 71st and Metcalf project.

Above: Aerial rendering of Union Hill development.

Left: Beachtown Galveston Village model home.

Below: Longfellow Court residential buildings.

Several residential projects show the firm's adaptation of traditional housing forms to specific circumstances. The 71st and Metcalf development in Overland Park, Kansas, proposes 24 townhouse and flat units, ranging from 650 to 2,000 square feet to serve different markets, on a 2.1-acre suburban infill site. Union Hill, Phase 3, in Kansas City includes apartments, townhouses, and retail on a two-city-block site complicated by steep topography. A single-family model home for Beachtown Galveston Village is meant to establish a design image for the community, dealing effectively with restrictions such as the raised first floor required at this beachfront location. Longfellow Court in Kansas City, developed by the firm itself, proposes 18 units, including detached single-family, townhouses, duplexes, and flats, in a scheme that achieved unanimous approval for 35 zoning variances.

Altoon + Porter Architects LLP

444 South Flower Street
48th Floor
Los Angeles, CA 90071-2901
213.225.1900
213.225.1901 (Fax)
apa@altoonporter.com
www.altoonporter.com

Altoon + Porter Architects LLP

Altoon + Porter Architects LLP

Knox Shopping Centre
Melbourne, Australia

As the first phase of a long-range plan for the 500-acre Knox City development, this 200-acre Shopping Centre contributes to a larger urban framework, incorporating a mix of retail, civic, and residential buildings, including existing mixed use buildings. Establishing linkages to wetlands and transportation, the overall plan also provides for sports, educational, and light industrial facilities. The Shopping Centre turns a familiar suburban retail form into an urban environment of streets and squares, with restaurants and cinema. Six separate precincts, each with a memorable name and visual personality, ease wayfinding within the centre and offer distinct merchandising opportunities. Calling upon the rich pictorial and metaphorical vocabularies provided by the site between Melbourne and the

Dandenong Ranges, the design evokes the Australian life style in the expression of native timbers and lodge forms, in the palette and patterns of the vineyards, in the broad verandahs and lawns of the town square, and in the bright lights of the urban scene. As a result, visitors enjoy a marked sense of place that is as diverse as the region itself.

Above: Two details evoking regional traditions of broad overhangs, industrial materials, and angular timbers.

Right: Traditional cityscape elements of urban square and pedestrian paseo.

Above: Intimate pedestrian passage opening into broader square.

Right: Activity along passage sheltered by tiers of canopies.

Far right: Retail interior.

Photography: Stuart Curnow.

Altoon + Porter Architects LLP

Victoria Gardens
Rancho Cucamonga, California

In a dramatic departure for a retail development, Victoria Gardens is conceived not as a project but as a town center reflecting the values of a multigenerational community. The design of the 1.2-million-square-foot development is rooted in the elements common to all towns and in the special qualities of this singular place. The plan is organized around a grid of streets, a town square, courtyards, paseos, pocket parks, and plazas. The individuality of shops and buildings thrives on the underlying sense of urban order. Two-story shops, second- and third-floor offices, and residential lofts above retail all contribute to the character and scale of a cityscape. Civic uses such as a children's performing arts theater, a conference center, and a central library around a public square all add a civic quality. The development occupies 12 city blocks at the heart of a 160-acre planned community and includes three major department stores, a cinema, and 150 specialty shops. The presence of residential development contiguous to Victoria Gardens reinforces its town-center role.

Top: Hi-tech building detail.

Above: Sleek Modernist loggia with characteristic street furniture.

Right: Cityscape recalling traditional towns.

Above right: Food Hall and other structures evoking old industrial districts.

Opposite, bottom left: Structure in Spanish Colonial spirit.

Opposite, bottom right: Interior of Food Hall.

Altoon + Porter Architects LLP

Fashion Show
Las Vegas, Nevada

A 20-year-old, well-performing but barely noticed retail center has been transformed into one of the most memorable landmarks on the Strip, a shopping environment that could hardly be replicated anywhere in the world. The complex has been doubled in size – without interrupting its retail operations – to 1,785,000 square feet, with eight department stores vs. the earlier five, and totally reconfigured to capitalize on the evolving pedestrian nature of the Strip. The enlarged center establishes its unique presence with a 600-foot-long high-tech canopy known as The Cloud. Suspended 180 feet above a 72,000-square-foot plaza, The Cloud provides visual entertainment as well as welcome shade. A sophisticated audiovisual system projects images to and from the plaza and The Cloud with a series of super-sized LED screens. Fashion shows from around the world and within the center are projected as they take place in real time, thus delivering a vivid embodiment of the project's name. Sophisticated controls allow projections of other world events, as well, in real time. Inside, a great hall,

Top: Whirling geometries of canopy and building.

Above: Projections on round screens in great hall.

Photography: Erhard Pfeiffer.

Above: Canopy known as The Cloud above plaza at center's entrance.

Right: Actual fashion show in great hall.

Far Right: Great hall's elevated, theatrically lighted runway/stage.

23

850 feet long and 150 feet wide, gives visitors a chance to watch real fashion shows on an elevated runway/stage. The complex now includes 4,800 parking spaces. It is bound to be on the "must-see" list of every visitor to Las Vegas.

Above: Canopy as unique evening landmark.

Left: Ample interior circulation areas.

Below: Dynamic building corner.

Photography: Erhard Pfeiffer.

annex|5
An Epstein Design Group

600 West Fulton
Chicago, IL 60661
312.454.9100
312.429.8175
312.559.1217 (Fax)
www.annex5.net
ametter@annex5.net

New York
Tel Aviv
Warsaw
Beijing
Shenzhen
Los Angeles
San Antonio

annex|5
An Epstein Design Group

Motorola Global Software Group
Krakow, Poland

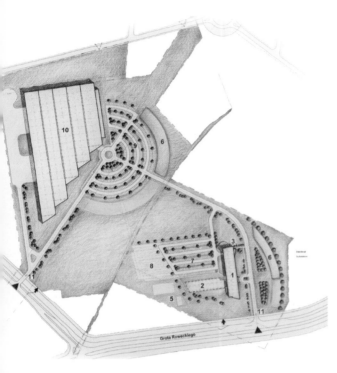

Left: Site plan with completed building and Phase II wing at lower right, proposed manufacturing facility at upper left.

Middle left: Entry detail.

Bottom: Long façade.

Facing page top: Building at night.

Facing page middle: Façade detail.

Facing page bottom: Narrow front facing street.

Photography: Christian Richters.

Intended for the development of proprietary software, this facility is located on the outskirts of Krakow as part of a master planned technology campus associated with the 800-year-old Jagiellonian University – Poland's equivalent to Oxford. Situated among high-profile institutions such as the nearby Papal Academy of Theology, this first private-enterprise building on the campus houses research and development offices, computer labs, and a cafeteria. The design addressed its relationship to these other complexes through its siting strategies and its external expression as an abstract, industrialized volume – in effect a metaphor of software development. The three-story, 5,500-square-meter (59,400-square-foot) structure takes the form of a narrow linear volume oriented perpendicular to the road, yet it provides a frontal reading as approached from the city. The narrow floor plate affords all employees access to daylight, views, and natural ventilation. Workstations are held back from the floor-to-ceiling, double-walled glass envelope to improve circulation and establish a non-hierarchical interior. Amenity spaces and interactive zones are highlighted through shape and location. Phase II will add a 5,000-square-meter volume at right angles to the initial one and parallel to the street, creating a screened car park.

Planning Design of Haikou West Coast
Haikou City, China

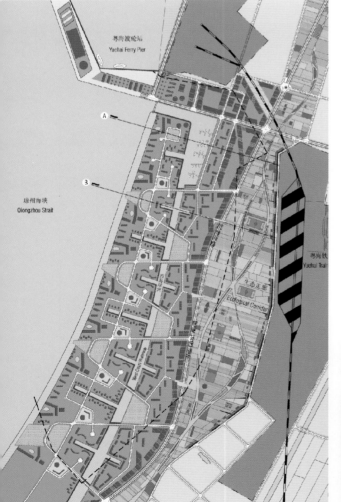

Above: Composite land-use plan.

Left: Detailed master plan of area at left in land-use plan.

Below: Aerial image of area in this master plan.

Awarded First Prize in an international design competition, this plan envisions environmentally responsible development along 26 kilometers of shoreline in Hainan province, an island just off the southeast China coast. Haikou is the political, economic, and cultural center of this tropical island. Considering the expressed goal of developing Hainan into a national four-season garden and holiday resort, Haikou has a unique opportunity to become an ecological showcase. While Haikou has seen tremendous growth, much of it has been unplanned, uncompleted, or unsuccessful. This master plan outlines a framework within which Haikou could implement a successful smart-growth strategy. It defines areas of medium- and high-density residential development, public open spaces, and resort accommo-dations, with creative architectural design guidelines. By properly harnessing the area's resources, the plan could make Haikou world-famous as a green international resort and metropolis.

Above: Bird's-eye view of area at right in land-use plan.

Below left: Concept image of "garden wall" residential units.

Below right: Concept image of beach villas.

Serta International Center
Hoffman Estates, Illinois

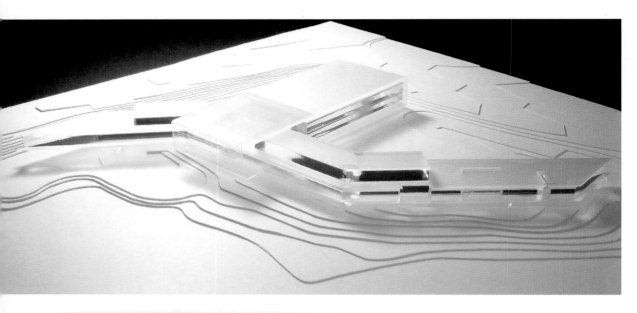

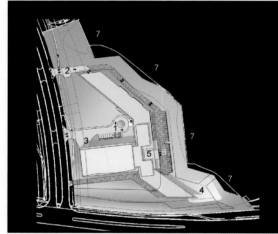

Top and bottom: Model of building in landscape.

Middle left Site plan: 1 main entry drop-off; **2** employee parking entry; **3** service dock; **4** retention pond; **5** outdoor deck; **6** grass paver/fire lane; **7** protected wetlands.

Facing page top: Rendering as seen from grasslands.

Facing page middle: Projection over retention pond.

Facing page bottom: Shading studies.

Model photo: Andrew Metter.

The 80,000-square-foot headquarters of the Serta International Center will be located on a seven-acre parcel in an environmentally sensitive business park. The site immediately adjoins a protected wetland that is essential for storm water management. All parking is located under the building, reducing impervious surfaces on the site and generating the 65-foot width of the office structure. The building appears to hover above a sea of grass, its glass walls shaded by horizontal louvers echoing the prairie landscape. Its massing reflects its two main functions: office space in the "bar" portion along the edge of the wetlands and research and development in a "box" volume. These two join at the center, where public spaces such as showrooms, lunch room, and training auditorium are located. The second level opens to a deck area covered by a canopy with a woven pattern that reflects Serta's interest in textures and fabrics.

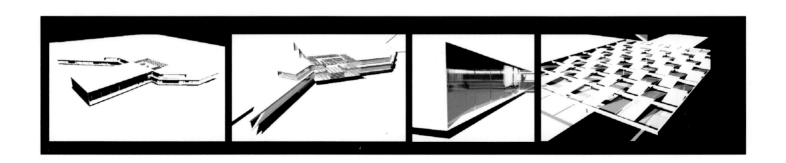

Brighton Village
Coolidge, Arizona

Located 53 miles from Phoenix, Brighton Village is a new planned community of 1,500 acres, projected to house a population of 25,000. Annex/5 was commissioned to design the 57-acre Town Center, which will include civic, small-scaled retail, and higher-density residential functions, along with support functions such as day care, college outreach, and YMCA facilities. A proposed 350,000 square feet of buildings will be organized for walkability, climatic response, and water management, using gray-water reservoirs, water courts, and cisterns. One of the major elements affecting the plan is a large "arroyo" channel, which will double as a greenbelt and open up views of distant mountains. The plan proposes community gardens and farmer's market stalls. The plan is based on solar orientation, composed of a grid of shaded pedestrian arcades oriented on a north-south axis. An additional shading layer of horizontal trellises allows for the generous use of glass, resulting in an intimate connection to the landscape.

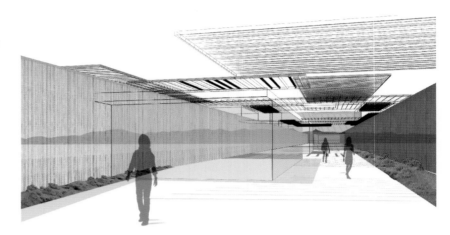

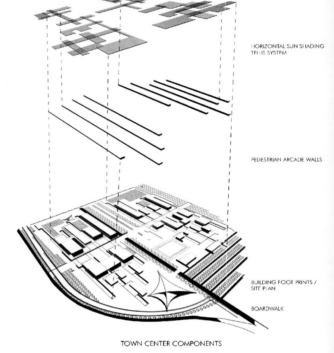

HORIZONTAL SUN SHADING
TELLIS SYSTEM

PEDESTRIAN ARCADE WALLS

BUILDING FOOT PRINTS /
SITE PLAN

BOARDWALK

TOWN CENTER COMPONENTS

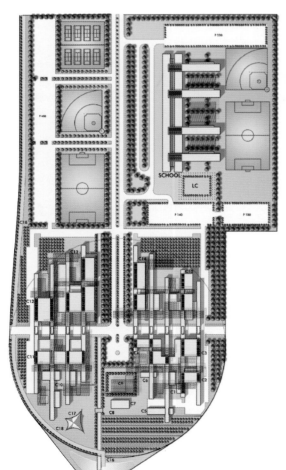

Top: Kit-of-parts concept image.

Middle right: Assembly of kit of parts into town center.

Bottom right: Model of town center.

Left: Plan of town center, including school/athletics campus.

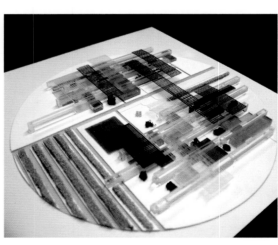

Austin Veum Robbins Partners

One America Plaza
600 West Broadway
Suite 200
San Diego, CA 92101
619.231.1960
619.231.1920 (Fax)

info@avrp.com
www.AVRP.com

Los Angeles
213.627.7170

Ventura
805.652.1129

Tijuana, Mexico
011.52.664.686.3986

Austin Veum Robbins Partners

Austin Veum Robbins Partners

Allegro Tower Apartments
San Diego, California

Above and right: Tower seen from harbor.

Top right: Details of exterior and balconies.

Above right: Eighth-floor pool deck.

Opposite: Tower seen from transit line.

Photography: David Hewitt and Anne Garrison Architectural Photography.

This 204,000-square-foot project was shaped in part by its impact on neighboring buildings. Much of the site is in parts of the Little Italy District where high-rise buildings are not allowed. In response to zoning restrictions and considerations of neighborhood context, the project's 201 apartments are divided into a slim tower which is flanked by an 8-story block on one side and a 5-story block on the other. By making the tower very narrow in its east-west direction, AVRP minimized its shadow on surrounding structures and streets. The tower floor plan is single-loaded, so that every unit faces the bay. Retail spaces at the street level help to activate the street, and there are four levels of parking below ground level. An eighth-floor pool deck offers ample natural light and views of the neighborhood city skyline bay. The cast-in-place concrete structure is clad partly in cast-in-place concrete and partly in GFRC panels.

**Austin
Veum
Robbins
Partners**

Egyptian Lofts
San Diego, California

Bush's historic Egyptian Theater is embedded in the heart of this mixed-use complex, scheduled for late 2005 completion. The aim of the design is to acknowledge the Egyptian Revival style of the theater's colonnaded entrance front and link it to the modern housing constructed around it. Dating from 1926 and originally serving as the foyer for the theater, the monumental entry is being fully renovated, with repairs to deteriorated features and reconstruction of missing but documented elements. The foyer will have the same appearance but play a different role as outdoor seating for a restaurant or café. The new surrounding structure includes retail at the street level, with 80 one- and two-bedroom condominium units on the upper floors. Defining architectural features of the residential construction allude to Egyptian style in the use of Art Deco elements, such as occasional round windows and planar projections that cast deep shadow lines. An angular fin reaching above the flat roof, reminiscent of the "blade" signs of historic movie houses, identifies the complex.

Above: Long facade, with niche at historic theater.

Right: Building corner, showing relationship to existing neighbor.

Photography: David Hewitt and Anne Garrison Architectural Photography.

Rendering: Jason Brown.

Left: Partial elevation view, with vertical fin sign.

Right: Restored Egyptian Theater façade between mixed-use wings.

**Austin
Veum
Robbins
Partners**

Park Laurel on the Prado
San Diego, California

Prominently sited along a broad approach to Balboa Park, this luxury complex includes two similar condominium towers turned at right angles to each other maximizing views. Each building is designed with four condominiums per floor, and condo elevators opening directly into units, creating a 90-percent efficiency above the second floor. Two-story penthouses crown the buildings. The lower two floors contain retail and office space, including an existing bank that has been moved to a new location within the complex. A canopied and vaulted entrance pavilion differentiates the residential entrance from the lower-floor commercial uses and recalls the landmark lattice house in Balboa Park.

Above: Rendering of two towers seen from boulevard.

Left: The completed tower, with entrance in foreground.

Below left: Tower two rising from the two-story commercial base.

Photography: AVRP.

Rendering: Laurel Watts.

**Austin
Veum
Robbins
Partners**

Smart Corner
San Diego, California

Located in San Diego's East Village, Smart Corner is intended as an ideal "smart growth" project. It includes a 19-story condominium tower, a 5-story office building, retail at the street level, and a trolley stop located between its two buildings. Altogether, the project includes 298,000 square feet of residential and 111,500 square feet of office space, plus four levels of underground parking. The project's public open space, including the trolley stop, amounts to 31,000 square feet. The basic 450-square-foot studio unit, starting at $185,000, is designed as flexible space or "morphable rooms," which can be divided by furniture, counters, or partitions. They are adaptable to Murphy beds or partial lofts over kitchens. The developers have set aside 25 units for buyers whose incomes qualify them for special mortgage terms under a first-time-owner program.

Top left: Complex's two buildings, with trolley stop in public space between.

Left: Residential building, showing two distinct architectural volumes.

Above right: Angular walls along trolley line.

Austin Veum Robbins Partners

This upmarket residential condominium is intended to share its Marina District site with the San Diego Children's Museum. A low-rise podium with retail spaces fronts onto three streets with office space above. A single tall tower was chosen in lieu of a lower and bulkier building to minimize obstruction of views from neighboring buildings. The 182 residences are accommodated in a slender 434-foot tower with open space to the south and southeast. The tower and its podium total 350,000 square feet of mostly residential space and 10,000 square feet of pool deck over retail spaces. There are three levels of parking below ground for residents and for the Children's Museum staff and visitors. The Children's Museum will total 32,000 square feet above ground plus basement level. The tower is located along the Harbor Boulevard trolley line and the Martin Luther King Promenade. It is also a short walk from historic and rejuvenated downtown destinations. The project is scheduled for completion in the fall of 2005. The incorporation of the Children's Museum and substantial open space adjacent to the development promises to promote a sense of community and enhance the environment for children and adults alike.

The Pinnacle Museum Tower
San Diego, California

Above: Pinnacle tower rising over public open space.

Left: Broad view of tower in urban setting.

Far left: Tower with Children's Museum at its base.

Photography: AVRP.

Beeler Guest Owens Architects, L.P.

4245 North Central Expressway
Suite 300
Dallas, TX 75205
214.520.8878
214.520.8879 (Fax)
bgoemail@bgoarchitects.com
www.bgoarchitects.com

Beeler Guest Owens Architects, L.P.

Beeler Guest Owens Architects, L.P.

The Highlands of Lombard
Lombard, Illinois

Located in a southwest suburb of Chicago, the Highlands is a high-density infill project with a total of 403 units. A change of elevation of 35 feet across the five-acre site posed design challenges. A five-story, seven-level scheme, with a unique combination of entries, stairs, and elevators, achieved the goal of 81 units per acre. At the center of the development, a six-and-a-half story parking structure is concealed by the surrounding residential buildings. Residents have direct-access parking on the levels where they live. Variations in the design of facades and the elevations of entries reduce the visual impact of this large-scale project on its neighborhood. Construction with light-gauge noncombustible steel turned out to be faster, more accurate, and safer than conventional wood framing. The precast parking garage was significantly faster to erect than cast-in-place construction. The Highlands is a success for the owners, is appreciated by residents, and is well received by the surrounding community.

Above: Typical street elevation.

Top right: Pool courtyard.

Above right: Interior public space.

Facing page: Exterior, showing variety of architectural features.

Photographs: Scott Brennan/ Hedrich Blessing.

Beeler Guest Owens Architects, L.P.

5225 Maple Avenue
Dallas, Texas

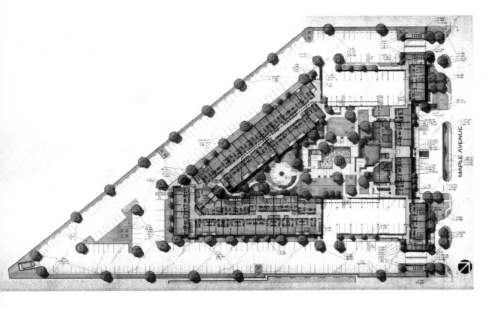

Left: Site plan.

Below left: Entry tower on main façade.

Facing page top: Lobby space and pool courtyard.

Below right: Details of pool deck and building exteriors.

Photography: Mark Guest & Jeffrey Massey.

Just a stone's throw from the center of Dallas, the Maple Avenue infill project provides luxury housing for young professionals who work downtown and in nearby hospitals. The complex fits 224 units and two parking structures on its 4.9-acre site, with a design aesthetic that borrows from the area's light industrial uses of wood, concrete, and steel. A monumental four-story steel-and-glass tower, along with two large arched automobile gates, creates a dramatic entry statement on the Maple Avenue façade. An interior courtyard with a pool and pavilion makes reference to the same rugged aesthetic. The interiors also play variations on the industrial theme, with dark-stained concrete floors, brick walls, and exposed steel structural elements. The project sets an instructive example for a neighborhood undergoing growth and change

Beeler Guest Owens Architects, L.P.

Easton
Dallas, Texas

Situated in a neighborhood first developed in the 1920s and 1930s, primarily with Craftsman-style houses, this three-story development is designed to focus attention on its compatible details and thus minimize its apparent bulk. Seen from the street, the highly articulated elevations divide the building into portions of single-family scale. The three-acre, 150-unit project is the latest infill effort in a 10-year-old process that is revitalizing older residential areas north of downtown along the North Central Expressway. The dwelling units surround a central precast parking garage, effectively blocking its view for neighbors. Also hidden from the community are the project's active pool courtyard and a passive courtyard with an outdoor fireplace. Inside the complex are luxurious interiors with many amenities. The development targets the growing population of young, single professionals who wish to be connected to the single-family lifestyle of the northern suburbs as well as the high-energy activities of downtown Dallas.

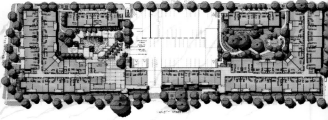

Above left: Craftsman-related details along street.

Left: Pool courtyard.

Above: Plan of Easton Development Site.

Photography: Mark Guest & Darren Dobbins.

Beeler Guest Owens Architects, L.P. The Davis Building
Dallas, Texas

Once a proud symbol of the Dallas financial district, this building has been adapted to house 183 distinctive residential lofts. Originally the headquarters of Republic Bank, the structure played a prominent role in the emergence of Dallas as a major city. It had been unoccupied for over a decade, vandalized and deteriorating. In order to qualify for historic tax credits the renovation had to meet the strict standards of the National Park Service. The individual units are designed as "hard lofts," revealing original building elements such as concrete framing and exposed ducts. Juxtaposed to them are new maple doors and cabinets, granite counters, and oversized oval bathtubs. The penthouse that includes the cupola has five interior levels, two private terraces, and a glass-bottomed hot tub.

Above left: Loft unit.

Above: Internal air and light shaft.

Below left: Building in cityscape.

Below: Cupola and penthouse terrace.

Photography: Mark Guest.

Beeler Guest Owens Architects, L.P.

Union Station
Union, New Jersey

The first transportation-oriented development (TOD) in the state of New Jersey, Union Station will have a 20-minute link to New York City via a metro rail station bordering the property. Its 227 corporate suites will provide limited views of the city skyline. Although surrounded by a residential community, the project draws architectural inspiration from the industrial and shipping facilities that have traditionally occupied the New Jersey shore of the Hudson River. The complex has one level of underground parking, with four levels of wood-framed construction rising from this concrete podium. On top of the garage is an open courtyard with a pool, water features, a fire pit, and private patios adjoining first-floor units. Amenities characteristic of a luxury hotel include a business center, a 50-seat theater, a cybercafé, a fully equipped and staffed fitness center, and a Great Hall for entertaining guests. To tenants, the complex offers a variety of furnished or unfurnished units, available by the week, by the month, or on one-year leases.

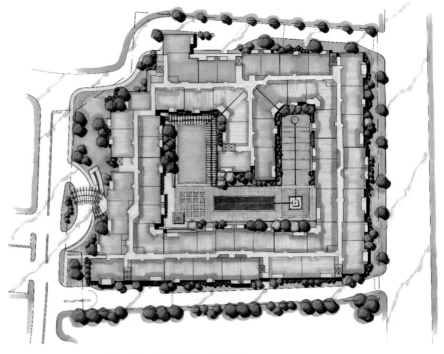

Top: Site plan.

Above: Closer view, showing architectural details.

Left: Overall view.

Callison Architecture, Inc.

1420 Fifth Avenue
Suite 2400
Seattle, WA 98101
206.623.4646
206.623.4625
info@callison.com
www.callison.com

Callison Architecture, Inc.

Callison Architecture, Inc.

Ayala Center Greenbelt
Makati City, Philippines

Greenbelt is a four-story open-air pavilion located within the Ayala Center mixed-use complex in Manila's central business district. While enclosed shopping centers are the rule in this tropical climate, this complex of buildings is interwoven with nature, providing a welcome oasis in a dense city. Louvers, canopies, overhangs, and ample ventilation protect patrons from the weather. The project fits around existing features — a park, a church, and a museum — and was laid out to save 440 mature trees. A "garden wall" concept allows the complex to meet a variety of needs. Its city side presents the unified street front that more fashion oriented retailers desire, and on the other side the park virtually grows into the terraced building, with opportunities for outdoor dining. The project's series of four-story pavilions offers a spectrum of environments, starting next to the museum with quiet bookstores and galleries, proceeding to home and fashion oriented tenants and terrace restaurants near an active intersection, then to a lively zone of music and video stores with dining, cinema, and nightlife.

Above and left: Retail pavilions around water garden.

Below: Entertainment and nightlife portion of project.

Facing page: Interpenetration of building and landscape.

Photography: Chris Eden.

Callison Architecture, Inc.

Grand Gateway
Shanghai, China

Adjacent to the Xuijahui subway station, one of Shanghai's major transportation nodes, Grand Gateway comprises a 1.1-million-square-foot, seven-level retail podium, two 34-story residential towers, two 52-story office towers and a nine-story service apartment. One of the first comprehensive collections of Western-style retailing in Shanghai, the shopping center introduces a variety of themed environments: an outdoor street of restaurants and sidewalk cafes modeled after those of Paris, a lively entertainment zone with Hollywood imagery, and shopping districts ranging from Chinese zones to fashion-oriented international areas. The design creates a synergy among uses for greater identity and impact. Connections to the subway pass through the shopping area to encourage retail volume; apartments are located near the outdoor dining zone as a convenience for residents and a benefit to restaurant operators; the entertainment component reinforces the shopping center and is an amenity for the service apartments and residential towers. The project was designed for flexibility to add or expand components as demand for such functions as offices and service apartments increases.

Above: Cylindrical retail atrium as city landmark and prominent entrance to project.

Top right: Interior of atrium.

Right: Towers exterior.

Below right: Multi-level shopping concourse.

Facing page: Pedestrian retail street within complex.

Photography: Chris Eden.

Callison Architecture, Inc.

Suwon Gateway Plaza
Suwon, Korea

As co-developer and anchor department store, Aekyung has become an industry leader pioneering a new type of retail destination for Korea. Suwon Gateway Plaza incorporates Aekyung at one end, a superstore/entertainment anchor at the other and specialty retailers that link them together, all built above one of the busiest transit centers in the country. Designed to enliven the tra-

ditional Korean shopping experience while capitalizing on the activity generated by the 30 million travelers who pass though the commuter station annually, Gateway Plaza represents the future of retail for the country. The 1,365,000-square-foot mixed-use complex also includes cultural facilities, restaurants, and office space. Responding to an increasingly competitive

retail environment in a previously under-stored nation, Aekyung was the first in Korea to modify the traditional department store format by taking specialty retailers out of the store and into the mall. And while Korean department stores have traditionally been self-contained and indifferent to their settings, Gateway Plaza opens outward to the city and has become a signature

feature of the city of Suwon. Integrating a unique merchandising mix and a strong architectural identity, the center is now being emulated across the country in numerous other developments and has set the standard for retail destinations.

Facing page: Main entrance to complex.

Above: Mixed-use development rising over existing transportation hub.

Far left and left: Interiors of retail mall.

Photography: Chris Eden.

55

Callison Architecture, Inc.

Metropolitan Tower
Seattle, Washington

Located at the edge of Seattle's retail core rather than in one of its established downtown neighborhoods, the Metropolitan uses hospitality-inspired design and service to attract residents to its uptown address. Flanked by office towers, upscale retail, restaurants, hotels and a new Federal courthouse, the location offers a mix of activities and uses. The 24-story, 386-unit luxury apartment tower rests on a seven-story podium that includes parking and street-front retail. Its dramatic architectural profile encases 47 different unit floor plans and the grand hotel style lobby sets the tone for amenities including concierge and valet service, a full-service health club, business and conference center, guest suites and a spacious, eighth-floor garden terrace. The tower's plan and distinctive form are derived from the unique angular geometry of the site. The design objective was a sleek, sophisticated hotel ambiance that would fit the neighborhood image and the likely preferences of those who would live here. The exterior limestone base, pre-cast panels, metal and glass echo the materials of neighboring buildings. The units stress elegant living accommodations and are laid out to take maximum advantage of spectacular views from cantilevered bays and recessed balconies. Residents ranging from their early 20s to mid-70s cite the array of services as well as proximity to social and work opportunities as reasons they chose to live at the Metropolitan. Despite its completion amid a sharp economic downturn, the building was nearly 90 percent leased when opened.

Above: Tower in its edge-of-downtown context.

Right: Glazed canopy providing pedestrian shelter.

Far right: Metal and glass details relate to surrounding non-residential buildings.

Photography: Chris Eden.

Canin Associates

500 Delaney Avenue
Orlando, FL 32801
407.422.4040
407.425.7427 (Fax)
design@canin.com
www.canin.com

Canin Associates

Grande Lakes Resorts
Orlando, Florida

A resort destination has been created here, knitting two hotels and the health club/spa structure between them into a complex with a distinctive ambience. But the elite Ritz Carlton and the less formal J.W. Marriott maintain their separate brand identities. The identity of the resort is established for arriving visitors by a mile-long road of picturesque landscaping designed to immerse the guest in the relaxed experience of a tropical resort. The amenities of the complex, in addition to the two hotels with their total of 1,600 rooms, include the health club and spa, two pools, and a golf course. One of the most memorable features of the 500-acre

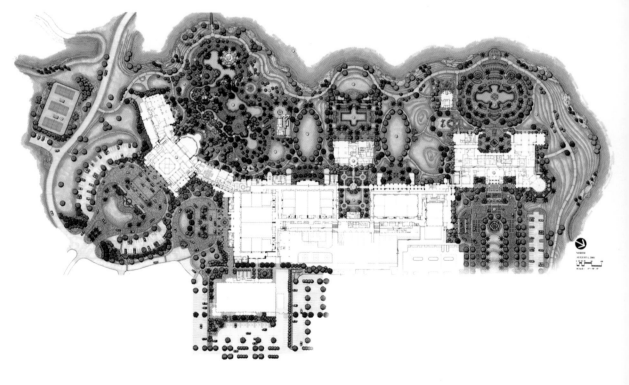

grounds is the lazy river, a convoluted and meandering watercourse running between rustic stone walls and under lush plantings, along which guests can be propelled, playfully splashing or passively observing the setting.

Facing page: Pool and spa area.

Above: Lazy river passing under footbridge and fountain.

Above right: J.W. Marriott seen from lazy river.

Right: Master plan of J.W. Marriott (at left on plan) and Ritz Carlton properties.

Canin Associates

Buena Vista
Bakersfield, California

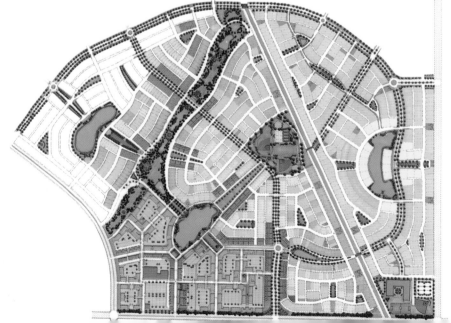

On a 2,182-acre site in a high-growth area dominated by conventional development, a distinctive urban community of 7,450 residential units has been planned. Traditional town planning principles have been applied to generate a sense of place and shared experience. The development has been laid out as a series of villages that are both self-contained and linked with a three-acre Town Center, which includes a recreation complex with a pool, exercise rooms, arts and crafts studios, etc. Plans also include four elementary schools and one middle school. All parts of the community are connected by an extensive and varied system of parks, totaling 200 acres, many of them featuring bodies of water.

Above left: Town center seen from residential balcony.

Far left: Master plan, with higher density areas shown predominantly yellow, Town Center in middle.

Left: Waterfront structures mixing ground-floor restaurants and retail with upper-floor condos.

Canin Associates

Solivita
Poinciana, Florida

"A sense of real community" was a primary goal in planning this age-restricted adult community. The completed first phase of the 3,300-acre, 6,500-unit development comprises a Village Center, which includes two restaurants, a coffee shop, some retail, and a Gathering Center for dances and special events. Further amenities such as a golf course, tennis courts, a grand ballroom, and a craft and fitness center provide centers of community activity that are not dependent on retail. There will be walking and biking paths and a canoe trail along the mile-long community waterway. Intensive landscaping includes thousands of flowering shrubs and numerous canopy trees, many of them relocated from within the site. The streets and architecture of the Village Center appeal through their traditional proportions and planning principles. So effective has this center been as an indication of the entire community that many residents have purchased residences before model homes were even built. Phase III of the community is being completed as this book goes to press.

Facing page, top: Main spine of Village Center.

Facing page, bottom left: Bridge over community waterway.

Facing page, bottom right: Village Center's main entrance.

Above: Characteristic buildings.

Below: Village Center master plan.

Canin Associates

Promenade Town Center
Pasco County, Florida

Top: Town center boulevard.
Above: Master plan.

The planning challenge here was to create an appealing mixed-use town center at the intersection of arterial roads that are designed for cars rather than pedestrians. The solution was to lay out two-way couplets to disperse traffic on pairs of one-way streets. Although one-way streets are not usually associated with traditional town planning, in this case they serve the necessary function of reducing street width and traffic flow to a level compatible with a pedestrian-oriented environment. Circles at intersections provide further traffic-calming effects. A pedestrian-friendly tree-lined boulevard – identifiable on the site plan by diagonal green band – runs through the core of the development. The 100-acre town center is planned to include 770 residential units, including townhouses, apartments, and condominiums, plus retail, a grocery store, office space, and a hotel.

Carter & Burgess, Inc.

Corporate Office
777 Main Street
Fort Worth, TX 76102
800.494.4082
design@c-b.com
www.c-b.com

Austin
Baltimore
Boston
Columbus
Dallas
Denver
Detroit
Fort Lauderdale
Houston
Las Vegas
Little Rock
New York

Oakland
Oklahoma City
Orlando
Phoenix
Raleigh
Sacramento
Salt Lake City
San Antonio
Santa Ana
Tampa
Washington D.C.

Carter & Burgess, Inc.

North Hills
Raleigh, North Carolina

North Hills Mall, one of the South's pioneering enclosed shopping centers, had served affluent Raleigh suburbs for decades, but was being upstaged by newer malls farther out. Developer John Kane saw the opportunity to convert the flagging retail complex into a new "downtown" for those suburbs, strategically located along a major expressway. The $200-million redevelopment started in 2001 with plans to transform the 15-acre North Hills Plaza into an upscale neighborhood shopping center. By 2002 the project had grown to include the 35-acre mall site across the street.

The project includes more than 770,000 square feet of retail and restaurants laid out around a town square and shopping streets with on-street parking. Other components of the project are a 14-screen cinema, a 200-key hotel with banquet facilities, 300,000 square feet of offices, a 300-unit residential building and a 65-unit luxury condominium tower over community-oriented street-level retail. Two levels of underground parking underpin much of the development. In both its planning and architecture, North Hills avoids the homogeneity of the typical lifestyle center, displaying the kind of variety found in a 1920s midtown. Building facades and details are highly varied but limited in color to the neutral tones typically seen in such older cores. The project's pedestrian-scaled streetscape will link its commercial facilities to condominiums on the periphery to form a highly walkable community.

Above left: Internal street, showing fountain and angled parking.

Left: Pedestrian area around central pavilion.

Photography: J. Brough Schamp and Eric Taylor (Right streetscape).

Top: Shopping street with offices above, retail and residential beyond.

Above: Aerial rendering of completed project.

Left: Shops in evening.

Carter & Burgess, Inc.

The Walk
Atlantic City, New Jersey

Left: Aerial panorama.

Below left: Retail shops and fountain.

Bottom left: Street scene showing graphics and landscaping.

Bottom right: Storefronts with bold signage.

Photography: J. Brough Schamp.

Although legalized gambling has spurred construction along Atlantic City's fabled Boardwalk, there have been few attractions to lure visitors away from the casinos and few family-oriented developments. The Walk addressed this problem by converting an eight-block area between the Boardwalk and the new Atlantic City Convention Center into a 320,000-square-foot pedestrian-friendly retail, dining, and entertainment environment. Also linking the city's intermodal transportation center with the Boardwalk, the site had been largely barren and uninviting. The Walk's tenants include shops, restaurants, entertainment facilities, and factory outlets, located in subgroups in an open streetscape enhanced by plazas, fountains, kiosks, and distinctive landscaping, lighting, and environmental graphics. The project was developed by the Cordish Company in collaboration with the city's Casino Reinvestment Development Authority, which made an initial $31-million investment. The two organizations are now researching the viability of adding residential development to the project.

Carter & Burgess, Inc.

Power Plant Live!
Baltimore, Maryland

Above: Overall view showing landmark fountain and identifying sign.

Left: Street scene with bold graphics and generous greenery.

Below left: Restaurant graphics that are lively yet respectful of historic building fronts.

Photography: J. Brough Schamp.

A two-city-block area of twentieth-century row buildings near Baltimore's lively Inner Harbor has been redeveloped as a colorful entertainment district. Adjacent to the established Power Plant retail project, the new district has been dubbed Power Plant Live! and features light shows, a 2,500-seat music hall for nationally known performers, and tenants such as the Improv, Babalu Grill, Maryland Art Place and Ruth's Chris Steak House. Originally, the area's landmark fountain was to be the focal feature, but Carter & Burgess judged that some-

thing was needed that would represent the concepts "power plant" and "live." Drawing on the imagery of electricity, the project's design and graphics represent high-voltage energy. The Power Plant Live! sign lights up in sequence, and there are bright marquees and bold neon signs. One entrance is dominated by the image of a workman holding a lightning bolt, which he crashes into an anvil once an hour to set off a light and sound show.

Carter & Burgess, Inc.

Citrus Plaza
Redlands, California

Orange groves, introduced to the area around Redlands in 1873, set off a second California "Gold Rush" and blanketed the area until recent decades, when the mild climate and striking scenery supported a population boom. Located at the intersection of Highways 10 and 30, the 125-acre Citrus Plaza site can draw on a pool of about one million residents. The 50-acre Phase One development, completed in 2004, includes 520,000 square feet, with nationally known retailers along broad landscaped walks. A central fountain and a signature 45-foot tower serve as focal points. Highly visible from the freeways, the project draws design inspiration from the Spanish Colonial architecture of the area. Discreet, abstracted citrus fruit motifs appear in the tops of the openwork metal domes and in lighting elements. The development is planned for expansion to a total of 1.9 million square feet.

Top: Central court and tiled fountain.

Above: Regionally inspired architecture in the landscape.

Left: Ample drives and walkways approaching shops and restaurants.

Photography: Larry Falke (top & left), Richard Leon (above).

Carter & Burgess, Inc.

The Shoppes at Blackstone Valley
Millbury, Massachusetts

For an integrated retail facility that includes big box, junior box, and lifestyle retail, the lifestyle component is laid out in a C-shaped plan that creates a central public space. Building design here is characterized by changes of plane on the relatively continuous storefronts and distinctive roof forms and turrets appearing at key locations. Purposeful over-scaling of the architectural elements and control of signage and lighting lend an air of restraint and dignity to the environment as a whole. The use of fieldstone and brick, along with well-pro-portioned moldings and eaves, connects the project to regional traditions. The streetscape is generously provided with raised and flush planting beds to humanize the experience of this large-scale complex.

Right: Typical walkway and storefronts.

Below: Buildings around central public space.

Photography: J. Brough Schamp.

Carter & Burgess, Inc.

Walkers Brook Crossing
Jordan's Furniture, Home Depot, IMAX
North Reading, Massachusetts

Above: Jordan's just before opening.

Photography: J. Brough Schamp (above), Anton Grassi (below).

Below: Jordan's Furniture store, IMAX theater, and Home Depot.

Jordan's has become one of the country's highest sales-per-square-foot furniture retailers by making every store a fully themed experience. This 252,000-square-foot facility carries the concept to a new level, with a "Beantown" entertainment area just inside the entrance, an ice cream stand, a full-service diner, and a 500-seat IMAX theater. Playing on Boston's nickname, Beantown exhibits replicas of the city's landmarks composed of over 11 million Jelly Belly jelly beans. While they eat, shoppers can watch a Liquid Fireworks display. The main selling floor resembles a street, its windows displaying complete rooms with coordinated accessories. A glazed volume facing Interstate 95 exhibits the interior activity to the highway. Additionally, this project includes a 165,000 square-foot Home Depot at the lower level.

Chan Krieger & Associates

8 Story Street
5th Floor
Cambridge, MA 02138
617.354.5315
617.354.3252 (Fax)
mhoward@chankrieger.com
www.chankrieger.com

Chan Krieger & Associates

Beth Israel Deaconess Medical Center
& Master Plan
Boston, Massachusetts

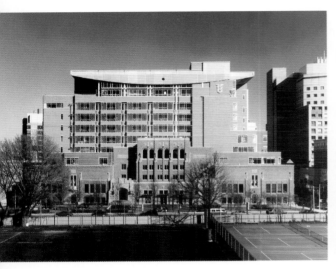

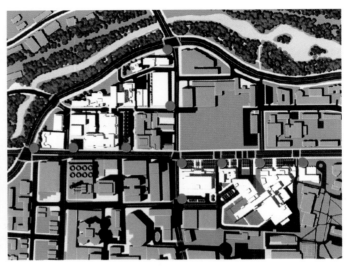

Above: New clinical center, which incorporates former Massachusetts College of Art building.

Above right: Master plan of two combined campuses, with entry points marked.

Right: Landscaped pedestrian link.

Photography: Peter Vanderwarker and Steve Rosenthal.

A $160-million redevelopment program is intended to consolidate the two existing campuses of the former Beth Israel Medical Center and the New England Deaconess Hospital, giving them a single identity. Chan Krieger drew up the master plan for this redevelopment, including design of open spaces, and served as design architect for the shell and core of the Carl J. Shapiro Clinical Center, a new building for the combined institution. The $100-million, 380,000-square-foot clinical center includes medical offices, research facilities, a center for shared technology, and a 500-car underground garage, and it incorporates the former Massachusetts College of Art building. Objectives of the master plan include improving the appearance and efficiency of the unified campus, introducing design features to define its entry portals, and distinguishing it within the larger context of the Longwood medical facilities area and the city.

Chan Krieger & Associates

City Hall Plaza Community Arcade and Government Center Master Plan
Boston, Massachusetts

Left: Arcade, showing cable-supported canopies.

Right: Overall view with Cambridge Street at left, JFK Federal Office Building beyond arcade.

Below: Seating platform built over granite plaza steps.

Photography: Chan Krieger & Associates, Patrick Whittemore/Boston Herald.

The arcade is the first phase of a larger City Hall Plaza redesign and renovation effort master planned by the firm. The arcade is designed to better define the curved Cambridge Street side of the plaza without closing it off. It will serve as a spine between two proposed projects: a new transit station at one end and the JFK tower garden at the other. Included in the arcade project are

three seating platforms, extending beyond the existing plaza steps to serve as public seating areas, stages for small performances and speakers, or stalls for periodical farmers' markets. An elaborate lighting scheme includes LED light tubes mounted on the arcade columns, which can be programmed to change colors. The plaza master plan entailed a four-year process of studies and public approvals. It seeks to improve the "Walk-to-the-Sea" from Faneuil Hall to the harbor, to create small-scaled gathering and lingering spaces, to enhance the amphitheater-like qualities of the plaza for public activities, and to reintroduce Hanover Street to make the plaza a more effective part of downtown movement patterns.

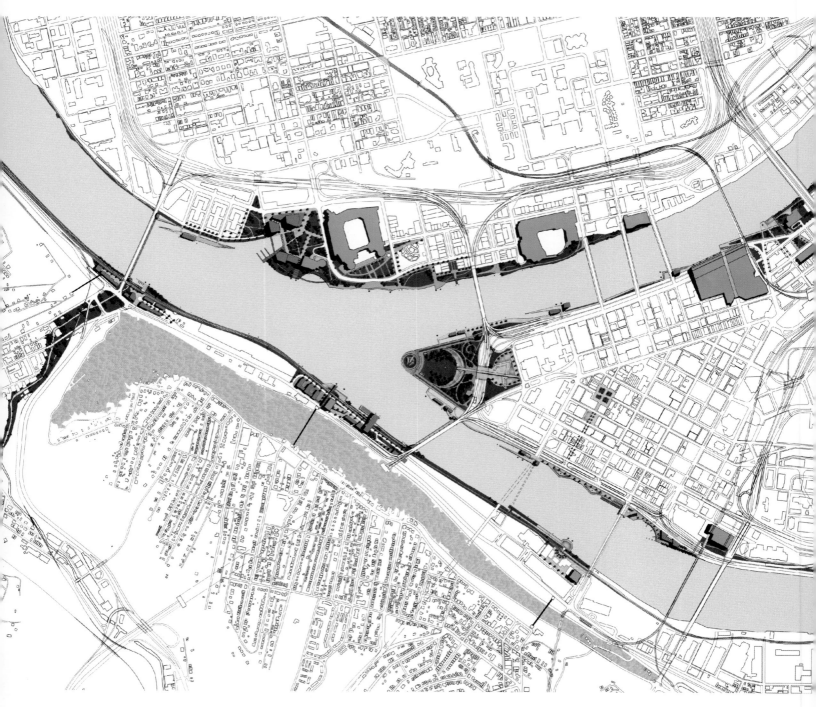

Top: Proposed north shore development.

Above: Master plan showing proposed public and private development.

Left: Bessemer Court Pedestrian Bridge on south shore.

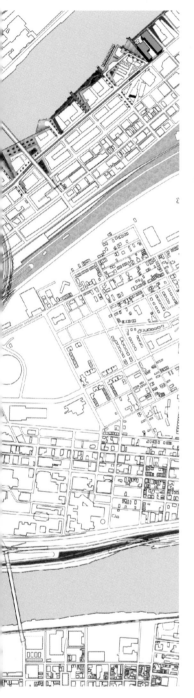

The RiverLife Task Force chose the firm to create a vision plan for energizing and directing development along Pittsburgh's three riverfronts. With two new stadiums, a new convention center, an extension of a light rail system, and several corporate buildings in design or under construction, a primary goal of this effort was to ensure that new private development and public investment will be carried out within a sustainable framework and to world-class design standards. New housing, water transit, and overall balance of public amenities and private investments were reviewed through an extensive public process. The resulting plan refocuses the Pittsburgh community on its rivers and proposes a great urban river park. With the backing of the city's major foundations, institutions, and corporations, the task force is charged with directing public and private investments totaling $10 billion over the next 10 years. The firm also designed the Bessemer Court Pedestrian Bridge, located at Station Square, a 52-acre entertainment development across the river from downtown Pittsburgh's Golden Triangle. The project includes $3 million in public funding for improvements,

including a pedestrian bridge spanning railroad tracks for access to the riverfront, which features a public marina, a floating boardwalk, and an entertainment venue called The Landing. Designed to provide views of Bessemer Court's fountains, the river, and the city, the bridge features contemporary industrial materials that also reflect the industrial heritage of the site.

Top to bottom: Tip of Golden Triangle, showing stadiums on north shore; Golden Triangle with lighted bridges; two aerial views of proposals for confluence of rivers.

Photography: Chan Krieger & Associates.

Chan Krieger & Associates

Fort Washington Way Highway Reconfiguration
Cincinnati, Ohio

Top left: Bridge over highway showing new design elements.

Above left: Benches and tree plantings along walkway.

Left: Mast and barrier on bridge.

Above: Bridge details.

Photography: Chan Krieger & Associates, Parsons Brinckerhoff, Hargreaves Associates.

This $160-million project is associated with the reconstruction of Fort Washington Way, part of an interstate highway along the edge of downtown Cincinnati. Covering 30 acres of highway and adjoining service roads, the project includes: five new bridges – two of them designed as new city "gateways"; over a mile of roadway walls providing visual relief for motorists and pedestrians; custom-designed light fixtures and railings integrated into the overall aesthetic yet complying with stringent federal highway standards. Linear parks along the surface boulevards flanking the highway, developed in collaboration with Hargreaves Associates, include: tree plantings, walls for sitting, special paving materials, protective barriers, and signage/banner standards.

Charlan • Brock & Associates, Inc.

2600 Maitland Center Parkway
Suite 260
Maitland, FL 32751
407.660.8900
407.875.9948 (Fax)
Butch@cbaarchitects.com
www.cbaarchitects.com

Charlan·Brock & Associates, Inc.

Williams Walk at Bartram Park
Jacksonville, Florida

Even though mixed-use developments are today's exciting housing types, there remains a strong market for stand-alone garden apartment communities. For developers, they offer the ability to respond quickly to changing local economic conditions. This 380-unit Williams Walk community represents this type of development and market situation. Residential buildings have been carefully sited to maintain the feeling of several villages. Views of the lake have been left unencumbered and parking has been sited to minimize its visual impact. The architecture of the project reflects modern design philosophies and historical influences, drawing inspiration from the nearby historic town of St. Augustine and the travels of the early botanist, William Bartram. The development's buildings are nestled among large existing oaks and pines. Outdoor spaces are designed as roofless rooms, furnished with elements that evoke history. A variety of cedar gateways are embellished with hand-painted botanical views. The Village Meeting Hall, or Clubhouse, evokes an earlier era of subtropical leisure. Without leaving the property, a resident can lounge in a hammock or club chair in a shady arbor, dine al fresco around an outdoor fireplace, indulge in a spa getaway, or swim laps in the community swimming pool.

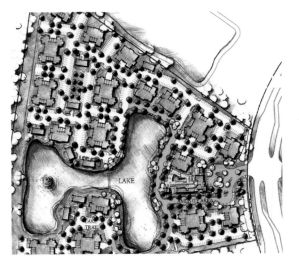

Above right: Site plan, with entrance at right, clubhouse nearby on lake.

Above left: Cedar gateway featuring botanical painting.

Left: Residential courtyard

Right: Clubhouse loggia overlooking pool.

Top: Community pool and club-house.

Above: Portion of pool area.

Right: Typical residential buildings and landscaping.

Photography: Beverly Brosius.

Charlan•Brock & Associates, Inc.

Aqua Condominiums
Panama City Beach, Florida

Left: Ground floor plan of tower and garage.

Below left: Beachfront view.

Below: Entrance front.

Renderings: Genesis Studios.

An unusually long, thin oceanfront site conditioned the design of this high-rise resort condominium. The 5.37-acre property was so restrictive that parking had to be located in a parking garage on the opposite side of a busy highway, with a safe, secure connection via a 200-foot-long bridge. The narrow configuration of the site also left inadequate space for the desired beach-front pool deck. This limitation was converted to an asset by carving some of the pool environment into the base of the building. Water was made an element of the Aqua theme with a series of fountains, pools, and runnels leading from the main entrance through to the pool deck. Other identifying features of the design are the broad trellises mounted on the rooftop, providing a play of light and shadow over the building surfaces. Another design focus was the use of salt-tolerant materials such as the split-face limestone cladding on the structure's lower floors. Budgeted at $55 million, the project is scheduled for completion in 2006.

Charlan·Brock & Associates, Inc.

Uptown Maitland West
Maitland, Florida

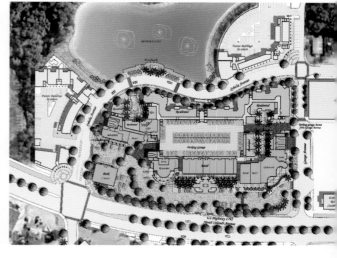

Above: Site plan.

Left: Perspective at major intersection, lower right on site plan.

Renderings: Genesis Studios.

Above: Partial elevation on George Avenue, right on site plan.

Below: Elevation on North Orlando Avenue, bottom on site plan.

Uptown Maitland West is an important step in revitalizing the downtown of Maitland, a suburb of Orlando. Located on 6.13 acres, this private development in the heart of the city is designed to contribute to a vibrant Town Center. It includes 300 condominium homes, 34,000 square feet of retail, 3 restaurants, and a bank. The development has been conceived as one where many residents will also work in the community's shops and restaurants. Planning has been fine-tuned to ensure that the pedestrian takes precedence over vehicular traffic. Estimated to cost $65 million and slated for completion in 2007, the project is envisioned as inspiring continued redevelopment of Maitland's core.

Charlan•Brock & Associates, Inc.

Rarity Pointe Lodge and Spa
Knoxville, Tennessee

Left: Aerial perspective of development.

Below left: Site plan.

Bottom right: Elevation of Lodge interior.

Bottom left: Inspiration for niches on interior elevation.

Renderings: Genesis Studios – Peter Chanakul.

A hilltop village overlooking Lake Tellico, just outside Knoxville, will evoke the qualities of English country estate of around 1900. Working with an interdisciplinary team, the architects have organized almost 200 condominium units on the five-acre site. Most of the units will be in two five-story structures flanking the central Lodge. The Lodge itself will include 13 condominiums above common facilities that will be open to the wider community: a 5,500-square-foot health club and spa, open to a wider public, a 20,000-square-foot conference facility, and a 7,000-square-foot first-class restaurant conceived in the spirit of the Biltmore estate in Asheville, North Carolina. The Lodge complex will include indoor and outdoor pools, and there will be extensive boating facilities along the lake shore.

Charlan·Brock & Associates, Inc.

The Flats at Rosemary Beach
Rosemary Beach, Florida

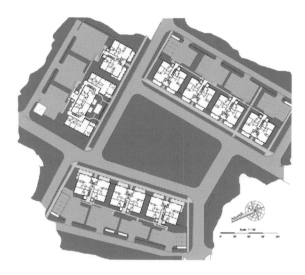

Above: Site plan.

Right: Typical exterior treatment, with turret on end unit.

Left: Walled ground-floor terraces and bracketed upper-floor porches.

Below: Shared central park.

Below right: Subtly varied row.

Photography: Charlan·Brock & Associates, Inc.

This 60-unit resort condominium development had to meet the stringent design guidelines of Rosemary Beach, which call for buildings recalling Florida and West Indian traditions. The detailing required under guidelines can be expensive, but the architects were able to interpret them here within the developer's target sales price range. One strategy was to build simple, repetitive volumes. Most of the buildings contain two mirror-image units per floor, stacked three high, each offering three exposures. An appropriately tropical exterior image, with generous porches, has been created using straightforward components. All of the units overlook a central park, with small-scaled parking areas on their opposite fronts.

Charlan·Brock & Associates, Inc.

Cheval Apartments on Old Katy Road
Houston, Texas

Left: Site plan, with fault line toward lower left.

Below: Main entrance front, with arched entrances to motor court.

Bottom: Overall front view.

Renderings: Genesis Studios.

As land values escalate, a client who had previously built simply-designed garden apartments took on a more demanding challenge, an old coffee mill on a 10.5-acre site that has a geological fault line running through it. The mill will be replaced by a 387-unit urban apartment development. The project will project the image of a single low-rise structure, wrapping discreetly around a central parking structure. Given the number of units, many will necessarily be oriented inward, where inviting courtyards have been created. The extensive corridors have been treated as pedestrian streets, with intersections designed to promote socializing and some routes passing through the club facilities. A motor court, just inside the entry arches, establishes a distinctive first impression and helps with orientation.

CBT/Childs Bertman Tseckares Inc.

110 Canal Street
Boston, MA 02114
617.262.4354
617.236.0378 (Fax)
www.cbtarchitects.com

CBT/Childs Bertman Tseckares Inc.

CBT/Childs Bertman Tseckares Inc.

Columbus Center
Boston, Massachusetts

Above: Project in city context.

Above: right: Mixed-use tower.

Left: Residential street.

Below left: Turnpike topped by residential buildings surrounding garage.

This 1.4 million-square-foot mixed-use development is proposed for three parcels — equivalent to three city blocks — over the Massachusetts Turnpike. It will knit together the historic South End and Back Bay neighborhoods. The parcels closest to the existing commercial development will include two high-rises with ground-floor retail, hotel floors above the retail, and several stories of luxury condominiums at the top. The third parcel will contain a 650-space parking garage surrounded by townhouses and retail. The project is designed so that it "looks like city streets and not like a mega project." Columbus Center buildings have individual, rather than group, identity — the high-rise is light and airy, and the lower buildings are detailed in masonry like the existing context. Bridging over the turnpike right of way posed major engineering and design challenges. In order to avoid elevated first floors, the huge support structures spanning the highway have to be concealed inside the buildings rather than under them.

CBT/Childs Bertman Tseckares Inc.

North Point
Cambridge, Boston, Somerville, Massachusetts

North Point is envisioned as a unique 21st century smart-growth, transit-oriented neighborhood that will transform 45 acres of under-utilized industrial land in the municipalities of Cambridge, Boston, and Somerville, MA, into a vibrant and integrated mixed-use community. The development consists of over 2.2 million-square-feet of commercial space, 2,700 residences and substantial retail to support 24-hour activities of residents, workers and visitors. The master plan also encourages a variety of built-form and architectural expression that is reflective of a true urban setting. Once complete, this 15- to 20-year project will have created 20 new blocks, a new Square for a state-of-the-art subway station, a multi-use bike and recreational trail, nearly one mile of new roadway and utility infrastructure, and a wide-range of public amenities. At the heart of North Point is the Central Park, 6.3-acres of green space designed to serve those that live and work in the neighborhood, as well as to attract visitors from the surrounding area.

Top: Bird's-eye view of entire project.

Above: Loft-style residences.

Left: Views of park and mixed-use buildings.

CBT/Childs Bertman Tseckares Inc.

The Residences at Kendall Square
Cambridge, Massachusetts

Left: Overall view of tower.

Below: Street level, with shops and residential entrance.

The Residences at Kendall Square will be one of the first projects built in a dynamic new 10-acre, mixed-use community in Cambridge, MA, conceived as a hub for biotechnology. Additional elements of the project are offices and laboratories for biotech companies, and extensive entertainment and recreation facilities, such as restaurants, outdoor parks, and a small kayak facility on a canal that feeds into the Charles River. CBT has designed the tallest building in the new development, a 332,000-square-foot residential tower that will include 330 rental apartments ranging from studios to two-bedroom units for employees and students of nearby universities and research centers, as well as 10,000-square-feet of retail space and a 15,000-square-foot health spa. While the top of the building animates the Cambridge skyline, the one-story base juts out and away from the tower and connects into a lively pedestrian network of open spaces, promenades, specialty shops, and restaurants at ground level.

CBT/Childs Bertman Tseckares Inc.

Rollins Square
Boston, Massachusetts

With a strong commitment to provide residential opportunities for families of all incomes, the Planning Office for Urban Affairs/Archdiocese of Boston developed Rollins Square as a model for a mixed-income community that combines market-rate, moderately-priced, and low-income housing in a high-quality condominium complex. CBT designed this award-winning project as a grouping of six-story elevator buildings and four-story townhouses to foster a sense of community for the residents. In addition to 184 residential units that vary in size from one-bedroom apartments to three-bedroom duplexes, the 376,000-square-foot project also includes a 200-space below-grade parking facility in an area where parking is scarce. Uniting the Victorian architectural traditions of the historic district with the industrial character of nearby warehouses that surround the site, Rollins Square harmonizes with the existing cityscape without overwhelming it. At the center of the project, the buildings wrap around a quaint exterior courtyard that captures the spirit of the surrounding district and gives the residents a shared sense of community, security and place. The complex also maintains a pedestrian orientation to the neighborhood by providing new ground-level retail and office space, and seating walls that serve as social gathering places for residents and members of the larger community.

Top: Complex seen along existing street.

Above: Aerial view.

Right: Buildings around central courtyard.

Photography: Robert Benson; Mark Flannery (aerial).

CBT/Childs Bertman Tseckares Inc.

The Prudential Center Redevelopment
Boston, Massachusetts

CBT is leading the effort on a 15-year, $1 billion expansion and redesign of the Prudential Center. Upon completion, the 27-acre site will feature 1.8 million square feet of new office, residential, and retail space that will give this 40-year old Boston landmark a new identity.

111 Huntington Avenue is a 21st-century icon that bolsters the Prudential Center's identity as a world-class commercial district in Boston. The 36-story office tower is the cornerstone of CBT's revised master plan for the southern portion of the complex.

The Winter Garden serves as the Prudential Center's dramatic new entrance for Huntington Avenue. The Garden is lined with retail shops, pedestrian connections and seating areas under a glazed façade and roof stretching 50 feet wide, 35 feet high and over 400 feet long.

The Belvedere is a 131,000-square-foot 11-story luxury condominium building that offers convenient 24-hour access to the Center's urban amenities and cultural activities in addition to a variety of other services that support a city lifestyle.

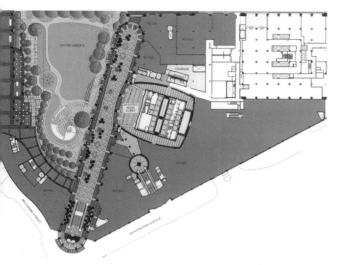

Facing page: 111 Huntington Avenue, Boston's newest addition to it's skyline.

Left: Partial master plan, showing Winter Garden, landscaped court, and lower floors of Belvedere and 111 Huntington Avenue.

Below: 111 Huntington Avenue in context, with original Prudential tower in background.

Right: The Belvedere.

Right middle and bottom: Exterior and interior views of Shaw's Supermarket.

Above: Huntington Avenue entrance.

Above right: A portion of the 400-foot-long Winter Garden.

Below: The Mandarin Oriental (rendering by Neoscape).

Photography: Jonathan Hillyer/Esto, 111 Huntington Avenue and The Belvedere; Edward Jacoby, Shaw's Supermarket.

The Mandarin Oriental will be a 450,000-square-foot building that will include a 150-room Mandarin Hotel, 50 individually planned condominiums, 35 rental apartments, street-level retail space, and guest amenities to define the highest standard of luxury in Boston. The Mandarin Oriental-Boston will be a microcosm of the 24-hour urban environment that has come to distinguish the Prudential Center as a place to work and live.

Shaw's Supermarket provides a vital urban amenity for the surrounding residential area. Situated in a prominent and accessible location within the Prudential Center complex, the 52,000-square-foot facility combines a range of amenities with the size of a superstore yet offers the convenience and breadth of product typically found in the suburbs.

Costas Kondylis and Partners LLP

31 West 27 Street
New York, NY 10001
212.725.4655
212.725.3441 (Fax)
info@kondylis.com
www.kondylis.com

Costas Kondylis and Partners LLP

Trump World Tower
845 United Nations Plaza
New York, New York

A neighbor of the United Nations Headquarters in Midtown Manhattan, this 860-foot-tall residential tower rises as a sleek rectangular form, without setbacks or ornamentation. Designed to appear as if sheathed in a single sheet of glass, the building was inspired by such nearby International Style landmarks as the Seagram Building and the U.N. Secretariat. Its curtain wall is composed of deep-bronze-colored glass, with a structural silicone glazing system, creating a subtle, incised grid that gives the walls scale and texture. On the interior, glazing extends from the ceilings — ranging from 10 to 16 feet in height — down to 20 inches above the floors, offering residents panoramic views of the Manhattan cityscape, the

East River, and distant landscapes. The uninterrupted verticals of the tower's form and an advanced structural system allow optimum layouts of the 370 apartments, without the obstructions of massive piers or setbacks. Street-level amenities include a 30-foot-high lobby, a generous porte-cochere, and a private garden. There is also a 72-car garage, an 11,000-square-foot health club with a 60-foot lap pool and a ground-floor luxury restaurant.

Facing page: Tower rising above nearby buildings.

Above: Building as high point on East Midtown skyline, U.N. Headquarters to left.

Left: Upper floors of shaft, showing curtain wall details.

Photography: Jeff Goldberg©. ESTO (facing page).

Costas Kondylis and Partners LLP   The Heritage
New York, New York

Above: Trump Place along Hudson.

Below and facing page: The Heritage, seen from Riverside Park with other Trump Place buildings beyond.

Photography: Chuck Choi.

Occupying a unique site, where the Manhattan street grid meets the Trump Place development in a sweeping curve, the Heritage is designed as the unmistakable cornerstone of the towered row. Rather than designing the building by fitting units into its curved volume and the square tower that rises from it, the architects took an "inside-out" approach in which the optimum apartment layouts were arrived at first. Features of the 174 units include foyer galleries, studies adjoining bedrooms, and luxurious bathrooms with "his" and "hers" dressing rooms. To make the most of dramatic views, window assemblies seven feet high and 16 feet wide were adopted. Recessing balconies into the façade creates shadowed variations in the façade pattern and provides occupants with outdoor spaces protected from wind and rain. Two full-floor units on the 30th and 31st floors feature loggias 30 feet long and 8 feet deep. Amenities of the Heritage, consistent with those of other Trump Place buildings, include meeting rooms, a children's play room, storage rooms, a 199-car garage, and a second-floor health club, with two indoor pools offering stunning views of Riverside Park and the Hudson River.

Costas Kondylis and Partners LLP

Morton Square
600 Washington St.
New York, New York

To build a full-block residential complex in an area traditionally zoned for manufacturing, the developers first went through a two-year process to get a special permit. An agreed-upon zoning envelope for the site allowed for three contiguous buildings of different types. A 14-story L-shaped tower contains 129 condominiums. A six-story block contains a row of six three-story townhouses, topped by an additional three stories with 12 loft units. A seven-story rental building houses 136 apartments. The three structures enclose a lushly landscaped shared garden over a two-level 133-car garage. A major design challenge was to link the diverse buildings with common architectural elements, principally horizontal bands of limestone-colored precast concrete, uniform metal panels and window frames, and transom glazing at the tops of windows. In the tower building, floor-to-ceiling glazing, curved corners, and glazed projections visibly express the goal of maximizing Hudson River views. The townhouses have bowed or projecting fronts, with private stoops, recalling the city's typical rowhouses. The fronts of the loft units above are compatible but clearly in the tradition of industrial lofts. The rental building is simpler in detail, while sharing the rusticated base and piers of the same precast material.

Facing page: View of townhouses with lofts above.

Above: L-shaped condominium tower, apartment block at right.

Right: View of rental building.

Photography: Chuck Choi.

Costas Kondylis and Partners LLP The Grand Tier
1930 Broadway
New York, New York

Sited prominently on Broadway opposite Lincoln Center, the Grand Tier contains 230 luxury rental apartments, street-oriented retail, a health club, and a parking garage. Total floor area is 448,000 square feet. The podium-and-tower massing was determined in part by a special zoning permit, required for its Lincoln Square area site. While the podium maintains the street line along Broadway to a prescribed height of 85 feet, the tower is set well back and configured as a cluster of bays, exploiting the extraordinary views east toward Central Park and west toward Lincoln Center and the Hudson. Exterior limestone and limestone-colored masonry were chosen to echo the hue of the performing arts center's travertine cladding. Because of the depth of apartments in the podium portion, they were designed as loft-type units, with high ceilings and broad windows facing Lincoln Center. Several of these units are duplexes, as are those in the top two stories of the tower. Amenities available to tenants include a swimming pool, a lounge and an outdoor roof deck.

Left: View across Broadway toward Grand Tier.

Photography: Chuck Choi.

Cunningham + Quill Architects PLLC

1054 31st Street NW
Suite 315
Washington, DC 20007
202.337.0090
202.337.0092 (Fax)
marketing@cunninghamquill.com
www.cunninghamquill.com

Cunningham + Quill Architects PLLC

The Mather Building
Washington, DC

Left: Restored terra cotta detail and new canopy.

Below: Restored street façade.

Right: Duplex apartment.

Below right: Penthouse details and view of Washington Monument beyond.

Photography: Maxwell MacKenzie.

This project set a precedent as Washington's first conversion of a downtown office building into housing. Constructed in 1917, the structure was occupied by the University of the District of Columbia from 1967 to 1989. The adaptive reuse completed in 2003 provides for arts spaces on the street level and residential uses above. About one quarter of the residential spaces are live/work units suitable for artists, the remainder market-rate apartments for contemporary living. A penthouse, added as an approved exception to the DC height restriction, offers spectacular views of the National Mall. As a contributing structure in the Downtown Historic District, the building required — and unanimously won — approvals of the DC Historic Preservation Review Board, the Board of Zoning Adjustment, and the Area Neighborhood Commission. The terra cotta of the notable Gothic Revival façade was painstakingly restored on the basis of historical research.

Cunningham + Quill Architects PLLC

Huntfield Master Plan
Charles Town, West Virginia

Left: Master plan.

Below: About half of 995-acre development, with rail line and possible station in foreground.

Right: Historic core of Charles Town.

Bottom left: Completed houses.

Bottom right: Huntfield Monument neighborhood.

Photography: Christopher Morrison, Greenvest LC.

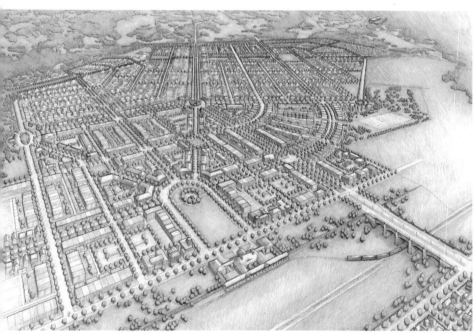

Following county rejection of the owner's previous plan for the 995-acre site, CQA was commissioned to lead a new master plan team. The site is about 1¼ miles from the center of Charles Town, immediately adjacent to Claymont, an impressive c. 1820 house built by George Washington's nephew. The plan reflects a study of communities in the region and embodies the principles of smart growth: compact design, mix of uses, and clear links to the existing community. Its neighborhoods are based on ¼-mile (5-minute) walking distances, with parks, retail, and civic facilities as neighborhood centers. Views of Huntfield from Claymont and other key vantage points will show house fronts rather than backyards, and high points will be occupied by public spaces rather than houses. The firm is exploring the possibility of extending an existing commuter rail along a track that traverses the site, with transit-oriented development around an on-site station. The first neighborhood is now completed and selling well.

Cunningham + Quill Architects PLLC

Caton's Walk
Washington, DC

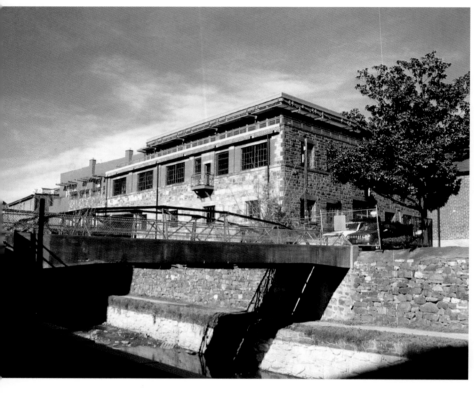

Located in Georgetown along the historic C&O Canal National Park, this building was constructed in 1929 as a commercial automobile garage. Although the street front is of brownstone, the walls exposed to the canal are of fieldstone with a brick upper story. Caton's Walk extends the redevelopment of old commercial structures that began decades ago with Canal Square. The immediate area is now the site of several interior furnishings showrooms. Approval for building modifications was obtained from the Old Georgetown Board and the U.S. Commission of Fine Arts, with support from the National Park Service and the local community. CQA oversaw the historic preservation of the structure and its conversion to retail, office, and residential uses, with two luxury units in a third-floor addition. Steel-framed windows and the steel-and-glass penthouse exterior were approved as in character with the building and its industrial context.

Above: Caton's Walk from canal.

Left: Stone wall and penthouse addition.

Below: Steel details on old masonry wall.

Right: Terrace outside set-back penthouse.

Photography: Christopher Morrison.

Cunningham + Quill Architects PLLC

The Alta
Washington, DC

Currently under construction in the downtown area near Thomas Circle, the Alta is a 13-story concrete-framed high-rise building with retail uses on the ground floor and 126 residential units above. Introducing residential uses to a formerly all-commercial district, the project is designed to appeal to young professionals who are interested in an urban setting and loft-like spatial qualities. The typical unit is divided by a linear core that includes all kitchen appliances and other mechanical requirements. Amenities include a community room and landscaped terraces at the second floor shared by all occupants, with private terraces at the top offering views of the National Mall. The exterior palette of stone, precast, metal, and glass is detailed to suggest urbanity and luxury. The design includes a planted roof, and the project team is working toward LEED certification for its environmental qualities. If approved it would be the first such recognition for a residential building in the District of Columbia.

Above: Exterior detail with loft-like residential unit.

Left: Typical unit plan

Below left: Rooftop terraces.

Below: 14th Street elevation.

Renderings: Interface

109

Cunningham + Quill Architects PLLC

National Cathedral School
Washington, DC

In a competition design for this well established girls' school, CQA proposed a phased process of demolition, remodeling, and new construction that reconcile the school's motley physical plant with the larger National Cathedral campus. The firm's design organized the school's upper, middle, and lower divisions around a courtyard open on its fourth side toward views of the hilltop cathedral and secluded from busy Wisconsin Avenue. Each of the three divisions would have had its own distinct entry. Proximity to a new theater was intended to facilitate use of the courtyard for performances. Arched openings, pitched roofs, and prominent clusters of chimneys recall historic precedents. The masonry walls were to be graduated from largely brick on the existing exterior of the lower school to brick with large areas of limestone on the new upper school wing — linking it visually with nearby Hearst Hall, which also houses much of the upper school program. Generous areas of glass brighten the interiors, at once expressing the buildings' modernity and its affinity with the cathedral's High Gothic.

Right: Cathedral and neighboring existing building.

Below left: Area plan of cathedral and outbuildings.

Below center: Site plan of school.

Below right: Perspective of school wings around new entry court.

Photography: David Bagnoli.

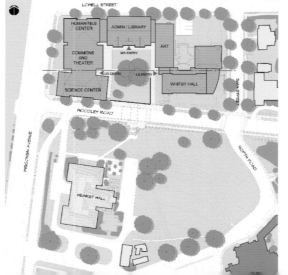

Cunningham + Quill Architects PLLC

Park Hill Condominiums
Washington, DC

This 29-unit condominium on Connecticut Avenue reconciles two very different architectural contexts: a street wall of masonry apartment houses, including some of Washington's official "best addresses", and a number of freestanding Modernist buildings across the avenue, including the Intelsat headquarters. The new building is composed of two five-story masonry "bookends" and a central volume with a metal and glass façade rising eight stories from a shallow entry court. The different portions of the building are unified by devices such as the proportions of the tall windows and the projecting metal balconies on the masonry blocks. Because the building is close to a Metro transit station, it was allowed to rise from the prevailing 60 feet to 90 feet over part of the site, affording the upper-floor units views of Washington's major landmarks and the National Mall. Modernist interiors with fluid spaces introduce a new paradigm to this traditionally "best address" residential area, anticipating the market for loft-like units that would soon follow.

Above: Duplex units on upper floors.

Below: Typical condominium interior.

Above right: Building front in context.

Right: Glass-canopied main entrance.

Photography: Daniel Cunningham.

Cunningham + Quill Architects PLLC

Fortnightly Neighborhood Master Plan and Herndon Senior Center
Herndon, Virginia

Working with the Fairfax County Department of Housing and Community Development, CQA planned a mixed-use neighborhood adjacent to the historic downtown and new municipal center of Herndon. Revitalizing 11 acres of mostly vacant and blighted industrial properties, the plan provides an urban village connection between the downtown and a newly constructed senior housing development. The plan proposes a variety of single-family town-homes, multi-unit housing and office/retail buildings along tree-lined streets, with alley access to garages. Rezoning of the area for mixed use involved garnering the support of community residents and leaders. To ensure high quality development, the design team created design guidelines covering a range of issues from building massing to fenestration and street furniture. Some prototype housing is now completed. A new senior community center by CQA has been completed and includes activity and meeting rooms, a commercial dining facility and double height multi-purpose room, and serves as a physical functional link between the senior development and the community as a whole.

Top left: Fortnightly Boulevard leading toward Senior Center.

Top right: Aerial view with Senior Center in foreground.

Center: Elevation of Senior Center.

Left: Neighborhood plan.

Above: New Senior Center by CQA.

Photography: Scott Matties.

Renderings: Luc Herbots.

Dahlin Group
Architecture Planning

5865 Owens Drive
Pleasanton, CA 94588
925.837.8286
925.837.2543 (Fax)

ddahlin@dahlingroup.com
www.dahlingroup.com

415 South Cedros Avenue, Suite 200
Solana Beach, CA 92075
858.350.0544
858.350.0540 (Fax)

Digital Imaging Studio
101 Townsend Street, Suite 209
San Francisco, CA 94107
415.538.0933
415.512.1313 (Fax)

18818 Teller Avenue, Suite 260
Irvine, CA 92612
949.250.4680
949.250.8002 (Fax)

Suite 502, Tower C
Heqiao Mansion
Jua #8, Guang Hua Road
Chaoyang District
Beijing 100026
China
011.86.10.6581.0466
011.86.10.6581.0470 (Fax)

Dahlin Group

Coyote Valley
San José, California

Coyote Valley is envisioned to be a high-density pedestrian and transit oriented urban community with a population of approximately 75,000 residents in the City of San José. A restored four-mile long Fisher Creek and a 50-plus-acre focal lake, park, a 1.8-mile canal/park system, a fixed guideway transit system and a multi-functional Parkway system are planned for the 7,000-acre site, of which 3,500 acres are planned for urban development. Originally conceived as a way of dealing with storm water runoff and flood control, the lake, canal, and creek have become defining features of the community. The heart of the Coyote Valley is envisioned as a mixed-use urban core focused on the lake that will include residential, office, commercial uses, plus plazas and parks. Circulation will follow a merge and loop parkway system linking grids of low-volume, pedestrian-friendly streets. The entire community will be within 1,500 feet of the fixed-guideway transit system,

initially using open style vehicles, linking the community to the regional public transportation system. Housing will range from high-density single-family detached units (10 dwelling units per acre) to 20-story towers (100 dwelling units per acre), with greater than 72% of the units at densities of 22 per acre or greater. Coyote Valley will also include a minimum 20 percent of the units as deed-restricted for affordable housing. The full build-out, over approximately 30 years, will include a minimum of 25,000 dwelling units and 50,000 industry-driving jobs with a total of about 60 million square feet of construction. Also included in the plan will be nine elementary schools, two middle schools and one collegiate style high school containing several smaller campuses.

Right: Master plan.

Opposite center: Rendering of full community, with creek leading to lake at center.

Below: High-density mixed use surrounding lake.

Bottom: Proposed street elevations.

Dahlin Group　Luxe Hills International Golf Community
Cheng Du, Sichuan Province, China

Left: Two-level driving range at public golf teaching center.

Below: Detached villas varying in configuration.

Photography: Wide Horizon Real Estate Development Company.

Above: Community center in the Wan An style, using local river stones, stucco, teak, and tile roofs.

Below: Overall master plan provides a community skeleton of networked and focal amenities. The circulation has been designed to capture powerful vistas of these amenities, key focal landmarks and unique site features.

Facing page, bottom: Community gatehouse.

An emerging generation of affluent, well-traveled people in China has generated a demand for living environments of international quality. To meet this demand in the Sichuan Province, Luxe Hills' master plan includes a championship 18-hole golf course with clubhouse and the widest possible range of residential densities, including single-family detached houses, low-rise patio villas, and high-rises of 20 or more stories. Also included, to serve a broader public, are a pedestrian-friendly town center with landmark office buildings, a variety of retail and restaurants, a conference center, a health club, a golf teaching center, and a hotel and resort. Since Luxe Hills' 667 acres must be developed in phases, it was crucial to establish a prestige identity and high market value from the outset. Contributing to this identity is the "Wan An" style adopted for the buildings, reflecting Asian character in forms and details, with a touch of Western relaxed elegance, using natural materials, warm colors, and patina finishes. Within this style, individual buildings are allowed a great deal of diversity. The layout of the site takes maximum advantages of appealing topographic features, such as, its many small hillocks, where groups of detached villas and other key building groups are located.

Dahlin Group

University Villages
Marina, California

While the closing of military installations can create immediate hardships to their localities, some can provide rare redevelopment opportunities. Such is the case for the site of Fort Ord near Monterey, across Highway 1 from a state beach. The 420-acre site consists of rolling hills with striking views of the Pacific, adjacent to the campus of California State University Monterey Bay. The proposed mixed-use community will include 1,237 residential units, 650,000 square feet of retail, and 650,000 square feet of office, research, and light industrial facilities. The plan is organized around two linear parks that cross at a central sculpture garden, one running east-west linking the university campus to an art district and the other forming a north-south link from the village center to a research/office area. Other large and small parks throughout the area provide community focal points. Traffic calming is achieved by narrow streets, narrowed intersections, and strategically located round-abouts. Readily accessible from Highway 1, the Village Center includes a mix of one-, two-, and three-story buildings, with a lively variety of storefronts, plus high-density and live/work housing. At the core of the Village Center, a one-acre Village Square forms a focal point for the village promenade, which evokes a classic main street atmosphere. The promenade normally includes parking along its wide, landscaped walks but can be cleared to accommodate special events. Homes will be of a "beach town character," largely clad with siding or shingles. Planting will be drought-tolerant native species, minimizing water demands. University Villages creates a true sustainable urban village.

Facing page, top: Site plan, with community area highlighted.

Facing page, bottom: Beachfront plaza.

Above: Live/work buildings.

Right: Houses of "beach town character" with native plantings.

Below right: Portion of research/office area.

Dahlin Group

Black Diamond
Pittsburg, California

A private development with support from the local redevelopment agency, Black Diamond is designed to bring residents back to downtown Pittsburg. The 7.3-acre mixed-use project will total 230,000 square feet, with 195 dwelling units occupying all of its upper floors. On portions of the street floors will be several sit-down restaurants, a coffee shop, a smoothie shop, retail shops, and boutiques – some widely known (Starbucks, Jamba Juice) and some unique – to create a downtown commercial destination. Street-level parking is wrapped with townhomes on three edges behind the mixed-use structures. Building design responds to the concerns of adjoining single-family neighborhoods and landmarks, including a historical church. The deeply sculpted exteriors are inspired by traditional styles found among historically significant structures in Pittsburg. The buildings recall numerous precedents, such as American Second Empire, with mansards and prominent window hoods, Art Deco, with smooth curves and low-relief details, and English Regency, with simplified Classical forms rendered in white stucco. A variety of canopies and arcades offer welcome weather protection along the first floor.

Below left and bottom: Architecturally varied mixed-use structures generating new downtown streetscapes.

Below: All-residential buildings with lower profiles, responding to nearby single-family areas.

Renderings: Digital Imaging Studio.

David M. Schwarz

1707 L Street NW
Suite 400
Washington, DC 20036
202.862.0777
202.331.0507 (Fax)
www.dmsas.com

201 Main Street
Suite 600
Fort Worth, TX 76102
817.339.1133

David M. Schwarz

David M. Schwarz

Fort Worth Master Plan
Fort Worth, Texas

Top: Computer model of Downtown.

Above and above right: Sundance East building with two floors of retail, one of offices.

Right: Sundance West apartment building with street-level retail.

Photography: Jim Hedrich/Hedrich Blessing.

Left: Sundance East restaurant building.

Below: Cinema entrance façade in mixed-use Sundance West block.

Right: Sundance East cinema building.

Since 1988, the firm has been involved in the revitalization of downtown Fort Worth, which had suffered economic setbacks after World War II, compounded by planning practices that only made the area less attractive and less safe. Beyond drawing up a sensitive and workable plan, the firm has been the architect for all of the key buildings and renovations discussed and illustrated on these pages, thus enjoying a rare opportunity to carry out its planning intentions and affect the character of a major urban core. The master plan initially focused on the 30 blocks around Sundance Square, but considered 150 blocks as significant context. Numerous parking lots, multistory garages, and set-back office buildings had interrupted commercial street life. Structures spanning streets had produced forbidding tunnels. The firm identified Third Street as one street with no major obstacles, recommending that it be restored to two-way traffic and lined with a mix of uses. To reintroduce residents essential to round-the-clock activity, the Sundance West

apartments and the Sanger Lofts were sited on Third Street, initiating a process that has so far produced 1,200 units. Sundance West contains about 90 apartments, above an 11-screen AMC cinema, with street-level retail and underground parking. Sanger Lofts is a conversion of a 1928 department store, carried out under Department of Interior guidelines for historic preservation. The Sundance East project occupies a full city block, designed as a group of buildings in scale with historic neighbors. It comprises the Palace cinema, designed in the Moderne style plus a 28,000-square-

foot Barnes & Noble store, some 26,000 square feet of dining places, and 11,000 square feet of office space. The expansion of the city's Central Library, including a new public entrance and lobby, extends the structure to help reconnect portions of the urban core. The Nancy Lee and Perry R. Bass Performing Hall for symphony, opera, and ballet companies — and the Van Cliburn International Piano Competition — seats up to 2,100 and is symmetrically laid out to fit its 200-foot-square city-block site, with its main entry at one corner to address the restaurants and shops of the Sundance

Top: Nancy Lee and Perry R. Bass Performing Hall.

Above: Bass Hall lobby.

Right: New main entrance to expanded Central Library.

Photography: Steve Hall/ Hedrich Blessing, top and above, opposite top left and bottom tight; Jim Hedrich/ Hedrich Blessing, right, opposite top right.

area. On a block next to Bass Hall, the Maddox-Muse Center houses recital, rehearsal, and other support spaces in a complex with the exterior appearance of four distinct structures. Two new office properties in the district, the Wells Fargo and Bank One Buildings, adopt the architectural character and the time-proven organization of historic commercial structures, built out to the sidewalk with retail at the street level. Today's Downtown Fort Worth has a wealth of commercial and residential resources that would hardly have seemed possible 15 years ago.

Below left: New Bank One Building.

Below: New Wells Fargo Building.

Bottom: Maddox-Muse Center, housing various performing arts functions.

David M. Schwarz

Southlake Town Square
Southlake, Texas

The master plan for a 135-acre site establishes a new downtown for a city that has never had one. The plan proposes a total build-out of 2.7 million square feet, of which the completed Phase 1 includes 300,000 square feet on 40 acres. For an area whose commercial development had been limited to strip commerce, the goal was a mixed-use, pedestrian-oriented environment that would appeal to residents countywide. Since most visitors would arrive by car, one objective was to accommodate cars without a negative effect on the pedestrian experience. The town has attracted numerous restaurants, shops, and offices, plus a town hall, and is the setting for many area celebrations and arts events. The mandated 21-meter right of way for its public streets was addressed with extra-wide sidewalks, generous plantings, angled parking, and necked-down intersections. Project is currently in Phase II which includes 150,000 square-foot retail/restaurant uses, a 14 screen cinema, a 200 room Hilton hotel, and structured parking for over 1600 spaces. Additionally, Phase I Residential is currently under construction and Phase II Residential is in the planning phase. The project has been praised by the Urban Land Institute and Landscape Architecture magazine, among others.

Top: Fountain in Town Square.

Far left: Sidewalk scene.

Left: Town Square, with bandstand/pavilion.

Below left: Street fronts seen from square.

Photography: Steve Hall/ Hedrich Blessing.

David M. Schwarz

West Village
Dallas, Texas

West Village is designed as a hub for Dallas's Uptown District, which has evolved over the past decade as a premier residential, shopping, and entertainment area. The development's 6.75-acre site is favored with exceptional public transportation. It is two blocks west of the Dallas Area Rapid Transit's (DART's) CityPlace station and is ringed by the Uptown Dallas Trolley's terminal loop. The project includes 178 luxury apartments and 125,000 square feet of high-end retail. Building heights range from one to four stories, with retail on the lower levels, residences above. Parking is provided by spaces along its streets and in an 800-space garage, hidden by mixed-use structures. Building heights and architectural treatments vary in response to neighboring development, with a loftlike structure facing the site of high-rise structures planned near CityPlace station, lower buildings facing lower-density areas, and a Mediterranean character along Cole Avenue, where this style was already prevalent.

Top: Retail street scene.

Above: View of village along one perimeter.

Above right: Main entrance to Cole Avenue apartments.

Right: Mixed-use frontage reflecting Mediterranean style of older neighbors.

Photography: Steve Hall/ Hedrich Blessing.

David M. Schwarz

Parker Square
Flower Mound, Texas

Before Parker Square was built, Flower Mound was a suburban locale – near Dallas-Fort Worth Airport – without any sense of neighborhood or community focus. For a 24-acre site previously approved for an office park with pad-site retail/restaurant along the highway, the architects worked with a new owner and town officials to produce zoning and development guidelines for a more pedestrian-friendly, mixed-use development that can serve as a focus for Flower Mound as a whole. Because site limitations and area demographics reduced the likelihood of large-scale tenants, the project is geared to neighborhood commercial tenants and smaller office users. Offices are located on the second level around the central square. Buildings are carefully laid out to screen the majority of the site's parking areas from the approach roads, the square, and the pedestrian streets. Building facades feature brick details in creative interpretations of regional Main Street architecture.

Above: View from square.

Above left: Plan of development.

Left: Square with pavilion.

Below left: Façade detail of domed building.

Below: Typical offices-over-retail buildings.

Photography: Steve Hall/Hedrich Blessing.

Dougherty Schroeder & Associates, Inc.

211 Perimeter Center Parkway
Suite 900
Atlanta, GA 30346
770.650.7774
770.650.7708 (Fax)
kdougherty@dsaarch.net
www.dsaarch.net

Dougherty Schroeder & Associates, Inc.

Destin Commons
Destin, Florida

The "New Urbanism" exemplified in the Florida Panhandle communities of Seaside and Rosemary Beach can now be experienced in the larger city of Destin, nearby. This retail and office development brings the same kind of pedestrian-friendly atmosphere and civic symbolism to a new commercial hub for the Emerald Coast. It is designed to appeal to a wide spectrum of the public. The 56-acre project includes 420,000 square feet of retail space, with 70,000 square feet of office at second-floor level. The generous use of natural stone, brick pavers, roof tiles, slate, and other traditional, durable materials lends the project a substantial feeling not common to commercial developments in the area. Landscaping is relatively formal, and outdoor lighting is of the subtly modulated kind found in high-end resorts. The project is the first phase of a larger development to include additional retail and office as well as an upper level hotel.

Top: Fountain plaza.

Left: Evening view of shops.

Above: Focal fountain.

Below: Destin Commons elevations.

Facing page: Two signature towers.

Photography: Craig Tanner and Dennis O'Kane.

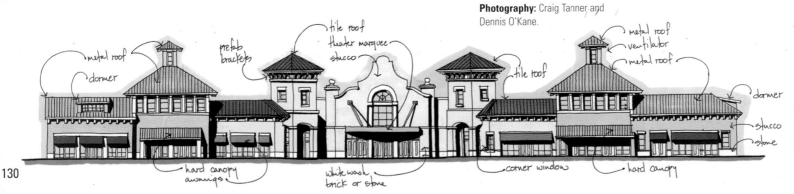

Dougherty Schroeder & Associates, Inc.

Pinnacle Hills Promenade
Rogers, Arkansas

Left: Plan of development.

Left center: two views of Central Park.

Below: Street scene.

Bottom: Typical building elevations.

The goal here was to create a new downtown for Rogers, which is experiencing explosive growth as the headquarters of Wal-Mart, the world's largest corporation. The development will include 1.1 million square feet of retail, a theater, and second-level office spaces, organized around a 1.33-acre park of urban character. The architects' first inclination was to base the design of buildings on the appealing 19th-Century precedents represented in nearby communities such as Eureka Springs and Fayetteville. Discussions with the developers, however, soon convinced them that the city's extensive international connections — attracting business people from all over the world — made a less regional, predominantly Modern design vocabulary more appropriate.

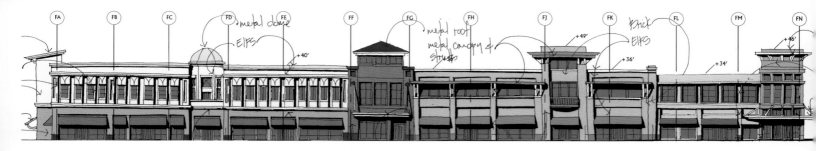

132

Dougherty Schroeder & Associates, Inc.

The Avenue East Cobb
Atlanta, Georgia

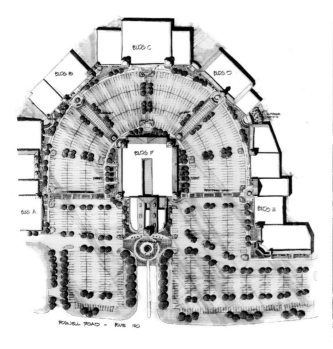

Far left: Horseshoe plan of center.

Left: Three views of shopping environment.

Bottom: Characteristic elevation, showing central tower and wings.

Photography: Dennis O'Kane,

A.O.R.: CMH, Inc.

This 240,000-square-foot lifestyle center in Atlanta's Cobb County suburbs established a signature look for subsequent Avenue retail projects. For this site, local zoning would not permit inclusion of residential functions. The layout and architectural design recall the pattern of an Antebellum town square, with a centrally located "transportation building" resembling a 19th-Century railroad depot, surrounded by lower structures. Lushly landscaped "pedestrian boulevards" linking the buildings modulate the passage from car to stores and encourage strolling around the project. Storefronts for some 50 retailers, many nationally known, are urged to display individuality within the unifying framework composed of red brick and traditional molding and belt courses. Fine materials such as tumbled brick pavers and standing-seam metal roofs maintain the center's appeal for both retail tenants and their customers.

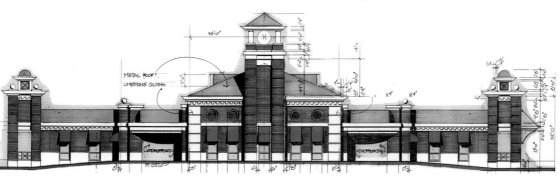

133

Dougherty Schroeder & Associates, Inc.

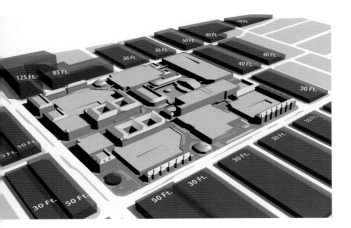

The Forum at Sunnyvale
Sunnyvale, California

Left: Massing model.

Below left: View from the main thoroughfare.

Bottom: Representative building elevations.

Facing page top: Typical street view.

Facing page bottom: Public open space.

Here the architects were challenged to recreate an urban core that had been decimated in the 1970's by the displacement of six city blocks by an in-town shopping mall. Their design replaces the mall with a more traditional layout of streets lined with mixed-use structures, including first-floor shops, a department store, and a three-level theater, with offices and housing units on upper floors. In accordance with local planning and zoning decisions, there will be 1.1 million square feet of retail, 250,000 square feet of offices, 330 housing units, and 5,000 structured parking spaces, along with 1.5 acres of public open space. Building surfaces will include stone, brick, and stucco, with slate and tile roofs. Generous landscaping will include some existing 100-foot redwoods and Monterey cypresses.

**Dougherty Schroeder &
Associates, Inc.**

Gulf Coast Town Center
Fort Myers, Florida

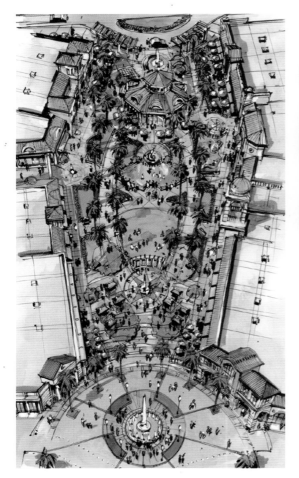

Spanish Colonial building fronts will surround formal plazas and subtropical water gardens in this 1,700,000-square-foot retail development in suburban Fort Myers. Its axial plan will focus on a column-topped circular fountain and a variety of garden towers, pergolas, and pavilions, with vistas delineated by tall palms. Generous arcades and awnings will protect patrons from sun and weather. Stuccoed retail structures will be topped with a variety of tile roofs. Signage will be restrained. Occupying approximately 204 acres, the complex will include a 770,000-square-foot life style center "Main Street" development, with restaurants and three anchor department stores, as well as a perimeter Big Box retailer and a cineplex.

Above: Fountain and main axis.

Above left: Aerial rendering.

Left: Central water garden.

Bottom: Building elevations.

Model: Pacificom Multimedia, Inc.

Duany Plater-Zyberk & Company

1023 SW 25th Avenue
Miami, FL 33135
305.644.1023
305.644.1021 (Fax)
www.dpz.com

Duany Plater-Zyberk & Company

Tannin
Orange Beach, Alabama

The plan for this coastal village on the Gulf of Mexico responds to several challenging characteristics of the site, including its irregular boundaries and the linear dune and wetland formation that run oblique to the main highway. Wetlands within the site have been transformed into linear lakes, while the swamp at its edges has been left wild, framed by residential lots and a public pavilion terminating the main boulevard. A town square at the highway gathers the public buildings including a village hall, post office, and regional fire station. Tannin's urban regulations prescribe the physical characteristics of traditional Southern building types, and architectural regulations specify construction materials and techniques that are economical and found in the local vernacular.

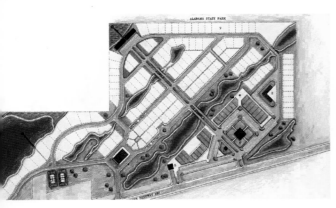

Top: Typical Tannin cottage with front porch, front yard of native vegetation, and picket fence along street.

Above: Houses along a lake.

Above left: Street leading to swimming pool pavilion.

Far left: Site plan.

Left: Public fountain with distinctive pump house.

Photography: George Gounares.

Duany Plater-Zyberk & Company

Amelia Park
Fernandina Beach, Florida

An exemplary infill neighborhood, the 106-acre Amelia Park is at the heart of a historic coastal city. Located close to existing community facilities, the development offers convenient housing for a wide range of ages and lifestyles, including single-family houses, rowhouses and apartments over shops. The master plan draws upon some of the best-loved towns in the region, particularly the city's own historic downtown. Understanding the value of this example, the city adopted the proposed Amelia Park Plans and Codes as part of a planned unit development ordinance and established a Community Development District to facilitate self-governance and financing. Now 55 percent completed, the neighborhood will contain about 450 residential units, 70,000 square feet of commercial space, 25,000 square feet of professional offices, and various public amenities, including a YMCA on a lakeside site.

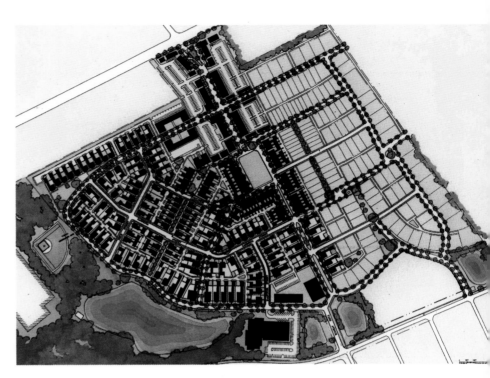

Top: Neighborhood plan, with streets and parks linked to adjacent areas.

Above and above left: Rowhouses along typical streets.

Left and far left: Variety of residential types from large homes to small cottages.

Photography: DPZ, Oscar Machado.

139

Duany Plater-Zyberk & Company

I'On
Mount Pleasant, South Carolina

Left: Charrette Master Plan.

Below left: A series of townhouses.

Below right: Porch houses fronting one of the man-made lakes.

Bottom left: Commercial buildings at central square.

Bottom right: Houses overlooking East Lake across public street, diverted to accommodate existing trees.

Photography: DPZ.

The 243-acre site near Charleston is bordered by a marshy creek to the north and a rural thoroughfare to the south, with residential subdivisions to either side. The property features three manmade lakes, a historic graveyard, and a monument to local hero Jacob Bond I'On. The master plan locates a village center close to the main road, with commercial uses around a central square. Neighborhood centers include one on the creek, which includes a community boat landing and a meeting hall. The smallest of the lakes is left as a wildlife sanctuary, and the others are surrounded by porch houses. Rowhouses and single houses are located in the more central areas, with porch houses in the more rural and marsh-front sites. The master plan was designed in collaboration with Dover-Kohl & Partners.

Duany Plater-Zyberk & Company

Habersham
Beaufort, South Carolina

Above: Town plan.

Right: Edge along wetlands.

Below right: Single-family houses among mature trees.

Bottom left: Rowhouses.

Bottom right: Boardwalk over tidal marshes.

Photography: DPZ.

Located on the water just eight minutes from historic downtown Beaufort, the new town of Habersham provides the Low Country with an alternative to suburban sprawl. The town's architecture respects the expert methods employed in traditional designs for ventilation and cooling and mandates them in the codes that accompany the plan. Porches within conversation distance of the sidewalk encourage socializing. An assortment of residential building types encourages a diverse population and permits a single development to address a variety of market segments. A neighborhood center at the main entrance to Habersham is designed to grow as demand increases, with buildings of the historic Main Street type, with office or residential spaces above street-level retail. The plan was a collaborative effort of DPZ with Steven Fuller Design Traditions, Moser Design Group, and Historical Concepts.

Duany Plater-Zyberk & Company

Rosemary Beach
Panama City, Florida

Located on the northwest Florida coast seven miles east of the famous 1980s New Urbanist community of Seaside, Rosemary Beach represents 15 years of growth in Duany Plater-Zyberk's urban design experience. The community straddles the coastal highway, which crosses the town through a linear park. The design team distinguished Rosemary Beach from Seaside in several ways. They inserted mid-block vehicular alleys, permitting pedestrian boardwalk promenades leading to the beach, and they created civic spaces at the water's edge to emphasize the connection to the Gulf. About half of the alley-fronting garages are topped by granny flats. The community's center features live-work and arcade buildings, a town hall, and a post office. In contrast to Seaside's Key West vernacular, the architecture here is based on models from the Caribbean and St. Augustine, with stuccoed or shingled walls, cantilevered balconies, and shuttered sleeping porches. Now 70 percent completed, the community includes 470 residential units ranging from studio flats to six-bedroom cottages and a substantial portion of the allotted 97,000 square feet of commercial space.

Above: Master Plan, with coastal highway in linear green swath.

Below: Beach-bound boardwalk between house fronts.

Right, top to bottom: Variety of houses along boardwalk promenade; community pool and beach house; Caribbean-inspired house details; town hall and post office with walled courtyard.

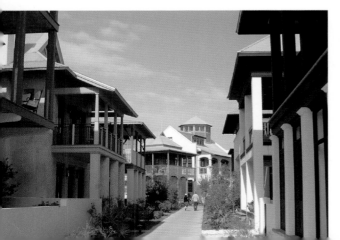

Right: Mixed-use buildings in a variety of types.

Below: Town center, Barrett Square, with town hall at one end.

Photography: DPZ.

Duany Plater-Zyberk & Company

Alys Beach
Panama City, Florida

A 160-acre resort community in the tradition of nearby Seaside and Rosemary Beach, Alys Beach is designed as a pedestrian-friendly community in harmony with nature and inspired by the graceful vocabulary of Bermuda's architecture. The planned 500 residential units range from above-the-shop apartments to family compounds, and the community will include 170,000 square feet of commercial and office space. Residents' front doors face footpaths tracing a network through the development. Courts on the interior of many blocks hide automobiles from view. Environmentally features include the use of permeable paving, natural storm drainage, wind energy, and cisterns. The community's white masonry walls and roofs, based on Bermuda models, contribute to energy efficiency.

Top left: Master plan, with Gulf to south, highway green belt through center, and wetlands to north.

Top right: Complex with walled courtyards, encouraged in plan.

Above left: Exterior view of the sales office featuring a distinctive Bermuda-style chimney and scalloped gable parapets.

Above right: Front entry of the sales office with a pedestrian friendly planter that doubles as a bench.

Left: Courtyard and loggia of sales office.

Bottom left: Detail view of Bermuda-inspired rooftops.

Photography: Alys Beach.

Elkus Manfredi Architects

300 A Street
Boston, MA 02210
617.426.1300
617.426.7502 (Fax)
www.elkus-manfredi.com
info@elkus-manfredi.com

Elkus Manfredi Architects

Elkus Manfredi Architects

35 and 40 Landsdowne Street
University Park at MIT
Cambridge, Massachusetts

Far left: Site plan.

Below left: Stone monoliths included in artwork by David Phillips.

Below: Quadrangle defined by 35 and 40 Landsdowne, left and center in photo.

Right: Entrance to 40 Landsdowne.

Far right: 35 Landsdowne and Quadrangle.

Historically, the intense chemistry lab has been low-rise, internally oriented and suburban. Driven by the desire for proximity to the resources of the Massachusetts Institute of Technology, 35 and 40 Landsdowne Street, on the "campus" of University Park at MIT, represent a new laboratory prototype: urban, high-rise, high-hazard-rated facilities for intense chemistry and biology use. Together, the buildings fulfill important urban roles: shaping open spaces, defining the public realm of surrounding streets, and energizing the adjacent sidewalks and park. Combined as the headquarters of Millennium Pharmaceuticals, one of the country's leading biopharmaceutical companies, the buildings serve as research facilities and corporate offices. The buildings

include a lecture hall and a cafeteria, as well as labs and offices. Design goals for the buildings were as follows: provide maximum flexibility for a rapidly changing science; encourage planned and unplanned interaction between scientists of different disciplines; draw employees from other buildings to foster interactions across the company. A commitment to sustainable design was implemented through a number of design strategies: reuse of a brownfield site; building-wide air-side management; lab waste management; maximum daylighting benefits; high-efficiency lighting and light controls; water conservation and gray water recycling; design for long-term adaptive reuse with minimal demolition and discarding of building materials; integrated systems commissioning. The 35 Landsdowne Street building has a total floor area of 220,000 square feet, and 40 Landsdowne, 225,000 square feet. The half-acre Landsdowne Quadrangle, defined by the buildings, features a 40-foot by 100-foot artwork by David Philips, which consists of granite monoliths up to 9 feet high, along with bronze inserts paving, granite and lighting installations.

Facing page: Entrance canopy, 35 Landsdowne.

Left: Cafeteria at 35.

Below left: Lounges at 40 Landsdowne.

Below: Overall view of 40.

Bottom: Night view of 40.

Photography: Justin Maconochie (35 Landsdowne), Bruce T. Martin (40).

149

Elkus Manfredi Architects

100 Cambridge Street/Bowdoin Place
Boston, Massachusetts

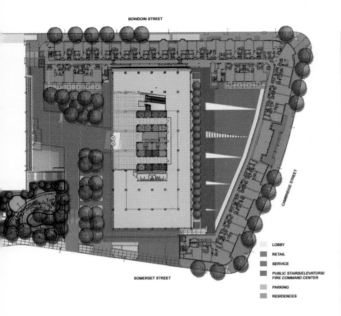

Far left: Site plan.

Near left: Entrance to Saltonstall Plaza and Garden of Peace, with Ibis Ascending sculpture by Judy Kensley Mckie.

Below left: Wall sculpture Freedom One by Howard F. Elkus over office building escalator.

Below: 100 Cambridge Street building lobby.

Facing page: Saltonstall Plaza, with Leverett Saltonstall building at right.

Rehabilitation of the 22-story Leverett Saltonstall State Office Building has yielded a dividend by mending the fabric of a historic neighborhood once divided by the tower's vacant plaza. When the Massachusetts legislature invited development proposals for the defunct structure, Elkus Manfredi, members of a team assembled by MassDevelopment, produced a winning scheme that wrapped five-story mixed-use buildings around three sides of the once-forbidding plaza. The proposal achieved much more than the state anticipated by including private components that carried much of the project's cost. Residential buildings and street-level retail and below-grade parking now line Bowdoin and Cambridge Streets, which are essential components of the Beacon Hill cityscape. The renovated office building now presents two distinct images and two addresses, successfully combining very different public and private identities and functions. The needs for building access and public space have been met by transforming the remaining plaza area into two parks: the Garden of

Peace, dedicated to victims of violence, and Saltonstall Plaza, honoring a public figure's legacy of service. Permanent art installations engage users and enhance the project's public areas. The completed project includes 133,000 square feet of residential construction and 34,500 square feet of retail, along with the 565,000-square-foot office building.

Above: Residential buildings along Bowdoin Street, with renovated Saltonstall building behind them.

Below: 100 Cambridge Street entrance to office building, with 60-foot Sol Lewitt mural, flanked by mixed residential/retail structures.

Below right: New mixed-use buildings along Cambridge Street, with Saltonstall building in background.

Photography: Woodruff Brown Photography.

ELS

Architecture and Urban Design

2040 Addison Street
Berkeley, CA 94704
510.549.2929
510.843.3304 (Fax)
info@elsarch.com
www.elsarch.com

ELS Architecture and Urban Design

California Theatre
San Jose, California

Existing
New

Above: Plans of existing and completed complex at left, site plan center.

Left: Addition with new entrance and support spaces opposite convention center.

Below left: New courtyard.

Below right Historic façade.

Above right: Renovated theater interior.

Facing page: Part of restored lobby.

Photography: Marco Zecchin (exterior and lobby), Rudolph & Sletten (courtyard), Tim Griffith (theater interior and historic façade).

With a combination of city and nonprofit funding, a historic movie theater has been renovated and expanded as a performing arts facility. The original 1927 building, presenting an exuberant display of ornamentation, has been carefully restored. Alterations to the theater interior include expansion of the orchestra pit and installation of a pit elevator, new lighting and sound systems, and re-raking of rear orchestra and balcony seating to improve sight lines. For required seismic upgrading, new supports have been added on the exterior of the structure to avoid disturbing historic interiors. To accommodate the needs of touring companies, opera groups in particular, the stage house

has been expanded, and that required relocation of a service alley serving adjacent buildings on the block. Other additions provide for dressing rooms, a green room, a conference room, and a large rehearsal space, restrooms, truck loading, and other back-of-house support spaces. Selected ancillary facilities added to the existing theatre formed a new outdoor courtyard along the main street, accessible to patrons at intermission and to the general public at nonperformance times. A second main entrance and lobby have been added across the street from the city's convention center to facilitate the theater's use in conjunction with meetings.

ELS Architecture and Urban Design

Church Street Plaza
Evanston, Illinois

Left: Aerial view of master plan development
1. Main Pavilion retail/entertainment
2. Public garage
3. Hotel
4. Office/retail building
5. Residential condominium
6. Retail
7. Northwestern University
8. Existing Saturday farmers' market
9. Metra Rail
10. CTA Rail

Below: Redeveloped Maple Avenue, with Main Pavilion on right, retail base and residential condominium on left.

Facing page: Two views of main pavilion, with street-floor retail and second-floor cinema. ELS--design architect, DeStefano + Partners--executive architect.

Photography: ELS (Maple Avenue), Timothy Hursley (Main Pavilion).

On a 7.5-acre tract between Northwestern University and Evanston's historic center, this development initiated the city's revival as an entertainment and residential center. Downtown eating and drinking places have increased from almost none to 85, new housing and a hotel have generated round-the-clock activity. ELS developed the master plan for the entire site and were the design architects for the main pavilion and parking garage. Strategically located between the garage and two regional transit stops, the pavilion houses retail and restaurants at street level with an 18-screen multiplex on its second level, its lobbies in dramatic glass-walled volumes. Retail and entertainment facilities for the whole development total 174,000 square feet. Other components include a 178-unit hotel; 190,000 square feet of office space; 207 housing units; and a 1,400-car garage. With original ownership of the site split between the university and the city, the redevelopment process was complex. After a lengthy selection procedure, the city agreed on one master developer, teamed with ELS, who offered a pedestrian-oriented plan, rather than an introverted mall, and proposed the second-level cinemas above retail.

The Village of Merrick Park
Coral Gables, Florida

Left: Central garden, with main retail arcade.

Below: Master plan.

1 Miraflores Arcade 3-level retail building

2 2-level retail pavilions

3 Department stores

4 2,000-car parking structure

5 Central garden

6 Residential buildings

7 Office building/parking structure

8 Rail line

Facing page, top: Two intimate fountain courts.

Facing page, middle right: Landscaped stairs connect housing to garden.

Facing page, bottom right: Central garden, with paired residential buildings at far end.

Photography: ELS (plan and facing page, lower photo), SWA (upper top photos).

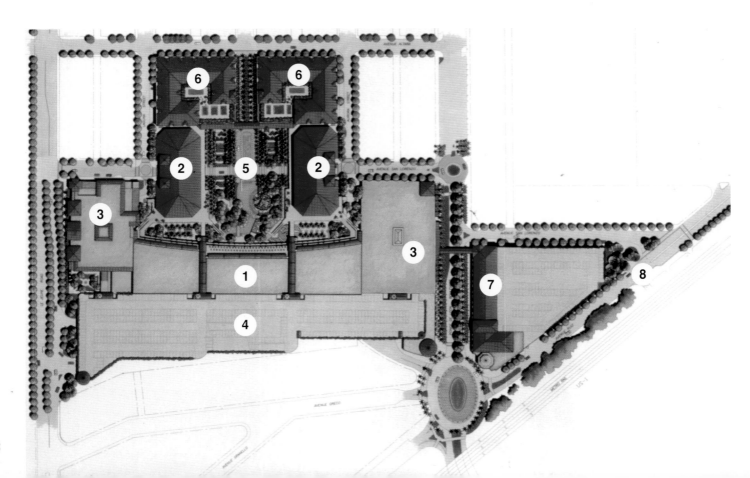

This mixed-use development organizes retail, entertainment, and residential uses around a central, pedestrian-scaled garden. Working closely with the developer, the architects designed retail structures that define a palm-lined green as a setting for round-the-clock, urbane activities. The main three-story retail building, the Miraflores Arcade, fronts on the central garden, which is flanked by a pair of two-story retail pavilions. At the end of the garden facing the main arcade are paired residential buildings. The Miraflores Arcade contains 280,000 square feet of retail, with a three-level Nordstrom store at one end and a three-level Neiman Marcus at the other. The two retail pavilions total 130,000 square feet. The Mediterranean-inspired architecture builds on Coral Gables' design guidelines that maintain a style established in the 1920s. The development opens itself up to the existing community with public streets running through it, following the historic city plan. The subtropical climate allows all circulation to be open-air, with a series of balconies, terraces, arcades, and loggias. Fountains and shade trees provide an appealing environment for outdoor eating and relaxation. A 2,000-car parking structure adjoins the main retail arcade. Perkins & Will designed the two residential buildings with 120 units and, adjacent to the roundabout, a 140,000 sf office building with parking structure.

ELS Architecture and Urban Design

The City of Sunnyvale Downtown Design Plan
Sunnyvale, California

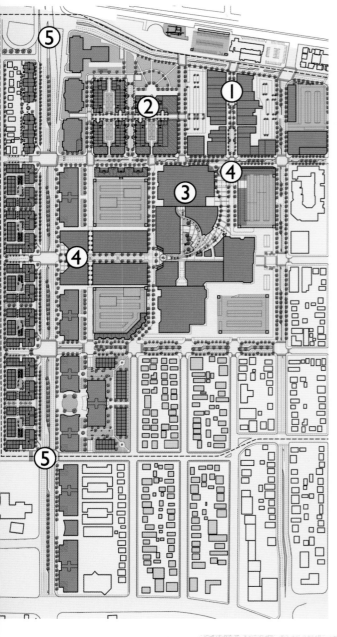

Left: Recommendations of Downtown Design Plan.

1 Defend and enhance historic districts

2 Add high-density housing downtown

3 Transform mall into open-air, mixed-use district

4 Reconnect historic street grid

5 Create a central boulevard lined with new offices and housing

(Red = retail; blue = offices; green = housing; gray = garages; cross-hatching for mixed uses.)

Below: Portion of new boulevard, lined with mid-rise office and residential buildings, lower housing bordering existing neighborhoods.

Bottom: Housing with some street-level retail around new park adjacent to train station.

Photography: Gerald Ratto (model).

Nine blocks at the center of Sunnyvale were demolished in 1977 for a shopping mall and surface parking, leaving only one block of the traditional shopping street intact. As new development pressures rose, the city commissioned ELS, working with an economist and a Downtown Stakeholders Advisory Committee, for an updated design plan covering 18 blocks. Workshops and public meetings helped shape the plan. Key goals are to reinforce the surviving commercial block and surrounding neighborhoods and to reestablish links in the disrupted city street grid. Anticipating renovation of the retail mall, the plan proposes transforming it into an open-air, mixed-use district. An existing arterial would be transformed into a central boulevard, lined with mid-rise housing and offices, a gateway to the downtown.

Field Paoli

150 California Street
7th Floor
San Francisco, CA 94111
415.788.6606
415.788.6650 (Fax)
architects@fieldpaoli.com
www.fieldpaoli.com

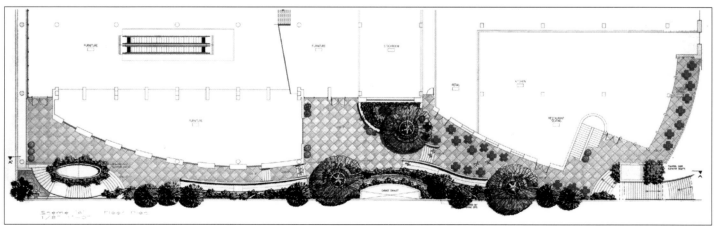

Located in one of the world's most fashionable shopping districts, this innovative mixed-use project was developed by the City of Beverly Hills to support the City's Strategic Plan. With a new anchor store and over 400 parking spaces, the project reinforces existing retail uses at the northern edge of the "Golden Triangle." Situated on a 48,000-square-foot infill property fronting Beverly Drive on one side and Canon Drive on the other, the complex includes 70,000 square feet of retail, 20,000 square feet of office space, and a four-level underground parking structure. Fulfilling the City's plan for enhanced pedestrian circulation, a landscaped plaza provides a continuous raised walkway over the mid-block service alley. Accessed by a number of stairways, ramps and elevators, this intimate urban oasis is open to the public at all times. The clean-cut geometric forms of the building are composed of limestone, plaster, glass and metal, creating a contemporary expression that reflects the optimism and self-confidence of this forward-looking city.

Facing page, top: Elevated walkway linking Beverly Drive and Canon Drive.

Facing page, bottom: Plan of walkway.

Above: Canon Drive elevation.

Above left: Fountain detail in walkway.

Below left: Diagram showing organization of project, with walkway crossing central alley.

Below: Beverly Drive elevation, showing elevator cylinder.

Photography: Jay Graham.

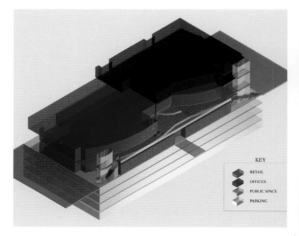

KEY

RETAIL
OFFICES
PUBLIC SPACE
PARKING

Field Paoli

On Broadway
Downtown Redwood City, California

Right: Cineplex entrance with flanking storefronts.

Below: View of proposed outdoor dining.

Below right: Cylindrical corner entrance at retail anchor.

Building a 160,000-square-foot retail/entertainment destination in the historic core of Redwood City required design sensitivity, community support, and resourceful teamwork. Landmarks such as the 1921 fire station (now a library), the 1930 courthouse, the 1912 Sequoia Hotel, and the 1928 Fox Theater contribute to a unique downtown environment. The Post Office and the City Hall are directly across the street from this full-city-block development.

To fit into this context, the cinemas are located on the second floor, allowing for the introduction of street level retail on the ground floor. Wrapping the theater with a glazed exit corridor and giving the ground floor retail a two-story expression has eliminated the blank walls typical of many of today's multiplexes. To produce a scale compatible with surrounding buildings, building facades are broken into discrete elements, with strong recesses and projections. Exterior details recall the Art Deco and Art Moderne commercial buildings of the 1930s, which were particularly congenial to storefronts and discreet signage. By bringing in new types of businesses, as well as the cinema complex, the project aims to increase the number and duration of visits to Downtown. With its close proximity to the Redwood City CalTrain station, On Broadway is a prime example of transit-oriented urban development.

Above right: Site plan, showing neighboring landmarks, with new development in red.

Right: "Flatiron" corner with canopied entrance.

Field Paoli

Victoria Gardens
Rancho Cucamonga, California

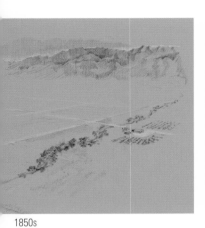

1850s

1900s

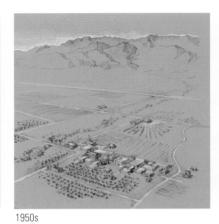

1950s

Today

Top: Conceptual sketches of community growth.

Right: Aerial view of Victoria Gardens.

Below left: New downtown.

Below right: Evening view of retail street.

166

Working closely with Forest City Development and the City of Rancho Cucamonga, Field Paoli created a Master Plan for a new 120-acre downtown. The open air town center is laid out with a new street grid designed to accommodate retail, housing and office uses, as well as a library and cultural arts center. During the master planning process, several architectural firms joined Field Paoli to provide distinct building designs for the initial retail phase of the project. The result is a rich aesthetic variety characteristic of evolving downtown streetscapes. In the central core, street widths were narrowed to slow traffic and provide an intimate shopping and dining environment. Specific sub-districts were identified for high-end fashion, lifestyle tenants and cafés around a central square. Smaller pocket parks and plazas enliven the street edges and create additional public gathering spaces. At the periphery, the Master Plan identifies surface parking areas that can be transformed into pedestrian-oriented city blocks as this Southern California city continues to grow.

Above: Public area off street.

Above left : Exterior window and façade detail.

Left: Pedestrian activity on street.

Below: Pocket plaza at night.

Photography: Jay Graham.

Field Paoli

The Streets of Tanasbourne
Hillsboro, Oregon

Above: Main Street.

Left: Central plaza at bend on Main Street.

Below left: Terraced gardens rising from central plaza.

Below: Gateway at perimeter boulevard.

Bottom: Site plan.

Located 10 miles west of Portland, The Streets of Tanasbourne was planned as a new retail neighborhood with a department store anchor and over 40 stores and restaurants totaling approximately 385,000 square feet. The project represents a more urban approach to suburban retail, with multi-level stores wrapping mid-block structured parking and fronting onto a curving "Main Street." Continuing Portland's long-standing tradition of pedestrian open space, a network of landscaped outdoor plazas includes a linear public garden that extends through the commercial center and connects to the regional park system.

FXFOWLE ARCHITECTS, PC

22 West 19 Street
New York, NY 10011
212.627.1700
212.463.8716 (Fax)
info@fxfowle.com
www.fxfowle.com

FXFOWLE ARCHITECTS, PC

The Helena Apartment Building
New York, New York

The Helena, a 37-story residential building with 600 studio, 1- and 2-bedroom apartments, is the first phase of the firm's master plan for the riverfront block at the Hudson River end of West 57th Street. A composition of interlocking elements – volumes, fenestration, and balconies – produces interesting and varied images of the building, which is visible from many vantage points. The design represents a reinvention of the conventional New York residential building, with floor-to-ceiling glass, wraparound windows, and sleek metal wall panels. Integrated high-performance technologies such as a blackwater treatment plant, efficient microturbines, and green roofs will earn the building a LEED Gold Certification.

Top left: Glass barrier around planted rooftop.

Middle left: Detail of corner balconies.

Bottom left: End view.

Below: Ground floor plan, with retail space in yellow.

Bottom: Continuous spandrels on long elevation.

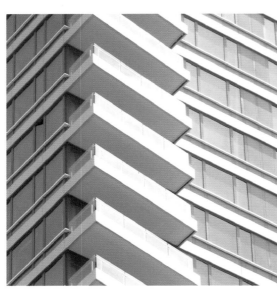

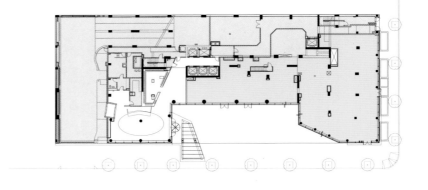

FXFOWLE ARCHITECTS, PC

The New York Times Building
New York, New York

Renzo Piano Building Workshop and FXFOWLE collaborated on the design of the new headquarters for The New York Times. Located on Eighth Avenue between 40th and 41st Streets, the structure will unite the company's employees under one roof in an exceptional signature structure. A grille of glazed terra cotta tubes will screen the floor-to-ceiling glazing. Increased ceiling heights and under-floor ventilation systems will ensure a new standard of comfort and efficiency for high-rise office space. The New York Times will occupy half of the building's 1.6 million square feet, with the remainder leased to retail and corporate tenants by the Forest City Ratner Companies, the project's developer. Construction of the building began in 2005, with completion expected in 2007.

Right, top to bottom: Base of tower and low-rise wing; signature sign across entrance front; exterior wall with terra cotta tube sunscreen; interior view of full-scale office mock-up.

Below: Building in Midtown Manhattan context.

FXFOWLE ARCHITECTS, PC

Whitman School of Management
Syracuse University
Syracuse, New York

The 165,000-square-foot Martin J. Whitman School of Management building is a crucial enhancement of the school's competitiveness. It contains classrooms, offices, and ample space for team meetings and collaborative activity among its 1,400 students, as well as dedicated distance-learning facilities and executive space. The primary design element, a central corridor with a grand staircase at its central lobby, maximizes program connectivity. Some of the many integrated sustainable features include under-floor air displacement, radiant heating and cooling, and highly efficient air filtration and distribution.

Left, top to bottom: Corridor linking facilities at all levels; detail of exterior cladding.

Below: Entry floor plan.

Bottom: Model, showing varied volumes flanking central spine.

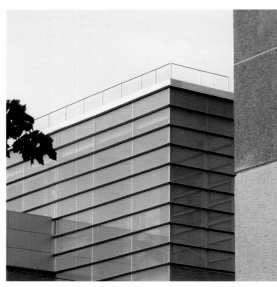

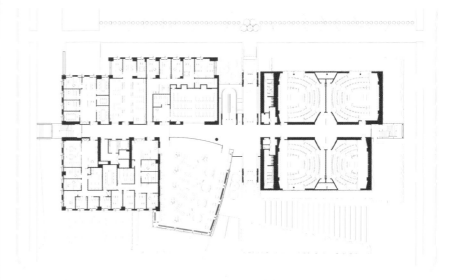

FXFOWLE ARCHITECTS, PC

Lincoln Center Redevelopment
New York, New York

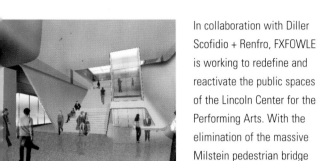

In collaboration with Diller Scofidio + Renfro, FXFOWLE is working to redefine and reactivate the public spaces of the Lincoln Center for the Performing Arts. With the elimination of the massive Milstein pedestrian bridge over 65th Street, the once-forbidding street will become a magnet of activity. A new transparent envelope for the Juilliard building at street level, along with new signage and graphics, will enliven the scene. The extension of the Juillard School and the renovation of the Alice Tully Hall lobbies will expose performing arts activities to both 65th Street and Broadway. Respect for the design character of the original 1960s buildings and public spaces has motivated interventions that will complement the existing while energizing the public experience.

Far left: New Juilliard lobby.

Top: Proposed Juillard Building Broadway front.

Above: New Juilliard School entrance.

Below: Allice Tully Hall after renovations, with 65th Street at left, Broadway at right.

FXFOWLE ARCHITECTS, PC

Tianjin Tower
Tianjin, China

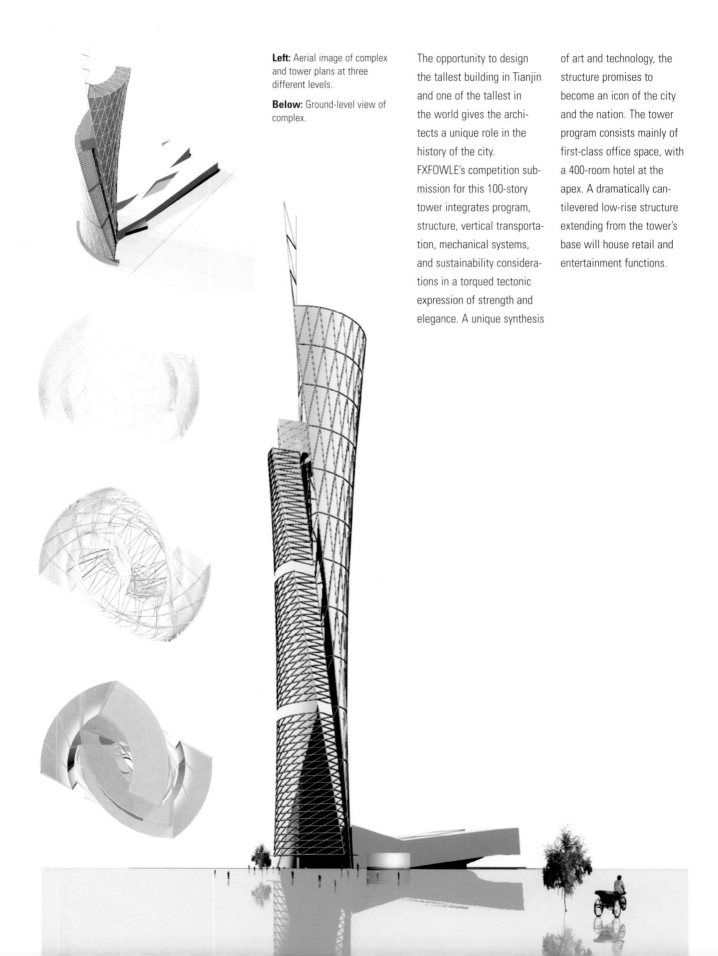

Left: Aerial image of complex and tower plans at three different levels.

Below: Ground-level view of complex.

The opportunity to design the tallest building in Tianjin and one of the tallest in the world gives the architects a unique role in the history of the city. FXFOWLE's competition submission for this 100-story tower integrates program, structure, vertical transportation, mechanical systems, and sustainability considerations in a torqued tectonic expression of strength and elegance. A unique synthesis of art and technology, the structure promises to become an icon of the city and the nation. The tower program consists mainly of first-class office space, with a 400-room hotel at the apex. A dramatically cantilevered low-rise structure extending from the tower's base will house retail and entertainment functions.

FXFOWLE ARCHITECTS, PC

Dosflota Multipurpose Complex Master Plan
Moscow, Russia

Right: Complex seen from riverfront promenade.

Below right: Main tower seen from glazed winter garden.

Below: Skyline view from water.

Bottom: Aerial view of complex.

The planned Dosflota Multipurpose Complex is a unique residential, recreational, and commercial development to be located in the northwestern part of Moscow. The site, once a sports complex, consists of 9.9 hectares (24.5 acres) on the west bank of the Khimkinskoye Vodokhranilishe. The master plan integrates various components to create a resort-like urban center in which hotel, office, conference center, residential, marina, and recreational uses are interconnected with a gracious network of interior and exterior public spaces and amenities.

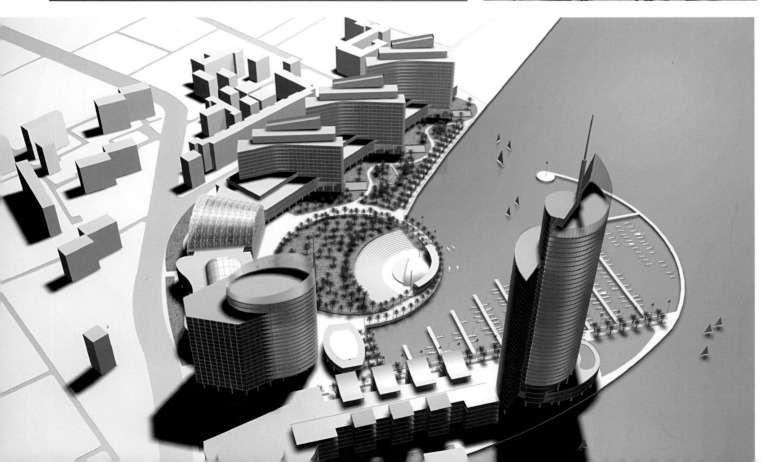

FXFOWLE ARCHITECTS, PC

Renaissance Place Redevelopment Plan
Naugatuck, Connecticut

FXFOWLE is developing a master plan for the 60-acre Renaissance Place site in the historic downtown of Naugatuck, a once heavily industrial city. With a mix of residential, retail, office, cultural, and educational uses, the plan creates an accessible riverfront, identifiable north and south gateways, and an extension of two main streets as spines of the development. An intermodal transportation center at the train station will connect the site and its 2,000 residential units to regional destinations. The latest sustainability technologies will contribute toward the project's goal of zero net energy use and educate the public on the benefits of energy-efficient design.

Left: Massing of new construction along waterfront.

Below: Diagram of conceptual approach.

Bottom: Aerial rendering of completed development.

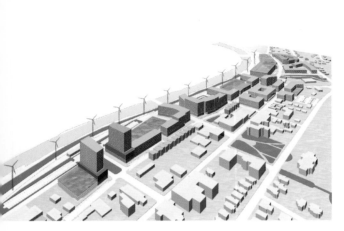

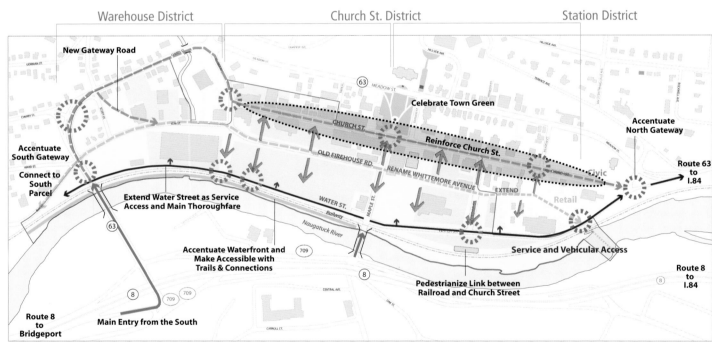

Glatting Jackson Kercher Anglin Lopez Rinehart, Inc.

33 East Pine Street
Orlando, FL 32801
407.843.6552
407.839.1789 (Fax)
corporate@glatting.com
www.glatting.com

1389 Peachtree Street, NE
Suite 310
Atlanta, GA 30309
404.541.6552
404.541.6559 (Fax)

222 Clematis Street
Suite 200
West Palm Beach, FL 33401
561.659.6552
561.833.1790 (Fax)

Glatting Jackson Kercher Anglin Lopez Rinehart, Inc.

Hollis Garden
Lakeland, Florida

Located within Lakeland's historic Lake Mirror Park, this new 1.2-acre garden is a gift to the citizens by the Hollis family. The city contributed in-kind work to the project. The garden's terraces are designed to negotiate the 14-foot drop across the site toward the lake. 16 individual Garden rooms display a spectrum of plantings selected to represent the development of Florida from wilderness through agriculture to formal landscaping. Architectural elements reflect the influences of both Addison Mizner's local interpretations of Spanish vernacular and Frank Lloyd Wright's version of Modernism at nearby Florida Southern College. A focal fountain plaza recalls Michelangelo's geometrical paving at the Campidoglio in Rome. A major work of sculpture installed in the garden is Jeremy Sobel's "Windows."

Above: The Swan plaza has become a favorite venue for outdoor weddings. The Lakeland skyline is featured beyond.

Left: Appealing plantings draw the interest of children.

Below: Fountain banks and runnels highlight a Wrightian theme and tie the garden together.

Right: Overall view.

Facing page, bottom: Lawn and border; Sobel sculpture.

Photography: Scott Wheeler/ City of Lakeland, Glatting Jackson Kercher Anglin Lopez Rinehart, Inc.

Glatting Jackson Kercher Anglin Lopez Rinehart, Inc.

Broad Street Park
Baldwin Park, Florida

Below: Central pedestrian bridge over lake, with relocated live oaks at ends and characteristic neo-traditional custom homes beyond.

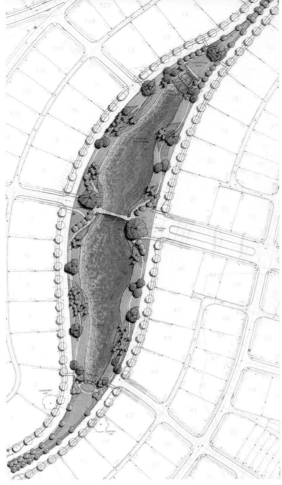

Left: Site plan.

Above: Pedestrian bridge and live oaks.

Below: Cantilevered trellis at south overlook.

Bottom: Perimeter walk approaching bridge.

Photography: Glatting Jackson Kercher Anglin Lopez Rinehart, Inc.

This 5.2-acre park is located in Orlando's Baldwin Park community, newly created by The Baldwin Park Development Company on the 1,100-acre site of the former Naval Training Center. The community plan follows neo-traditional town planning practices, exhibiting a consistent approach to architecture and open space design. This park serves as the central gathering place for the new community's first neighborhoods, located along the main boulevard leading to the Village Center on the shores of Lake Baldwin. The park design focuses on three formal nodes where people can experience the 2.2-acre man-made lake: an overlook featuring a cantilevered trellis at the south approach to the park; a pedestrian bridge at the center that is the primary link between neighborhoods to the east and west; and a formal green at the north end that serves as the principal gathering space. On-site specimen live oaks that were saved and relocated anchor the ends of the bridge and shade its approaches. The formal lawn of the north neighborhood green overlooks the weir fountain that contains the upper source pool and animates the area with the sound of falling water. A walk encircling the park has occasional side paths that provide a more intimate contact with the water's edge. The perimeter path passes through the dense shade of several "cypress domes" that recall the great wild landscapes of Florida.

Glatting Jackson Kercher Anglin Lopez Rinehart, Inc.

Park Avenue Streetscape
Winter Park, Florida

Designed to "right size" the streets through the prestigious Park Avenue shopping district, the master planning and phase I construction of Winter Park's streetscape project was carried out by Glatting Jackson Kercher Anglin Lopez Rinehart, Inc., in association with architects Dover Kohl & Partners. In all, 4,200 feet of pedestrian ways were improved at a cost to the municipality of $4,100,000. Travel lanes were narrowed and sidewalks widened, and traffic calming was effected. Improvements were made to landscaping, paving, site furnishings, and utilities. Specific features include additional live oaks, reused brick street paving, and new standardized trash receptacles. The project has distinctly enhanced the charm and economic health of this unique urban village.

Top left: Accessible crossing.

Middle left: Typical street scene.

Below: Plantings and awnings shading sidewalk.

Facing page top: Sidewalk dining.

Facing page bottom: Scene showing sheltered seating, planters, and streetcorner bump-out.

Photography: Glatting Jackson Kercher Anglin Lopez Rinehart, Inc.

Glatting Jackson Kercher Anglin Lopez Rinehart, Inc.

The Heights
Tampa, Florida

A vibrant mix of commercial and residential development is proposed on this 40-acre, post-industrial site. Through dead-end street and over-sized waterfront parcels, the underutilized site has become disconnected from the City of Tampa. The proposed plan will reconnect the area's streets in a grid pattern similar to Downtown Tampa and reopen the district to the water. "Great Streets" will lead to a new Riverwalk, with docks and outdoor cafés, designed to connect to a comprehensive riverfront walk planned by the City. The new townhouses and residential high-rises, which are intended for a diverse population, will enjoy views of the Hillsborough River and the Downtown skyline. The plan features the reuse of the old Tampa Armature Works building as a residential tower including a possible site for a history museum. The plan also revives the existing Waterworks Building as a place for civic functions and a small café. The adjacent Waterworks Park is energized by incorporating it into the Riverwalk and creating places for active and passive recreation within this urban neighborhood.

Top left: The Heights in relation to Downtown Tampa.

Above left: The revived Waterworks Building and café.

Left: Riverwalk.

Above: The Heights plan.

Goody Clancy

334 Boylston Street
Boston, MA 02116
617.262.2760
617.262.9512 (Fax)
arch@goodyclancy.com
www.goodyclancy.com

Goody Clancy   Fort Point Channel
Boston, Massachusetts

Once a neglected industrial waterway, the Fort Point Channel is being reinvented as a 50-acre water park enlivened by creative uses of its "watersheet." It is being envisioned as a major public destination linking downtown Boston with the South Boston waterfront, the city's newest development frontier. The plan builds on the strengths of existing destinations around the channel, including the Boston Children's Museum, which plans a major expansion of its building there, the Boston Tea Party Ship and Museum, several waterfront restaurants, and New England's largest resident arts community. Between six and eight million square feet of mixed-use development is planned for the edges of the channel over the next several years. Proposed uses of the watersheet include floating classrooms for the Children's Museum, an "art basin" for temporary and permanent works, barges for musical and artistic performances, boat rentals and water rides, model boating, water transportation facilities, transient berthing for educational vessels, and other uses serving residents, downtown workers, and visitors. The plan results from a collaborative effort involving the city, surrounding landowners, environmental advocates, the local arts community, and residents of adjoining neighborhoods. It was jointly

Above: Plan showing proposed features.

Above left: Aerial view looking toward downtown.

Left: Inner "Urban Industrial Wild" portion of channel.

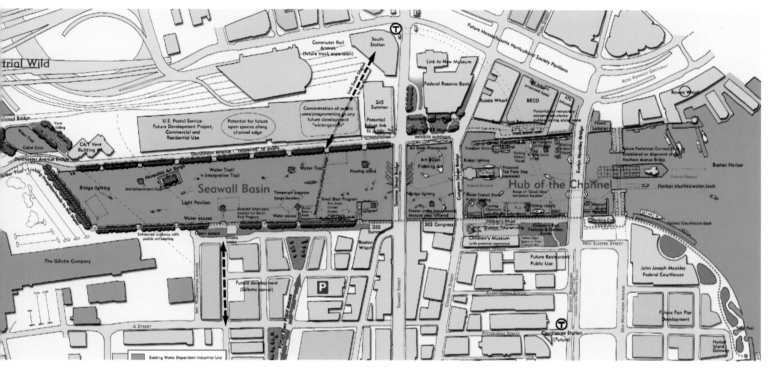

Top left: Completed area of waterfront park.

Top right: Channel as seen from downtown high-rise.

Left: Art installation in channel.

Below left: Potential recreation on "Seawall Basin" part of channel.

Left: Northern Avenue Bridge over channel, site of seasonal farmer's market.

Below left: Dining deck outside Boston Children's Museum.

Bottom left: Performance event along channel.

funded by the city with the Fort Point Channel Abutters, a group that includes the area's museums, major Boston developers, corporations, and real estate interests, and government bodies including the Federal Reserve Bank and the U.S. Postal Service. In 2004, the Friends of the non-profit Fort Point Channel was established to help implement the plan, and it has taken on the long-term programming and maintenance of the waterway and its edges. Water quality improvements are underway, and visitors are already able to enjoy new promenades and open spaces being built in connection with the vast Central Artery/Tunnel project, which adjoins part of the channel. Improved pedestrian connections will be incorporated in the rebuilt Boston Tea Party Ship and Museum, and an additional acre of open space will be provided on

the downtown side with the redevelopment of Russia Wharf, 500 Atlantic Avenue residential and hotel project, and Independence Wharf. New waterfront restaurants will be incorporated into 500 Atlantic Avenue and the existing buildings that flank it. Interpretive displays are being placed at key locations to remind visitors of the harbor's maritime history.

Goody Clancy Assembly Square
Somerville, Massachusetts

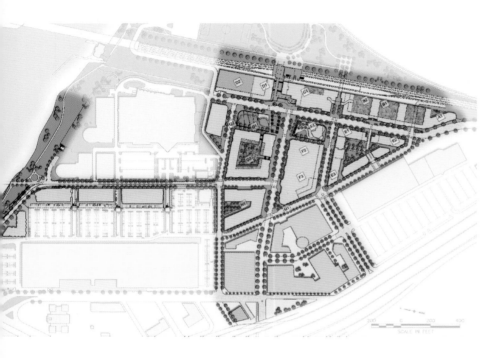

Left: Site plan, showing existing big-box retailers surrounded by mixed-use development.

Below: Phase I conversion of failed strip mall into walkable mixed-use environment.

Facing page, top: Assembly Square, showing transit station and surrounding mixed-use buildings.

Facing page, bottom left: Street-level view of Assembly Square.

Facing page, bottom right: Aerial view of overall development, with Assembly Square at center; view from square toward riverfront.

Renderings: Dongik Lee.

One of the few underdeveloped tracts close to the Boston core, this 140-acre brownfield site has recently attracted big-box retailers. But the current accessibility of the site, combined with its potential for an on-site transit station, argue for mixed-use redevelopment at urban density, which will support a lively public realm lined with street front retail and will justify the costs of site clean-up, the transit station, and other needed improvement. The plan proposes a new urban district, with a strong sense of place shaped around streets and squares, yet successfully integrates existing and proposed big box tenants, locked in place for now by current leases and ownership. Starting with a 26-acre failed retail mall, Phase I will include residential and office development over ground-floor retail, centered on a new pedestrian-oriented "Main Street." Phase II, located on 35 acres of city and privately-owned land, approved by the city of Somerville, will include the Assembly Square public urban space and transit station, with a potential 4 million square feet of development, including 1,300 housing units, over ten years. Eventually, the grid pattern of streets and public squares will be extended over the remaining site.

Goody Clancy   North Allston Strategic Framework for Planning
Boston, Massachusetts

In early 2000, Harvard University announced its intention to concentrate its future growth on approximately 100 acres of commercial and industrial land it had acquired in the North Allston section of Boston, across the Charles River from its historic Cambridge campus. The announcement raised concerns that the neighborhood's small-to-medium-sized industrial businesses and established residential areas would be threatened. Recognizing that a move of this scale held major implications for the neighborhood, the city, and the university, the city and North Allston community

members agreed to collaborate with Harvard on a four-year planning process, involving many interviews, workshops, public meetings, and other sources of input to produce this Strategic Framework. Setting forth principles for housing, open space, transportation, and economic development, the Framework creates a model of growth, change, and preservation to reshape a newly blended academic, residential, commercial, research, and recreational neighborhood; it embodies a desire, agreed to by all stakeholders, for full integration of "town" and "gown."

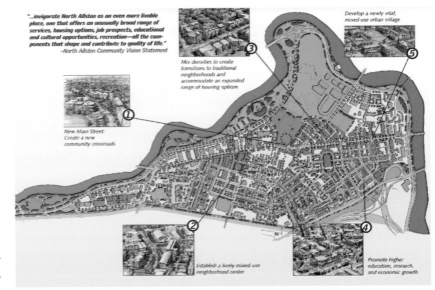

"...invigorate North Allston as an even more livable place, one that offers an unusually broad range of services, housing options, job prospects, educational and cultural opportunities, recreation—all the components that shape and contribute to quality of life."
—North Allston Community Vision Statement

Develop a newly vital, mixed-use urban village

Mix densities to create transitions to traditional neighborhoods and accommodate an expanded range of housing options

New Main Street: Create a new community crossroads

Establish a lively mixed-use neighborhood center

Promote higher education, research, and economic growth

Above: Plan with parts of existing Harvard campus along river at upper right.

Below left: Proposed development near center of plan.

Below right: Mixed institutional and residential district.

Bottom left: Presenting the Framework to the public

Bottom right: Mixed-use development along major avenues.

Lessard Group Inc.

8521 Leesburg Pike
Suite 700
Vienna, VA 22182
703.760.9344
703.760.9328 (Fax)
info@lessardgroup.com
www.lessardgroup.com

Lessard Group Inc.

Trump Plaza
New Rochelle, New York

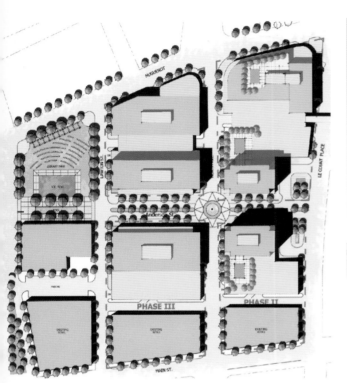

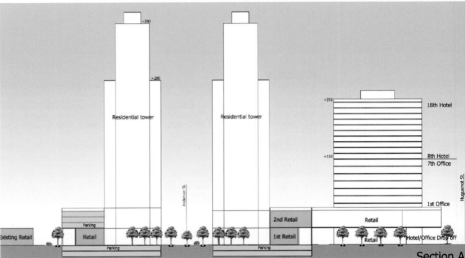

Above left: Long-range plan, with Phase I in upper right quadrant.

Above: Schematic elevation, with Phase I at right, matching Phase II tower at left.

Left: Curved entrance volume at key intersection.

Situated on a 1.9-acre site in the center of downtown New Rochelle, this 320,000-square-foot mixed-use structure is a key component of the city's plan for revitalization and redevelopment. The design was inspired by the idea of creating a signature building in the heart of New Rochelle, a growing market just outside New York City. The project features a 32-story high-rise of about 149,600 square feet, containing 181 residential units, with retail on the first two floors and 240 underground parking spaces for residents' use. Parking for the retail is provided in an adjacent municipal garage, reached via a pedestrian bridge. The massing and detail of the buildings complement and enhance the existing commercial district. Phase I of development is scheduled for completion in 2007. Future phases are planned to roughly quadruple the initial square-footage, with a varying mix of residential, office, retail, and parking facilities, and will include a twin to the Phase I residential tower, the two flanking a landscaped public mall.

Above: Main entrance to tower containing apartments above retail base, with pedestrian bridge to retail parking in existing public garage.

Right: Perspective and elevation drawings of mixed-use tower.

Lessard Group Inc.

Springfield Town Center
Springfield, Virginia

Located at the intersection of I-95 and the Capital Beltway, this mixed-use urban center is well situated to revive and expand the retail and residential resources of Springfield. The master plan of the 8.86-acre site is organized to reduce the impact of noise on the residential component. A parking structure and a hotel form a continuous barrier to buffer the noise of the highways. Internally, public plazas and retail along the streets will help make the development pedestrian-friendly. The completed project's residential component of 912,715 square feet will provide the consumers that are vital to pedestrian-oriented retail. The total 1,157,715-square-foot program includes 100,000 square feet of retail, 100,000 square feet of hotel, and 40,000 square feet of offices, plus 2,044 required parking spaces. An allocation of 5,000 square feet of interior community space, along with extensive public open space, will enhance the development as a center for the existing community.

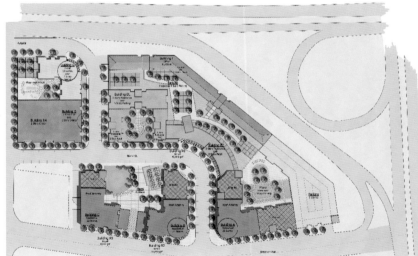

Opposite top: Aerial view of completed development, with highway interchange at lower left.

Opposite middle: Master plan, with hotel and parking structure buffering internal residential buildings, plazas, and pedestrian-friendly streets from highway noise.

Opposite bottom: Streets at core of development.

Above: Mixed retail, office, and residential buildings along curving street.

Below: Plaza and skylighted arcade between residential high-rises with mixed-use lower floors.

Lessard Group Inc.

Canton Crossing
Baltimore, Maryland

Situated along the edge of the Patapsco River, this 32-acre waterfront development introduces a mixed-use urban cityscape to an existing predominantly industrial location. The development features a variety of high-rise buildings that include multi-family, commercial office, retail, and hotel components. A central polygonal office tower marks the project's highest point. The massing and heights of surrounding buildings respect a hierarchy of forms. The building masses typically sit atop four-story parking garages that are masked at ground level by retail and restaurants. View corridors extending into the site from the waterfront allow for optimum views from most buildings. Streets are activated with wide sidewalks that serve as outdoor sitting areas. The waterfront edge is energized by a boardwalk lined with restaurants. A cruise ship terminal and customs station share the waterfront with a marina that is proposed to have a luxury residential component.

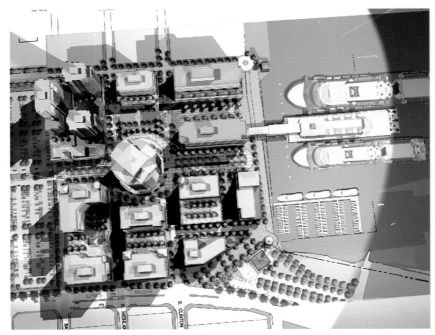

Opposite top: Development as seen from Patapsco River.

Opposite bottom: Aerial view of developed site.

Left: Residential tower complex at lower right in master plan.

Below: Master plan.

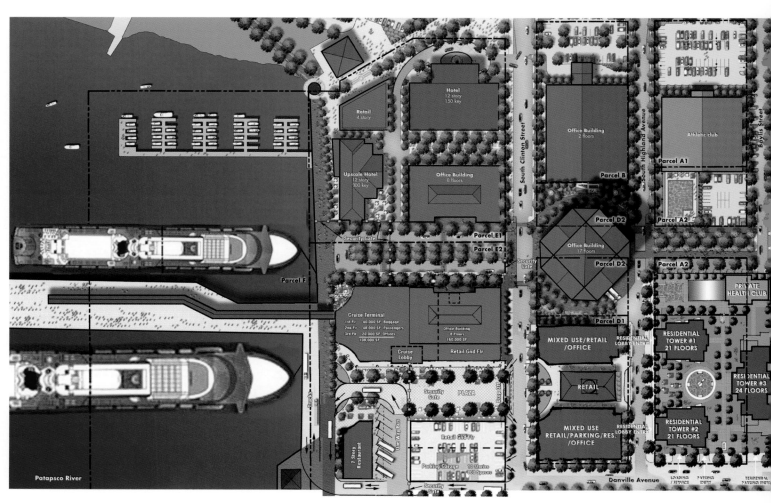

Lessard Group Inc.

National Harbor
National Harbor, Maryland

This mixed-use development will serve as a gateway project for Prince George's County, introducing an urban lifestyle to the area's existing suburban fabric. The site along the Potomac River offers impressive views across to Alexandria, Virginia, and up-river to Washington, D.C., and the sloping terrain facilitates view corridors toward the water. The overall master plan proposes 2,500 residential units in a mix of high-rise, mid-rise and low-rise structures, which are supported by substantial retail, restaurant, and office components. A convention center and a hotel complete the urban mix. The plan divides the 130-acre site into three distinct areas, known as Downtown, Midtown, and Uplands, each identified with a lifestyle and a market segment — with commercial uses concentrated in the Downtown, luxury residential in Midtown, and active adult units in the Uplands. A dedicated tree preserve at the center of the development acts as a central park. The waterfront is activated by restaurants, a theater, and public amenities such as a ferry terminal.

Right: Conceptual master plan.

Below: Uplands residential buildings rising beyond central park and clubhouse.

Bottom: Elevation of a Downtown mixed-use block.

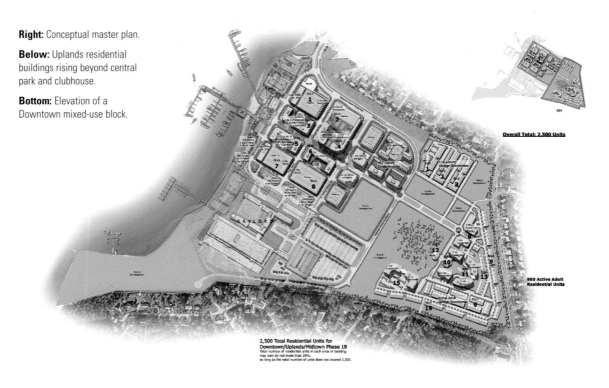

Looney Ricks Kiss

175 Toyota Plaza
Suite 600
Memphis, TN 38103
901.521.1440
901.525.2760 (Fax)

info@lrk.com
www.lrk.com

209 10th Avenue South
Suite 408
Nashville, TN 37203
615.726.1110
615.726.1112 (Fax)

182 Nassau Street
Suite 201
Princeton, NJ 08542
609.683.3600
609.683.0054 (Fax)

31 Main Street
Rosemary Beach, FL 32461
850.231.6833
850.231.6838 (Fax)

671 Front Street
Suite 220
Celebration, FL 34747
407.566.2575
407.566.2576 (Fax)

Looney Ricks Kiss

Jefferson at Providence Place
Providence, Rhode Island

The first luxury housing development in downtown Providence in over 20 years, this 330-unit project is meant to fill the unmet needs of young professionals. At the same time, it is designed to respect the character of historic brick warehouses in its district. The detailing of the facades, with broad arches, storefronts, bay windows, awnings, and individual stoop entries to some street-floor units supports a traditional urban atmosphere. Land costs in this location dictated the density of 75 units per acre, with garage parking. The four-story parking structure aligns at each floor with the

double-loaded corridors of the apartment building. The existing street has been improved with new sidewalks, landscaping, and street lighting and provides a direct pedestrian connection to the city core. The apartments follow 14 different floor plans, ranging in size from 563 to 1,421 square feet. Most of the top-floor units have "loft" studio layouts, with upstairs bedrooms overlooking two-story volumes. Shared amenities include an outdoor pool, a spa, a fitness center, a coffee bar, concierge services, a business center, and a well-equipped club room available for resident functions. Construction on land contaminated with mercury imposed several restrictions. This new construction had to accommodate itself to factory foundations and footings that could not be removed because of contamination. Landscaped areas that could not be capped with impervious construction had to be topped with 18 inches of clean fill.

Facing page: Street views of residential buildings.

Above: Club room.

Right: Interface with city.

Below: Lobby.

Photography: Frank Giuliani.

Looney Ricks Kiss

FedExForum
Memphis, Tennessee

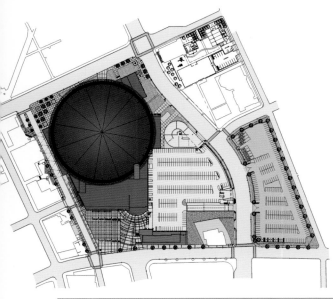

The revival of downtown Memphis has been given a major boost by this $200-million sports and entertainment complex, the largest public building project in the history of Memphis. It is home to the Memphis Grizzlies NBA team plus the Smithsonian Institution's Rock 'n' Soul Museum. The arena seats 18,200 on five levels, with the team's offices on the upper floors of the adjoining four-story office building and the museum on its street floor. Sinuous rerouting of a major street allowed for a 1,500-car parking structure adjoining the arena, which helps fill parking needs for the adjacent Beale Street musical entertainment district. Outdoor entertaining and party areas are accommodated on 35,000 square feet of plaza. Designed by Ellerbe Becket in association with Looney Ricks Kiss, the complex has been adjusted to the scale of historic Beale Street and the surrounding area. The height of the arena was lowered by depressing the event floor 33 feet below street level, simultaneously improving circulation by placing seating areas both

above and below entry level. Also minimizing the impact of the project are the smaller annexes surrounding the central drum, which create the impression of incremental development over a period of time. The arena drum is clad in aluminum panels, its lobby largely in glass, and the smaller structures in a variety of traditional brick. Artwork throughout the development represents the Memphis area's rich cultural and musical heritage. The complex was completed in 2004 on time and within budget.

Facing page: Site plan and aerial view.

Above: View toward entry, showing low wings in scale with surroundings.

Below: Entry plaza.

Photography: Timothy Hursley/The Arkansas Office.

Looney Ricks Kiss

Ave Maria Town Center
Collier County, Florida

The new town of Ave Maria is proposed for 633 acres of land adjoining the developing new campus of Ave Maria University. A prominent oratory, designed by others, is to be the main symbol of the university, at the same time linking it to the town. Looney Ricks Kiss's contribution is the planning of the town center, embracing and radiating from the Ellipse Road around the oratory. Town center planning calls for buildings that complement the central landmark, generate intimate open and covered spaces, and reflect regional traditions. LRK is designing four of the initial six mixed-use buildings in the town core, accommodating 77,800 square feet of retail/commercial space and 70,000 square feet of residential. Construction is to start in 2005, with completion in 2006.

Left: Plan of town center.

Below left: Town center street scene.

Below: Mixed-use buildings along Ellipse Road.

Bottom: Streetscape elevations.

Looney Ricks Kiss

Ross Bridge Village Center
Birmingham, Alabama

The new American resort town of Ross Bridge is anchored by a new 400-acre Town Center, located along the edge of a scenic parkway. The Town Center is entered through its main green and is composed of 75,000 square feet of commercial/retail space, 108 higher-density single-family residential units — cottages and townhouses — and 25 live-work type buildings. The town's architectural vocabulary is defined by that of local and regional villages of the early 1900s. This is evident in the community's town hall and welcome center, patterned after a vintage railroad station. Paired parks of 80,000 and 86,000 square feet will provide open space at the entrance to Ross Bridge, with the Town Center serving as a transition to the surrounding residential areas.

Top: Town Center plan.

Top right: Town aerial view.

Middle right: Market Street buildings.

Above: Town Center residential street.

Right: Main street into town.

Looney Ricks Kiss

Thornton Park
Orlando, Florida

This 809,000-square-foot mixed-use building with 311 condo units serves as a connector between downtown Orlando and the historic residential neighborhoods that line Lake Eola and its parks. The building's five-story mixed-use podium harmonizes with the surrounding low- to mid-rise neighborhood, and the residential tower rising from its corner joins the downtown skyline. A private club, with pool, and rooftop villas are located on the fifth-floor setback. The ground-floor retail was designed to comply with the city's mixed-use ordinance developed for the district. The main retail occupant, a food market, is given a prominent corner presence, with much of its bulk behind the streetscape of smaller retail spaces. By locating the garage entrances on opposite streets, access to underground parking for the retail has been clearly separated from the motor court entry and resident parking.

Above left: Condominium rising at intersection of Central and Lake Avenues.

Left: Corner Grocery entry.

MBH Architects

1115 Atlantic Avenue
Alameda, CA 94501
510.865.8663
510.865.1611 (Fax)

1300 Dove Street, Suite 100
Newport Beach, CA 92660
949.757.3240
949.757.3290 (Fax)

www.mbharch.com

MBH Architects

West Hollywood Gateway
West Hollywood, California

Above: Project's signature night-lighted curves.

Above right: Identifying lighted tower above plaza.

Left: Outdoor dining on widened sidewalks around complex.

Opposite bottom: Plaza with escalators connecting two retail levels.

Photography: RMA Photography.

This complex sets a valuable precedent for integrating big box retailers into an urban, pedestrian-oriented setting. Target and Best Buy have leased space in the development which includes 254,000 square feet of retail on two levels, with space for additional retailers, restaurants, and a 70,000-square-foot community meeting area, all organized

around a landscaped public plaza. Widened sidewalks with space for outdoor dining add further to the public realm, and two levels of parking are provided under the complex. The historic Formosa Café is retained and integrated into the design of the project. Both retailers have experienced exceptional sales in this unaccustomed setting. Located at a highly visible intersection, the project has already inspired upgrading of nearby properties. The 4.84-acre site came with several liabilities: multiple ownership, soil contaminants from a former rug-cleaning plant, and existing hard-to-relocate occupants (a car wash, an auto repair shop, and a cast stone manufacturer).

Working with city and federal authorities, the development team was able to get a grant and a favorable loan through HUD and to acquire some property through eminent domain.

MBH Architects

200 Brannan
San Francisco, California

This 191-unit residential complex, located in the historic South Beach neighborhood, has an exterior composition of red brick, white plaster, and metal-framed glazing that blends well with the area's warehouse tradition. Facing inward toward a lush central court, 79 of the units have transparent envelopes of sheer glazing, two-stories for each unit, forming a serrated boundary that expresses the individual residential module. Thirteen penthouse units have private balconies with sweeping views. Structural systems are pulled back from exterior walls to leave views unobstructed while meeting stringent seismic requirements.

Left: Interior court, with serrated edge of glazed walls.

Opposite left: Glazed walls revealing two-story unit heights.

Opposite top right: Street elevation, with areas of brick and plaster.

Opposite top center: Elegant complex identification signage.

Opposite bottom: Façade view from street.

Photography: Farshid Assassi.

MBH Architects

The Town Center at Levis Commons
Perrysburg (Toledo), Ohio

The Town Center is the first phase of J. Preston Levis Commons, a 200-acre urban village that will include offices, residential buildings, and recreational areas. This 319,000-square-foot mixed-use center is the focus of a master-planned street grid. The center is anchored by a twelve-screen cinema. Specialty retail, a variety of restaurants, 70,000 square feet of upper level offices, and entertainment venues overlook a town green that includes fountain, benches, and other amenities. Architectural design elements reflect the scale and tradition of the region, with varied building envelopes inspired by Georgian, Federal, Italianate, and Queen Anne precedents.

Opposite top: Building facades of varying form in consistent muted color.

Opposite bottom left: Central fountain on town green.

Opposite bottom right: View of Town Center from Archway.

Above: Town green and flanking buildings, showing on-street parking.

Right: Fountain and retail row with corner turret.

Photography: Tom Ethington.

215

MBH Architects

Marina University Villages
Marina (Fort Ord), California

Developed adjacent to California's beautiful and historic coastline highway, Marina University Villages is the evolution of the regional lifestyle center. Totaling 700,000 square feet the project contains a collection of restaurants and entertainment venues, specialty and large retailers, along with area suitable for civic events and public art. Marina University Villages is the anchor and first phase of an overall 270-acre master-planned community that ultimately will include single- and multi-family housing, additional neighborhood retail and office space connected with pedestrian and bike friendly streets, open space linkages, transit corridors and vistas to civic landmarks.

Top: Activity in mixed-use town center.

Far left: Town center's mix of automobile and pedestrian traffic.

Left: Portion of town center, showing buildings of various heights.

Below: Elevation of town center.

McLarand Vasquez Emsiek & Partners

1900 Main Street
Suite 800
Irvine, CA 92614
949.809.3388
949.809.3399 (Fax)
info@mve-architects.com
www.mve-architects.com

350 Frank H. Ogawa Plaza
Suite 100
Oakland, CA 94612
510.267.3188
510.267.3199 (Fax)

McLarand Vasquez Emsiek & Partners

McLarand Vasquez Emsiek & Partners

Fruitvale Village
Oakland, California

A number of smart-growth design and land-use concepts are embodied in this transit-oriented, high-density, mixed-use project, which is intended to revitalize Fruitvale's business district. The 10-acre development brings to life an existing BART station by replacing the on-grade parking lot with a commercial, retail, and entertainment paseo that accommodates community-related uses. Capitalizing on the pedestrian traffic generated by the BART station, Fruitvale's redevelopment plan includes over 30,000 square feet of retail and restaurant space, 60,000 square feet of offices, a 40,000-square-foot health clinic, a 12,000-square-foot community resources center, 5,000 square feet library, and 47 live/work units. The two buildings house retail on the first level, community facilities on the second level, and innovative loft housing on the third level. The atmosphere of a lively Mediterranean village is recalled in the project's use of simplified traditional architectural forms, a variety of warm colors, palm trees, and fountains. Circulation on third-level terraces, reached by broad stairs, adds a third dimension of activity and visual interest.

Above: Identifying signage at one entrance.

Left: Site plan.

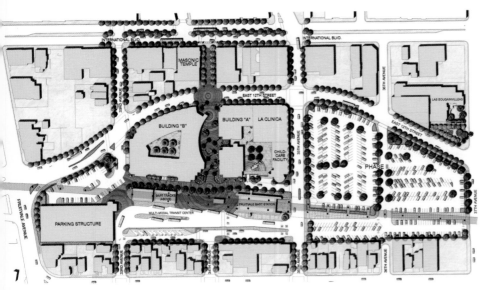

Above: Plaza approach to BART station.

Top right: Tiered building defining plaza.

Far right: Observable playground.

Right: Library

Photography: Keith Baker Photography; Evelyn Johnson Photography (opposite left).

McLarand Vasquez Emsiek & Partners

The Promenade at Rio Vista
San Diego, California

The Promenade is a 13.8-acre mixed-use community that exploits the site's light-rail transit and riverfront trails. It consists of six structures of four stories over a two-level subterranean garage, with commercial and retail activities surrounding a commons. The commons serves as the heart of the community for residents and transit riders alike. The space is enlivened by arcades fronting on the commercial uses, with patios for outdoor dining and a large fountain as a memory point. Based on the architecture of Irving Gill, the light-colored rectangular forms of the buildings, pierced by round arches, acknowledge the benign climate and design traditions of the area. Trellises, pergolas, courtyards, and patios tie the interiors to the landscape. A network of private streets and pedestrian passages connects destinations inside and outside the project. Retail parking is parallel to the streets or integrated into guest parking of the garage, with access to the commons through the building lobbies.

Above: Commons, with axial tower marking trolley station.

Below: Central fountain.

Right: Commons by day, showing plantings and parallel retail parking.

Photography: Robert A. Hansen Photography.

McLarand Vasquez Emsiek & Partners

Hollywood & Vine
Hollywood, California

Above: Alternative Vine Street treatments.

Below: View with Vine Street at left.

With one of the most famous intersections in the world as its address, this mixed-use development will deliver a Hollywood experience. One of Los Angeles' many MTA transit villages, the project will incorporate an existing subway terminal. The development responds to historical Hollywood with the use of colorful materials and established cornice heights. It also expresses the present and future of Hollywood through its incorporation of large-scaled wall graphics. In addition to MVE & Partners, the project design team includes HKS Architects for the 300-room hotel and the 140 condominiums. A transit plaza located on Hollywood Boulevard at the key subway entrance is lined with shops and restaurants and provides a forecourt for the hotel and condominium buildings. Vine Street is the primary address for the 350 apartments, designed in an urban loft aesthetic, which will range from 550 to 1,150 square feet each. Below these will be neighborhood retail space at street level.

McLarand Vasquez Emsiek & Partners

Uptown
Oakland, California

Located just north of the recently renovated Oakland Civic Center, this 14-acre project will transform under-utilized parking lots into a community designed to attract residents downtown. It will include 60,000 square feet of retail/commercial space, 1,200 mixed-income apartments, 400 off-campus graduate student housing units for U.C. Berkeley, and 900 condominiums. The corridor along Telegraph between the landmark Paramount Theater and the future Fox Theater renovation will accommodate live events, a food court, and a revitalized existing skating rink. Low-rise rental units and loft-style apartments, intended for young professionals, will be linked to the entertainment district by pedestrian paseos. The high-rise towers along Telegraph will house for-sale units. Loftlike units will be created by renovating existing structures, thereby maintaining the historical character of the site.

Top: Birds-eye view of site.

Above: Renovated Fox theater on Telegraph entertainment corridor.

Left: Park at center of development.

McLarand Vasquez Emsiek & Partners

Douglas Park
Long Beach, California

MVE & Partners worked with Boeing Realty Corporation in master planning their 260-acre former aircraft factory property adjacent to Long Beach Airport. The production site for Douglas Aircraft during World War II, the factory later turned out McDonnell Douglas jet-liners. As the reuse of this tract was of great interest to the community, MVE participated with Boeing in a series of public workshops soliciting comments and support from stake-holders, while also working closely with city officials and staff. The master plan features 3.3 million square feet of job-generating commercial uses ranging from offices and research and development to light industry and distribution. A 100-acre residential district with about 1,400 dwelling units will include a variety of detached and attached types along tree-lined streets. A mixed-use district with key retail amenities will serve as a focal point, as will numerous parks and open spaces.

Top right: Conceptual land use plan.

Below: Aerial perspective of entire development.

Middle right: Neighborhood park.

Bottom right: Residential street.

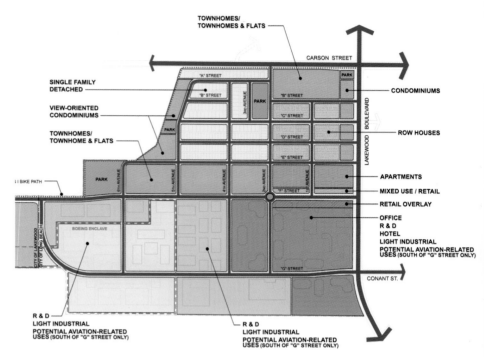

223

McLarand Vasquez Emsiek & Partners

Tralee
Dublin, California

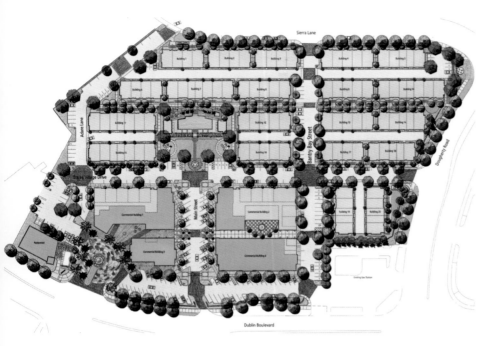

Left: Village plan, with mixed-use retail center at lower left.

Below left: Residential street.

Bottom: Mixed-use activities and on-street parking in Village Center.

A mixed-use urban village will be developed on the ten-acre site of a vacant retail center, adjacent to Dublin's civic center, sports park, and business district. The project is composed of two distinct parts. The Village Townhomes area will consist of 103 rowhouses, ranging in size from 1,350 to 1,930 square feet, organized on a grid of streets and pedestrian mews. Each unit will be articulated, with its own front porch or stoop, within an overall envelope that maintains the street edge. The Village Center will contain 130 townhouses, flats, and lofts, from 600 to 1,550 square feet in size, above 35,000 square feet of retail and restaurant space. Parking for the retail will be provided on the streets, and residents will park in a single-level garage below the Village Center. The architecture of the village evokes the forms of historic California towns, farms, and canneries, with vaulted and pitched roofs, numerous bay windows, and generous use of brick. Metal canopies will provide shelter and incorporate signage, as they have traditionally in local towns.

Pappageorge/Haymes Ltd.

814 North Franklin
Suite 400
Chicago, IL 60610
312.337.3344
312.337.8009 (Fax)
email@pappageorgehaymes.com
www.pappageorgehaymes.com

Pappageorge/Haymes Ltd.

The Glen Town Center
Glenview, Illinois

Left: Aerial perspective, with control tower at center.

Right: Mixed-use row, with broad sidewalks and angled parking.

Below: Navy Park and mixed-use façade.

Photography: Pappageorge/Haymes Ltd.

As the high-density, mixed-use focus for the 1,100-acre redevelopment of a former naval air station, Glen Town Center is designed to evoke the classic shopping districts of nearby Lake Forest and Winnetka. On its 45 acres, it includes 110,000 square feet of retail, restaurants, and movie theater, 181 apartments above street-floor commercial, and 154 townhouses. Two groups of gabled townhouses are located at either end of the center, curving around quiet greenswards, and others are "laminated" onto parking garages to screen them from view. The main retail street follows a graceful arc, linked at either end to the area's main boulevard. Centered on this arc and set off by the new Navy Park are the restored 1930s air control tower and hangar.

Facing page middle: One of residential ovals; reused air station building facing Navy Park.

Facing page, bottom: Axial entry to center, aligned with control tower.

226

Unifying the development is a vocabulary of red brick walls, slate roofs, punched residential windows, and projecting bays and balconies. Once established, this vocabulary has been varied by irregularities in rooflines, window placement, and signage. The curved mixed-use buildings facing the historic air station structure responds to its Modernism with extensive glazing and transparent canopies.

227

Pappageorge/Haymes Ltd.

600 North Lake Shore Drive
Chicago, Illinois

Above: Lake Shore Drive entrance.

Left: Paired towers flanking vine-clad garage wall.

Bottom left: Towers near left end in skyline view.

Occupying a pivotal position on Chicago's lakefront, this pair of towers is convenient to the urban activity of its Streeterville neighborhood yet offers the detachment of unobstructed lake views. On a site of about one acre, the project contains approximately one million square feet. Its 401 residential condominiums are divided into two slim shafts — of 40 and 48 stories — to limit the shadow cast on the neighboring beach. The concept of twin towers recalls Mies van der Rohe's world-famous paired apartment buildings nearby at 860-880 Lake Shore Drive, although the new pair is quite different in form and scale. Unlike Mies's rectangular towers, set back from adjoining streets, these building follow the boundaries of their site, reflecting the angular relationship of Lake Shore Drive to the prevailing Chicago grid. The tower walls facing outward consist of sleek expanses of blue-tinted glazing, divided into three-story horizontal bands. The walls facing inward to the 60-foot gap between the shafts present grids of punched windows in metal-paneled surfaces. The upper floors rise from a 500-car parking garage, the top of which is gardened between the towers, providing a shared sculpture garden and private terraces. The green theme is continued on the exposed walls of the garage between the towers, which will be clad with vines

Pappageorge/Haymes Ltd.

Block X
1145 Washington
Chicago, Illinois

Set in a context of industrial buildings and loft housing, this dense complex presents distinctly different images toward the streets outside and the court at the interior of its 1.77-acre site. Toward the streets, walls are regular, with large glazed bays echoing those of surrounding buildings. Toward the inner courtyard, volumes break down into a variety of balconies and projections, with exposed steel framing and fascias painted a lively blue. Structures containing a wide variety of flats and duplexes are pushed to the edges of the site to make room for the gardened court. The court — and the first floors of apartments — are a half level above grade, allowing for under-the-court parking, which is accessed from two streets without crossing pedestrian routes.

Top: Evening and daylight views of inner court.

Above: Street fronts echoing nearby buildings.

Left: Court fronts, with terraces stepping back between projecting stair towers.

Right: Court-level plan.

Photography:
Pappageorge/Haymes Ltd.
night view, The Thrush
Companies.

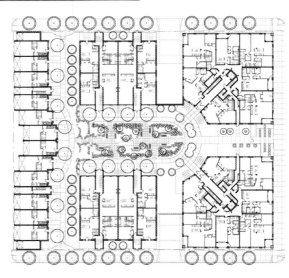

Pappageorge/Haymes Ltd.

Museum Park
Chicago, Illinois

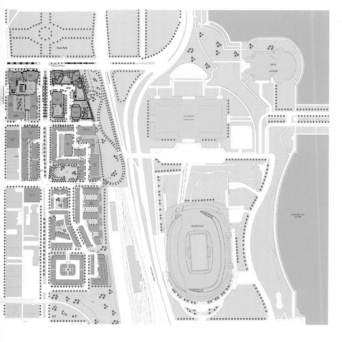

Until 1989, the 80-acre tract on Chicago's Near South Side known as Central Station was the vacant land of a former railroad yard. Adjacent both to Grant Park on the north and the recently reconceived Museum Campus on the east, the area presented a unique opportunity to create a new community responding to its prime location and the traditions of its surroundings. Occupying the largest part of Central Station, Museum Park includes a wide range of residential types: rental apartments, townhouses, condominiums, and loft units, along with a variety of community facilities, laid out along tree-lined streets and intimately scaled parks. To provide a strong sense of place and urban activity, all residential buildings front directly on streets. Generally speaking, taller buildings are sited toward the north and east edges of the site, facing large park areas and the lake, with low-rise buildings bordering established urban blocks to the west. Future construction proposed for Museum Park includes a 62-story residential tower with a distinctive organic prow-like form that is to rise at the northeast corner of the site, overlooking Grant Park, the Museum Campus, and Lake Michigan.

Top: Site plan.

Above: Townhouses facing a landscaped square.

Right: Residential loft structure.

Facing page, top left: Community recreational center.

Facing page, top right: Proposed residential tower at northeast corner of development.

Facing page, bottom: Large portion of project, seen beyond marina and Museum Park.

Photography: Pappageorge/Haymes Ltd.

Pappageorge/Haymes Ltd.

Kinzie Park
Chicago, Illinois

The master plan and architectural design of this development take advantage of a prime waterfront property while dealing with its difficult edge conditions. The project's 4.3-acre site offers exceptional views of the Chicago River but is hemmed in by intensively used rail lines and major roadways. In response, the site plan organizes townhouses around two brick-paved internal streets, creating an enclave of traditional masonry and stone façades. Mid-rise apartment structures at the ends of the site buffer the development from train and traffic noises and offer broader vistas to their residents. Available to all residents is a riverwalk with carefully chosen plantings, benches, lighting, and sculpture. A central fountain plaza provides a pivotal link between the townhouse streets and the riverwalk.

Above: Townhouses facing Chicago River.

Left: Site plan.

Below: Mid-rise structure and townhouses at one end of site.

Below right: Passage to riverwalk between townhouse rows.

Photography:
Pappageorge/Haymes Ltd.

Perkowitz + Ruth Architects

111 West Ocean Boulevard
21st Floor
Long Beach, CA 90802
562.628.8000
562.628.8005 (Fax)

lglick@prarchitects.com
www.prarchitects.com

Las Vegas, NV
702.892.8500

Portland, OR
503.478.9900

NW Arkansas
479.271.8090

Washington, DC
703.668.0086

Orange County, CA
714.850.3400

Studio One Eleven
at Perkowitz + Ruth Architects
562.901.1500
www.studio-111.com

Perkowitz + Ruth Architects

Bridgeport Village
Tualatin, Oregon

Above: Intimate passage evoking urban streets.

Below: Outdoor living room in central courtyard.

Right: View of main corridor lined with Italian kiosks.

Photography: Paul Turang Photography (above and right); Stephen Jones Photography (below).

Emerging from an abandoned rock quarry site, Bridgeport Village opened up the region to new high-end retail shopping opportunities. After a 20-year moratorium on large-scale retail development in the Greater Portland market, the new 500,000-square-foot open-air specialty village offers the latest in outdoor shopping concepts and technology to its regional consumers. Generating sales competitive with the top lifestyle centers in the nation, Bridgeport Village has become a place for friends and families to meet, shop and be entertained. The project emulates the urban nature of downtown with urban blocks, two story façades, and strategically placed narrow streets. As an extension of the urban architectural heritage of the greater metropolitan area, the design incorporates a wide spectrum of materials and façades from different eras. A fountain and play center inspire activity in the central courtyard, and an authentic imported gazebo is the site for outdoor afternoon concerts. Imported Italian kiosks line the main central aisle that ends with a large cinema, which serves as a dramatic yet elegant backdrop for the center. Fine dining options and coffee shops are easily accessible on outlying pads with curbside parking and valet options. Elegant landscaping and ambient lighting adorn the narrow meandering passageways. Complementary umbrellas and sheltered areas provide rain protection. Strategic placement of a parking structure behind the village places 1,140 cars in close proximity to shops.

Studio 111

at Perkowitz + Ruth Architects

Infill & Mixed Use

Studio One Eleven is an architecture and urban design practice dedicated to smart growth principles as an alternative to conventional suburban development models. From high-rise housing, mixed-use infill, hospitality and civic buildings to downtown revitalization, streetscape and storefront design, each endeavor aims at making a walkable, humane and sustainable larger urban whole.

Figueroa Central Downtown Los Angeles, California

Located adjacent to the Los Angeles Convention Center, Staples Center and the future L.A. Live and Nokia Theater developments, Figueroa Central, designed in collaboration with Johnson Fain International Inc., brings an ambitious program of retail and residential uses into the city's burgeoning downtown. With two residential towers defining the skyline, the development focuses flagship and neighborhood retail with restaurant uses along sidewalks, plazas and paseos to engage the public realm and avoids the street-deadening effect of inward-facing retail promenades. An environmental graphics program contributes to an exciting atmosphere reminiscent of Times Square.

Right: Aerial view highlighting the project's integration within the emerging entertainment district.

Studio 111
at Perkowitz + Ruth Architects

Above: Central green of Echelon is defined by a formal building edge.

Above right: Passive cooling tower, which captures breezes and cools them as they descend into intimate courtyards of Echelon, allowing for outdoor activities year round.

Echelon I, Las Vegas, Nevada

Echelon I is a 15-acre, 372-unit component of a larger residential campus. Buildings are arranged around linear quads and courts to maximize outdoor living and views of the Las Vegas strip and surrounding mountains. In response to the hot dry climate, the orientation of the buildings, cooling towers, trees and fountains are designed to cool and shade courts. To mitigate the desert heat gain, adjustable canopies, louvers and screens allow residents the ability to control individual environments.

Milan Lofts, Pasadena, California

Located within walking distance from Old Town Pasadena and Del Mar Station, Milan Lofts is designed as four buildings arranged around communal courts. Through massing and stylistic variety the mixed use transit oriented development integrates into the fine grain of the surrounding urban fabric.

Above: Development of Milan Lofts is consciously articulated as several buildings.

Perkowitz + Ruth Architects

Mercantile West
Ladera Ranch, California

Left: Gateway to development's Main Street, which can be closed to traffic for community events.

Below: Shop fronts evoking individual buildings on a traditional commercial street.

Photography: Paul Turang Photography.

This 320,000-square-foot development is the community shopping center for Ladera Ranch, a 4,000-acre planned community in Orange County. The 14.5-acre project combines functions of the neighborhood center and a pedestrian-oriented "Main Street." Retail shops want the intimacy of a Main Street, while restaurants, pharmacies, and supermarkets prefer outparcels with the best accessibility by car. In this case, conflicting needs were reconciled by laminating the supermarket with Main Street storefronts. The Main Street itself, flanked by shops, with diagonal parking along a central linear island, is located for convenient pedestrian and bicycle access from an adjacent community park and residential area. Storefronts in a variety of natural materials recall the architecture of the mid-century downtown core of traditional California communities.

Perkowitz + Ruth Architects

Buena Park Downtown
Buena Park, California

Above: Site plan.

Right and below: Central plaza under different lighting conditions.

Photography: Paul Turang Photography.

Once a successful, though typical, suburban mall, the development saw its market slip away as other destinations attracted its customers. It has now been reinvented as a vibrant town center with 138,000 square feet of new or renovated building space, adding a strong entertainment component to the revitalized shopping facilities. The design encourages pedestrian flow between the existing enclosed mall and the open-air zone, with the prominent theater lobby sited on axis with the main mall entry. Perkowitz + Ruth Architects created an urban setting that blends Modernist and Neo-Traditional styles to infuse the feeling of a place developed over time. Many amenities in the public open spaces enhance the community feeling. The central plaza combines a series of elegant fountains, a reflecting pool, seating areas, a café kiosk, and large shade trees.

Perkowitz + Ruth Architects

The Lakes at Thousand Oaks
Thousand Oaks, California

Above: Project elevation that highlights strong tower element, alternating facades, and dramatic landscape and lighting.

Left: Perspective of the pedestrian experience.

Photography: Paul Turang Photography.

The Lakes is a newly opened lifestyle destination created by the collaborative talents of Caruso Affiliated, Perkowitz + Ruth Architects, Lifescapes International Inc. and Francis Krahe Lighting Design. This refreshing outdoor location offers multiple options for family entertainment, featuring a mix of restaurants and specialty stores. The Lakes also has a seasonal ice rink incorporated into a new lake replete with playful water features.

The building design offers alternating façades orchestrated along the perimeter of the lake. Embedded within a sophisticated interplay of elegant landscape design and pedestrian paseos, the integration of dining opportunities and specialty shops will draw patrons to this new, stunning destination.

Retzsch Lanao Caycedo Architects

137 West Royal Palm Road
Boca Raton, FL 33432
561.393.6555
561.395.0007 (Fax)
www.rlcarchitects.com

Retzsch Lanao Caycedo Architects

Royal Palm Office Building
Boca Raton, Florida

The distinctive architectural tradition of Boca Raton, established by Addison Mizner and his contemporaries in the 1920s, has been respectfully reinterpreted in this 5,600-square-foot office building. Located in the city's redevelopment district, the building contributes to its urban character by defining the street edge and recapturing the porch, a typical Florida architectural feature. The towers at the building's corners enhance its one-story scale and lend it a consistent identity when seen from its most visible sides. The wood trellis filters daylight entering the interior and casts an intricate pattern of shadows on exterior walls. A plaza at the rear of the building, framed by the building envelope and lush landscaping, serves as a gathering place and entry court not unlike the traditional courtyards of Mediterranean architecture.

Top: Building seen from street.

Above: Lobby.

Right: Identifying tower.

Facing page: Trellis.

Photographs: Chuck Wilkins Photography.

242

Retzsch Lanao Caycedo Architects

Cypress Park West, Phase II
Fort Lauderdale, Florida

Above: New structures reflected in pond.

Below: Lobby interior.

Bottom: Walkway canopy.

Bottom right: Entrance façade.

Facing page: Aerial showing garage, office building, and new landscape design.

Photography: Chuck Wilkins Photography.

The second phase of Cypress Park West has transformed a single office building into a true office park, attracting a major tenant that might otherwise have moved its large workforce out of the Fort Lauderdale area. A new 116,000-square-foot office building and the existing building, renovated to match its class A standard, now accommodate Microsoft's Latin American headquarters and Nextel offices. The redesigned five-acre site now pulls together the two office buildings, a full-service Marriott, and a six-level parking garage into an attractive and functionally effective composition. New construction is sited well away from an adjacent eight-acre nature preserve to minimize impact on its natural growth and wildlife. The renovation of the Phase I office building was accompanied by the redesign of its plaza, the latter enhanced as an entrance to the development by royal palms relocated from other parts of the property. Lighting was designed to create a campus atmosphere, with bollards along walkways and plant lighting in the plaza. Construction was completed on time and within budget. Tilt-up concrete walls for the office buildings yield smooth white surfaces that contrast appealingly with green glass and surrounding foliage. The garage was constructed with twin tees and other precast components.

Retzsch Lanao Caycedo Architects

Fifth Avenue Place, Phase II
Boca Raton, Florida

Building on the success of the firm's Fifth Avenue Place development, completed in 2001, the proposed second phase will add the nine-story Fifth Avenue Tower. The 52,995-square-foot structure will have retail and restaurant space on the street floor, a recreation deck with a community pool on the second-floor setback, and condominium units above. An urban infill project, Fifth Avenue Place is located in the community redevelopment area of downtown Boca Raton, between a commercial area and a single-family residential district.

The first phase included townhouses that maintain the street line along Boca Raton Road and serve as transitional elements between low- and medium-rise neighbors. A parking structure in that phase of construction was located behind the townhouses and partially topped by two floors of offices, which offer views of the ocean and the Intracoastal Waterway. The new tower is expected to be completed in 2006.

Left: Phase I complex.

Below: Plan and elevation of phase I and II.

Facing page: Rendering of proposed tower.

Photography: Chuck Wilkins, phase I.

Fifth Avenue Residential Building · Fifth Avenue Parking Garage · Townhomes

SECTION "A"

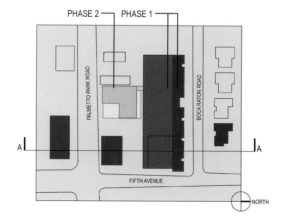

PHASE 2 — PHASE 1 —

PALMETTO PARK ROAD

BOCA RATON ROAD

A — A

FIFTH AVENUE

NORTH

Retzsch Lanao Caycedo Architects

The Pointe at Middle River
Oakland Park, Florida

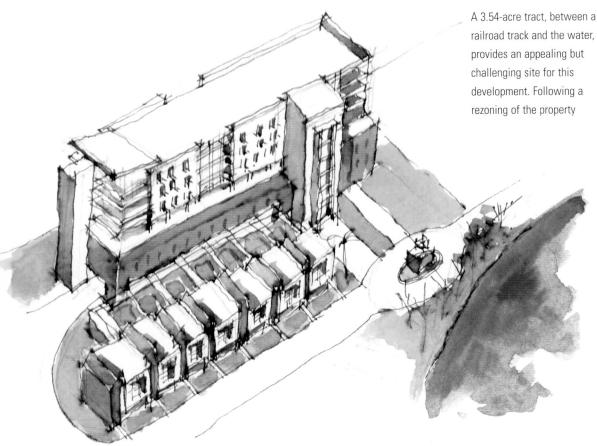

A 3.54-acre tract, between a railroad track and the water, provides an appealing but challenging site for this development. Following a rezoning of the property from business to residential, the architects organized the development with a high-rise residential structure rising above a three-story parking garage along the railroad side, shielding the rest of the development from rail activities. The 68 one- and two-story loft units in this building will offer views out to the water above the 37 three-story townhouses, with two-car garages, that extend out to the water's edge. The open site area of 92,322 square feet will include a clubhouse and pool. Construction will be of post-tensioned concrete, with CMU walls, some of which will be highlighted in vivid colors. The project is scheduled for completion in 2008.

Above: Sketch of high-rise structure with adjacent townhouse units.

Below left: Site plan.

Below right: Elevation of high-rise.

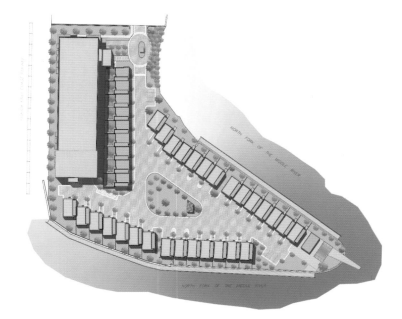

RTKL

Baltimore
410.537.6000

Chicago
312.704.9900

Shanghai
86.21.6122.5922

Dallas
214.871.8877

Miami
786.268.3200

Madrid
34.91.426.0980

Washington
202.833.4400

London
44.207.306.0404

Los Angeles
213.627.7373

Tokyo
81.33583.3401

www.rtkl.com

RTKL

LaQua Tokyo Dome City
Tokyo, Japan

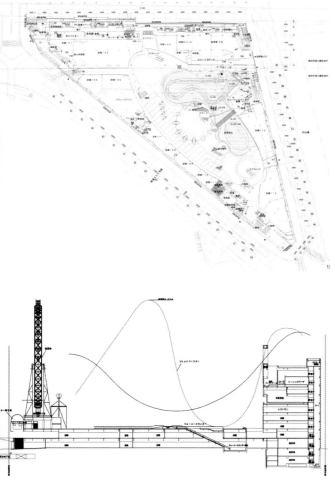

Fun is visibly the function of this entertainment center adjoining a domed arena in Tokyo. An iconic ferris wheel and a roller coaster that snakes through the complex are the most visually compelling elements of a development that includes a water slide, a haunted house, a concert stage, a spa, and over 70 shops and restaurants. Zoning requirements stipulated that the main structure be located at the back of the site, along a railroad line. There a multistory building houses retail and dining facilities on the lower levels and a state-of-the-art spa on the three upper floors. The architects' objective was to weave the active and passive functions together in a single coordinated experience. The outdoor rides and their support spaces are laid out around a roughly elliptical landscaped court. Subtle cues of lighting and design create segues from intensely active areas such as the roller coaster to the tranquility of the spa. A design challenge was integrating the necessary, but traditionally unsightly, safety accommodations of the rides into the project's aesthetic. The solution included designing the catchments for the ferris wheel to look like ships' sails and crafting safety barriers from stained wood to recall the hulls of historic ships.

Above left: Plan and section of complex.

Left: Central court and nautical-looking slab building.

Right: Entertainment center with domed arena at left.

Bottom right: After-dark view.

Photography: Courtesy of Takenaka Komuten KK.

RTKL

Downtown Brea Development District
Brea, California

Approached to develop a master plan for an ambitious mixed-use project in the Southern California city of Brea, RTKL collaborated with municipal planning and development agencies and the city council to design a district with memorable identity and market flexibility. The project occupies 25 acres in the heart of Brea's downtown and includes 220,000 square feet of retail and restaurants, nearly 100 residential units of various types, parking structures, and civic spaces, supplemented by a year-round events program. Its neo-traditional master plan recalls the ambiance and round-the-clock vitality of a classic Main Street. Pedestrian amenities include street trees, seating areas, fountains, and public art. On-street parking protects pedestrians and slows traffic. A district-wide parking authority allows shared parking solutions, thus reducing total demand requirements. Design criteria for building design encouraged individual expression for commercial properties, while establishing a distinctive overall character for the district and integrating key civic elements that celebrate Brea's unique history.

Left: Gateway to the district.
Below left: Aerial view of street.
Below: Night view with lively signage.

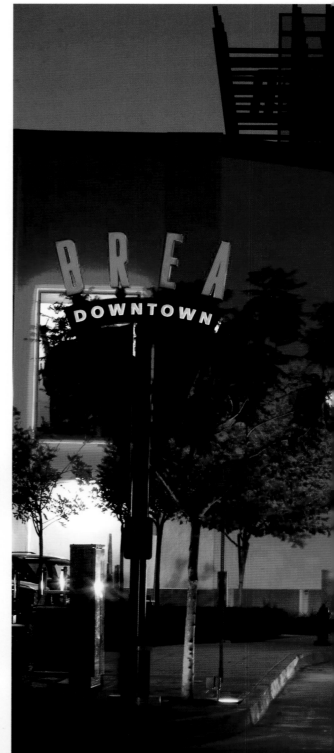

Left: Sidewalk activity and signs in pop tradition.

Right: Pedestrian environment.

Photography: RTKL Associates.

RTKL

Principe Pio
Madrid, Spain

A new 110,000-square-foot retail development has been created at an existing transportation hub in the dense core of Madrid. The project juxtaposes 70 high-end shops, a multi-screen cinema, and restaurants to a complex of rail, subway, and bus facilities, plus an 840-car underground garage. All transportation lines had to be kept running during construction. Architecturally, the clearly modern elements had to be integrated with the existing train station to form a cohesive environment. By moving several train tracks out of the existing station, it was possible to enclose the area under the old canopy that had sheltered the platforms. Innovative engineering techniques allowed excavation below this canopy to make space for a multilevel retail center with parking under it. A new central glass dome, with a different but related aesthetic, serves as an entranceway and a connection between the reused railroad station spaces and a new entertainment wing anchored by a cinema complex. Principe Pio is one of the most successful retail projects in Spain, with an average of 60,000 visitors monthly, and is 100 percent leased at rates 20 percent above the Madrid average.

Above: New entertainment wing and glass-dome entry.

Below: New parapet under old station canopy.

Below right: Multilevel retail inside historic shell.

Facing page: Domed rotunda, retail beyond.

Photography: David Whitcomb, RTKL.

RTKL

Zha Bei/The Hub International Lifestyle Centre
Shanghai, China

For an underdeveloped area of Shanghai still showing the scars of World War II bombings, this project will provide an essential mixed-use urban center. The 55,422-square-meter (599,000-square-foot) site will accommodate nine buildings totaling 202,199 square meters (2,184,000 square feet), with 8,000 square meters (86,400 square feet) of public open space. The mix of functions will comprise offices, an entertainment center including a cinema, a hotel, residential and mixed-use lofts, shops, and restaurants, all linked together by a network of pedestrian-friendly streets and extensively landscaped open spaces. Care has been taken to integrate the new development with the existing urban fabric so that it becomes a part of everyday local life, rather than an enclosed and alien presence.

Above: Aerial view of complex.
Left: Evening view along street.
Below left: After-dark aerial.
Below: Shops around landscaped court.

Sasaki Associates, Inc.

64 Pleasant Street
Watertown, MA 02472
617.926.3300
617.924.2748 (Fax)
info@sasaki.com
www.sasaki.com

77 Geary Street
Fourth Floor
San Francisco, CA 94108
415.776.7272
415.202.8970 (Fax)
sanfrancisco@sasaki.com

Sasaki Associates, Inc.

Addison Circle Park
Addison, Texas

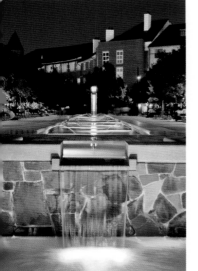

Top: Aerial view of park during a major event, showing high-density housing along some bounding streets.

Above: Central portion of park, showing transverse colonnade.

Left: Fountain near residential area.

Photography: Paul Chaplo (aerials), Craig Kuhner (others).

Located near the Dallas North Tollway, the park is the focus of a rapidly growing high-density community. For this key open space, the town wanted an inspiring urban park that would be ideal for the everyday use of residents yet be adaptable as a setting for regional festivals of over 100,000 people. Initial planning set the boundaries of its 10-acre site and located a new street with parcels for future mixed-use development along a light-rail transit corridor to the south. Numerous meetings with the town's events coordinator and potential operators determined the park's technical needs. The practicalities of public events were considered in the layout and regrading of the flat land for good sight lines, while preserving key trees. Provisions were made for a raised stage — allowing for operators to set up appropriate stage configurations and lighting for specific events. Locations of tents for food and beverage vendors were established, and underground electrical, water, and sewer hook-ups and paved ramps were provided. A pavilion building, with kitchen, restrooms, and sheltered seating is designed as the headquarters for events and can be rented out for wedding receptions and other festivities. The resulting park can accommodate such celebrations as an annual Octoberfest as well as intimate jazz and classical concerts.

Sasaki Associates, Inc.

Thu Thiem New Urban Center
Ho Chi Minh City, Vietnam

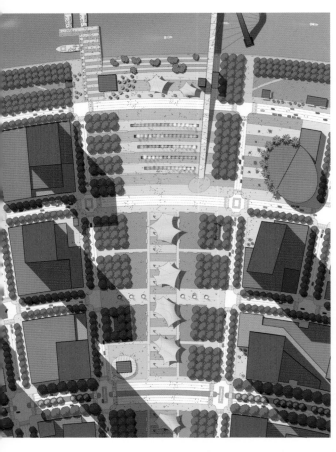

With an ultimate build-out of 68 million square feet on 1,840 acres, this new urban district is sited across the Saigon River from the center of the existing city. It will ease development pressure on the historic core and transform the river – now largely an industrial "back door" – into an important asset. The new development will feature waterfront open spaces and promenades. An iconic pedestrian bridge will connect a new central plaza to Me Linh Square in the old city. The new master plan responds to the bend in the river, and its primary road, Crescent Boulevard, echoes the curve. The plan recommends that a proposed highway through the district become an urban boulevard, with major traffic diverted onto a regional expressway. A system of canals and lagoons running through the new area will connect directly to the river. Areas of flood plain will be retained for tidal and storm-water management. The high density of built areas will favor pedestrian and transit access.

Approximately 60 percent of the new district's housing and other facilities will be within a 15-minute walk of the central plaza.

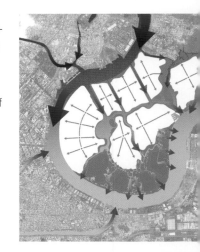

Facing page left: Detail plan of new central plaza, with end of footbridge and flanking buildings.

Facing page right: Thu Thiem hydrology concept.

Facing page below: New riverfront, with end of vehicular bridge in foreground; footbridge linking plazas in new and existing districts in middle distance.

Right, top: Urban design plan of the mixed-use core area district.

Right, bottom: Model of New Urban District.

Sasaki Associates, Inc.

Charleston Waterfront Park
Charleston, South Carolina

Charleston is a city of rare charm with an exceptional architectural heritage, yet the decline of its older port facilities had left vacant properties and rotting piers within a ten-minute walk of its downtown core. To revitalize the historic area, Charleston has carried out a long-term plan to reclaim the waterfront for the public. The Waterfront Park at the foot of Broad Street is part of the mayor's vision of a continuous promenade along two rivers, and is meant to redistribute some tourist activity from other heavily traveled parts of the core. Engaging key street corridors, the park allows views of the water and is designed as a destination place of civic stature. Its main entrance leads to an interactive fountain on a plaza that serves as a forecourt to a new wharf extending 365 feet into the Cooper River. A raised lawn scaled for large gatherings centers on another fountain, which takes the form of a pineapple, a traditional symbol of Southern hospitality. Bosques of live oaks along the city edge provide welcome shade. Restored salt marshes along the water's edge support wildlife and give visitors an appreciation of the area's marine ecology. Federal regulations required that publicly accessible parts of the park be raised 6.5 feet to the 100-year flood level. Unstable site conditions necessitated state-of-the-art stabilization of the landfill and 60-foot piles to support the pineapple fountain.

Left: Overall view of park.

Above: Entry plaza fountain in foreground, live oak grove, lawn centered on pineapple fountain, and palmetto-lined promenade.

Above right: Pineapple fountain in action.

Right: Portion of riverfront promenade.

Below right: Adger's Wharf gardens.

Photography: Landslides (left), David S. Soliday (above), Sasaki Associates (others).

263

Sasaki Associates, Inc.

Detroit Riverfront Civic Center Promenade
Detroit, Michigan

The Promenade meshes an active waterfront with recreational uses to link the city and its riverfront. Extending 3,000 feet along the Detroit River and a mere 55 feet wide in places, the site had previously been used mainly for surface parking. Key elements of the plan are: a grand stair linking Hart Plaza, the city's major public space, with the promenade; historic plaques marking Cadillac Landing, where the city was founded; and parallel bands of lawn recalling the area's 18th-century "ribbon farms." The 12-foot-high helix platform, reminiscent of a mariner's coiled rope, unwinds to form the serpentine seatwall. Undulations in the seatwall embrace the 20-foot-tall columns of a public transit viaduct, helping to integrate it with the promenade. Concave segments of the seatwall accommodate seating, and sections of the steel railing can be removed to accept gangplanks from visiting vessels.

Above: Downtown Detroit with promenade in foreground, bordering Joe Louis Arena and COBO Conference and Exhibition Center.

Photography: Landslides (aerials), Christopher Lark (others).

Below left: Corner of promenade showing night lighting and visiting vessels.

Below center: Close-up of seating helix and undulating seatwall.

Below right: Boats tied up along modular railing.

SEH (Short Elliott Hendrickson Inc.)

100 North 6th Street
Butler Square Building
Suite 710C
Minneapolis, MN 55403
612.758.6700
612.758.6701 (Fax)
866.830.3388 (Toll free)
www.sehinc.com

SEH (Short Elliott Hendrickson Inc.)

SEH (Short Elliott Hendrickson Inc.)

Mound Public Safety Facility
Mound, Minnesota

Left: Main entrance facing intersection.

Below: Vehicle bays flanking identifying tower.

Photography: ©Bob Perzel.

Left: Fire equipment on front apron.

Right: Fire station interior with exhibit wall and vintage fire truck.

Below right: Details of precast concrete exterior panels and balcony railing.

On a 3.72-acre site, the architects have combined fire and police stations in a way that offers the economy of shared facilities, yet maintains a clear-cut identity for each. A subtly night-lit tower announces the structure from a distance. A bold curved front, facing a major intersection and approached by a flagpole-adorned podium, indicates the main public entrance. Inside, the fire station occupies 23,084 square feet, the police station, 12,000 square feet. For public events, a commercial kitchen can provide meals for 5,000 people over a four-hour period. A glazed arcade on the front of the building provides a base for an open balcony facing the street. Exterior panels of precast concrete give the structure an appropriately dignified yet unpretentious image.

SEH (Short Elliott Hendrickson Inc.)

Heart of Anoka Commuter Rail Village
Master Plan
Anoka, Minnesota

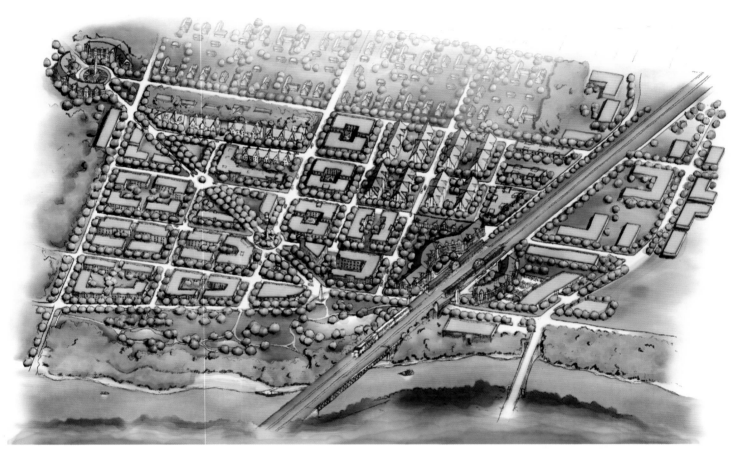

The objective for this 150-acre site was development that will support future commuter rail but is not dependent on it for its success. The resulting plan is based on solid market research and deep understanding of community preferences regarding development and design. Railroad station program elements such as parking and support services are integrated into mixed-use commercial and residential buildings. Medium- and high-density housing is organized around the station, making compatible transitions at the site boundaries to existing residential areas. Some existing buildings would be retained, including one industrial structure converted to loft housing units. Streets and bridges would be enhanced, new grade-separated railroad crossings created, and the riverside trail system extended. The community will demonstrate the possibilities that exist where there might otherwise be just a railroad platform and a parking lot.

Facing page, top: Aerial rendering of development.

Facing page, bottom: Residential blocks.

Above: Master plan, highlighting specific uses.

Right: Commuter station and related mixed-use buildings.

SEH (Short Elliott Hendrickson Inc.)

Loring Bikeway and Park
Minneapolis, Minnesota

The bikeway was needed to make a cohesive connection for cyclists and pedestrians across complex street and highway geometries, using public right-of-way. The bridge and the remainder of the one-mile-long bikeway have been designed to respond to their context, including the cultural and architectural traditions that define the neighborhood. The bridge will follow a long curve in plan, with visually engaging barriers on either side. Joining it at either end will be linear trails threaded through and aligned with the predominant street grid. A pocket park is planned for a vacant, neglected triangular lot adjoining the bikeway. Its green space will provide a rest area for trail users and a gathering spot for local residents, and a perennial garden within it will serve as a neighborhood activity. The project had to meet various standards of the state and federal transportation departments as well as accessibility requirements. The city, county, and state contributed to its $1.5 million cost.

Above: Bridge with decorative screen wall and railing design.

Below left: Bicyclists on bridge access ramp.

Below: Plan of pocket park serving also as trail head for bikeway.

Below right: Photographic map of area with trail and bridge routes superimposed.

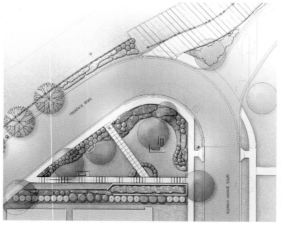

SEH (Short Elliott Hendrickson Inc.)

I-35W Access Project
Hennepin County, Minnesota

This freeway improvement project will help mend the urban fabric so drastically damaged by the highway's original construction. When the I-35 corridor was slashed through 70 blocks in the 1960s, it divided neighborhoods, obstructed access, and contributed to the concentration of poverty in some areas. Led by a partnership of landscape architects, the I-35 Access Project grew out of years of input from neighborhood residents and business and institutional groups. The focus is on mitigation of the freeway's negative effects and enhancements to the public realm, including noise abatement and integration of public transit. Adjacent redevelopment parcels will be developed with neighborhood-compatible structures. A comprehensive streetscape and traffic-calming program is included for adjacent city streets. The

highway bridges will be opened to local streets below, letting in light and air and providing opportunities for public art and fountains. Along a one-mile stretch, the center lane will be used for bus rapid transit, with multi-level stations to bring passengers from the city streets to the freeway level. The design had to meet federal and state highway and bridge standards and federal guidelines for context-sensitive design. The project does more than put a new face on the mistakes of the past. It builds a strong case for public involvement in creating wider freeway crossings, with inviting pedestrian lanes, as well as new landscaping and parks along and adjoining freeway routes.

Above: Elevated highway with masonry towers for transit station access.

Right: Proposed highway overpass and bus rapid transit station.

Far left: Early alternative for bridge over I-35 at 38th Street, showing pedestrian walkways, landscaping, and public art.

Left: Final, preferred "Ellipseabout" design for 38th Street bridge, with bus rapid transit station below.

SEH (Short Elliott Hendrickson Inc.)

Gateway Centre
Longmont, Colorado

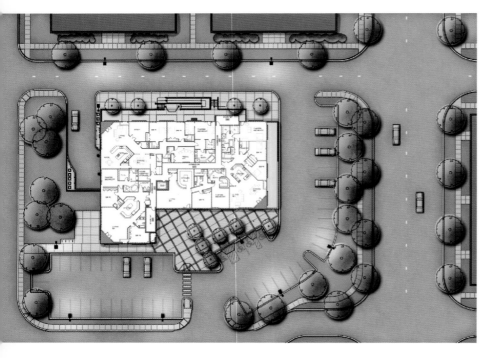

This development will introduce residential units as one element of a mixed-use program on a site where its immediate neighbors are all commercial. The project will contain retail and offices on the street floor, offices on the second, and luxury lofts on the third. Exterior walls will be a combination of concrete block, brick, and stucco. The building entrance, reached by way of a paved and planted front terrace, will be identified by a two-story-high glazed wall. Three of these lofts will have corner balconies, defined by the 45-degree geometry of their living rooms. Residents will enjoy views of the Front Range of the Rockies, visible from upper floors at this location. Loft residents will have basement storage areas and private parking spaces in the garage under the building. Spaces there will also be available to some commercial occupants.

Above: Plan of residential third floor.

Below: Four elevations, with main street front at lower right.

West

North

East

South

SWA Group

2200 Bridgeway Boulevard
PO Box 5904
Sausalito, CA 94966
415.332.5100
415.332.0719 (Fax)
www.swagroup.com

Sausalito
Laguna Beach
Houston
Dallas
San Francisco
Los Angeles
Shanghai

SWA Group

Lite-On Electronic Headquarters
Taipei, Taiwan

For its corporate headquarters, Lite-On wanted its building and landscape integrated to create a "green" complex. As soon as the architects were commissioned, they brought in SWA to work closely with them. The concept developed by this team was to place the private work spaces in a 25-story tower and the public facilities in a podium with a gardened roof. Under the podium is a four-level below-grade garage. The gardened plane became the focus of the project, sloping from the second level down to street level toward Gee Long River. Garden planting had to be chosen to flourish in shallow soil, areas of deep shade, and exposure to winds. Watercourses are organized to collect storm water, which is stored and used for irrigation. The direction of view from the building toward the river is emphasized with linear planting beds and walkways that bridge over a sunken light well/courtyard planted with camphor trees.

The tower-and-podium concept gave the project a distinctive image in its crowded urban area, opening up welcome space and views. The owner's endorsement of environmental principles yielded the first green roof built by a private developer in Taipei.

Above: Planted rooftops.

Left: On-site waterfall.

Right, top to bottom: Sign at road; building from road; entrance sunken into podium; pools cascading toward river.

Facing page, top: Aerial view of landscaped podium roof.

Facing page, bottom: Bridges where sloping landscape crosses sunken courtyard.

Photography: Tom Fox.

SWA Group   PPG Place
Pittsburgh, Pennsylvania

A failing plaza at a landmark city-center complex has been transformed into a success. Recognized as an icon of Post-Modernism from its opening in 1984, PPG Place is a 5.5-acre, 1,570,000-square-foot development composed of six Neo-Gothic glazed towers topped by 231 glass spires. While its skyline image is powerful, its central plaza, a half-acre of paving with no trees, constructed over a parking garage, turned out to be forbidding and unpopular. In 2001 PPG Place's new owners commissioned SWA to reinvent the plaza as a pedestrian destination that would attract upscale tenants to the complex's street-level retail arcade and encourage investment in surrounding blocks. Key to making the plaza attractive are locust trees in stainless steel planters, outdoor dining areas under 12-foot-wide umbrellas, and a 140-jet computer-choreographed fountain. Since the tree planters are movable and the water jets flush with the pavement, the plaza can be quickly cleared for the numerous concerts and festive events scheduled there. In the winter, a 9,586-square-foot skating rink is installed around the 40-foot central obelisk, using low-tech layers of sand and Styrofoam to level it on the sloping surface. Philip Johnson, renowned architect of the PPG Place buildings, judged the revitalized plaza "marvelous."

SWA Group Hangzhou HuBin Commerce & Tourism District
Redevelopment Master Plan
Hangzhou, China

A city of 3.3 million people, Hangzhou is located on the shore of West Lake, an internationally recognized recreation and tourist destination with ancient temples, teahouses, and moon bridges. But a major thoroughfare separated the lake from the core of the city. The first phase of a master plan, completed in 2003, has transformed the relationship. One key strategy was construction of a 1.5-kilometer (0.93-mile) tunnel beneath the lake, diverting traffic from the lakefront road, which has been redesigned as a pedestrian-friendly boulevard bordering an expanded waterfront park. "City Stream," a pattern of water courses, still pools, and waterfalls passing through mid-blocks, courtyards, and plazas, recalls rivers that once flowed through the district. Historic buildings have been preserved and adapted as cultural and art centers, and a new 10,000-square-meter (108,000-square-foot) focal plaza overlooking the lake has been created.

Top: Lakefront boulevard and park.

Above, left and right: "City Stream" waterway; boulevard in use.

Far left and left: Commercial district with new lighting.

Photography: Tom Fox.

SWA Group
Lewis Avenue Corridor
Las Vegas, Nevada

Above: View along avenue.

Below: Two views of stream bed.

Bottom: Quotations from local poets and writers at footbridge.

Right: Rock-rimmed pool, federal courthouse beyond.

Bottom right: Waterfall "source" at courthouse.

Photography: Tom Fox.

In a city known for fantasy, the design of Lewis Avenue affirms the real-world nature of its district. As part of a downtown revitalization effort, the city asked SWA — already engaged in two major projects along the avenue — to redesign a three-block corridor linking key governmental buildings. At the outset, the avenue presented a four-lane roadway and narrow, unshaded sidewalks. Working with city departments, SWA found that two traffic lanes could be eliminated, making room for 20-foot sidewalks with double rows of trees. It was possible to remove surface parking from one key block and turn it into a plaza.

Influenced by the rugged regional landscape, the redesign places trees much as they would appear at an oasis and uses water sparingly as in a desert wash. A dramatic 10-foot waterfall from the level of the federal courthouse entrance is the apparent source of the stream below.

SWA Group

Santana Row
San Jose, California

For the development of a neo-traditional town center near downtown San Jose, SWA provided landscape architectural services. At full build-out, the 42-acre site will contain 680,000 square feet of retail space, including shops and boutiques lining the main street, 1,200 residential units, a 231-room luxury hotel, 15 to 20 restaurants, and open-air cafes, along with parks, plazas, and landscaped streetscapes. Apartments, condominium units, lofts, and the hotel are located above street-level commercial spaces. The design intention, for both buildings and landscape, was the use of a variety of styles to create the impression of growth over time. The project included complete upgrading of infrastructure, transportation circuits, parking, access to nearby highways, and wireless internet access throughout.

Top: Ample outdoor dining areas.

Above: Planting as traffic calming device.

Left: Active plaza with passage into courtyard beyond.

Below: Typical streetscape and signage.

Far left: Streetscape with intended "European" character.

Photography: Tom Fox, Bill Tatham.

Swaback Partners pllc

7550 East McDonald Drive
Suite A
Scottsdale, AZ 85250
480.367.2100
480.367.2101 Fax)
info@swabackpartners.com
www.swabackpartners.com

Swaback Partners pllc

Swaback Partners pllc

DC Ranch
Scottsdale, Arizona

The master plan for this 8,300-acre development is the fortunate outcome of a process marked earlier by conflict. At one point a legal dispute between the property owner and the city was settled by the Arizona Supreme Court with the imposition of a court-mandated plan that would have damaged both the environment and the resulting development. Five years later, the process was redone, with the developer and city collaborating on a plan that respects the land and assures a cohesive community through comprehensive architectural controls and governance. A mix of residential types is located within walking distance of a range of services and amenities, all of them linked by a system of paths and trails. The open space designed as part of the development combined with land set aside for city ownership amounts to 74 percent of the total acreage. Of the remaining 26 percent, about half is in private gardens and other non-building uses. Architectural guidelines recognize the need for texture, shade, and shelter in the desert environment. The siting of all buildings must be topography-sensitive, all plantings drought-tolerant, and watercourses treated as amenities. Public elements such as streets, bridges, lighting, signs, and fences must contribute to a coherent environment.

Above left: Partial master plan.

Left: Entry marker.

Top right: Portion of a trail system.

Above: Architecture combining openness with durable shelter.

Photography: DMB.

Top left: Golf course.

Above left: Sculpture in rock garden.

Left: Retail structure with discreet signage.

Right, top to bottom: View to city lights; community event; swimming oasis; clubhouse.

Swaback Partners pllc

Biosphere 2
Oracle, Arizona

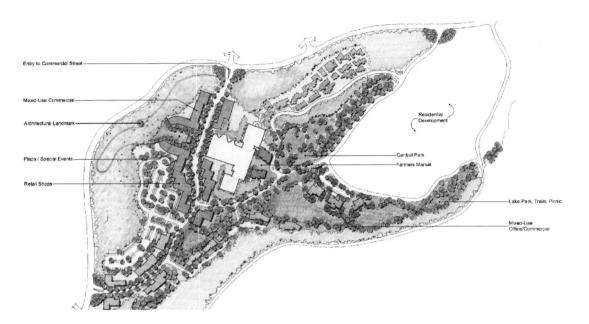

In January 2005 Swaback Partners was asked by developers to draw up a series of conceptual planning alternatives for the future development of an area centered on the world-renowned Biosphere 2. The land consists of the 140-acre Biosphere campus and two adjacent ranch tracts, which total 1,660 acres, and it offers striking panoramic views of the Santa Catalina Mountains. Alternatives proposed include: a hospitality complex, including resort hotel, health spa, retreat, and conference facilities; a cultural center, including performing arts, library, museum, and botanical garden; a research park, including a university annex and corporate facilities; a recreation complex, including an Olympic training center, an extreme sports center, and an ice rink; a local mixed-use development, including a town center, playground, amphitheater, and public plaza. Plans for the 1,520 acres that would surround any of these alternatives include a residential component of 1,553 homes, with 1,800 more approved for an adjacent 2,203 acres of State Trust land.

Top of page: Plan for local mixed-use alternative.

Above left: Biosphere 2 structures.

Left: Possible hotel uses inside Biosphere.

Above: Renderings of possible gateway design and resort pools.

Swaback Partners pllc

Scottsdale Hangar One
Scottsdale, Arizona

Top: Entry courtyard, showing signature rooftop "paper airplane."

Top right: Canopied entrance near apron.

Above: Car showroom.

Above right: Canopies cantilevered from hangars.

Left: Entry past distinctive steel-tube structural grid.

Photography: Paul Warchol.

This 129,000-square-foot facility combines airplane hangars, offices, car showroom/storage, and aviation/automotive repair shops. It can accommodate up to 15 aircraft in its two 30,000-square-foot hangars. An approximately 68,500-square-foot multipurpose facility adjoining the hangars includes premium office space, entertainment space, and below-grade parking, as well as a unique high-end automobile showroom. The unique mix of uses has caused the project to be dubbed "a spa for jets." Hovering over the roof, a 108-foot-long aluminum "paper airplane" symbolizes the complex and is one of several exceptional structural accomplishments visible throughout the complex.

Swaback Partners pllc

The Village of Kohler
Kohler, Wisconsin

Swaback Partners has been involved for more than 25 years in the master planning and urban design of Kohler, a community originally planned in the early 1900s by the renowned Olmsted firm. A master plan drawn up in 1978 was updated in 1980 and again in 1990. The plan includes preservation of an 800-acre riparian open space zone and trail system, an astrophysical observatory, and golf course communities. In the early 1970s, the center of Kohler was being vacated as retail activity moved to a nearby mall. Now a village center provides a full range of goods and services, along with a lakeside inn. The American Club, a structure built in 1918 to house immigrant workers, has been restored

as a highly-rated resort. Two 18-hole golf courses, created under the evolving master plans, are internationally known.

Left, top to bottom: Partial aerial view; open space along river; winter activity.

Above: Community event along Kohler's central lake.

Below: Golf course along Lake Michigan.

Bottom: American Club resort.

Photography: Kohler Co.

Swaback Partners pllc

Las Palomas
Puerto Penasco, Mexico

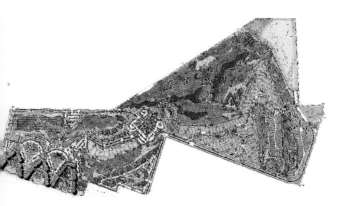

Left: Master plan.

Below left: Courtyard between high-rises.

Bottom left: Retail area at the base of towers.

Right: High-rise cluster seen from ocean.

Below right: Pool overlooking sea.

The master plan design placed high-rise residential complexes to take full advantage of ocean views. Amenities include golf, recreation, dining, lounging, and a variety of residential types. The clusters of towers define intimate pool and patio spaces. The architecture of the development includes contemporary design elements consistent with high-rise construction and modern technology, as well as traditional materials and forms that create a "village" experience, with narrow brick-paved passages, thick wall masses, and trellises as shading elements. The use of regional landscape materials and native stone, with work by local artists and craftsmen, contributes to a sense of timelessness and a connection to the place.

Swaback Partners pllc

Marana Master Plan
Marana, Arizona

Traditionally a small farming community near Tucson, Marana has grown to a population of 30,000 over the past decade, and demographic projections indicate an increase of 100,000 over the next 25 years. Swaback Partners has been retained to plan a 100-acre mixed-use town center that will establish a new identity for Marana and act as a guide for the character of future development. The planned urban village core will encourage higher-density housing and provide for public open space and industrial, office, and retail uses, along with civic and governmental services. The firm is also assisting the town in preparing residential design standards and overall land use scenarios for over 38,000 acres of undeveloped land in its total of 76,000 acres.

Top drawings, clockwise from top left: Master plan; overall view of town center; two views of proposed pedestrian environment.

Left: Aerial view of government buildings.

Thomas Balsley Associates

31 West 27 Street
New York, NY 10001
212.684.9230
212.684.9232 (Fax)
info@tbany.com
www.tbany.com

Thomas Balsley Associates

Thomas Balsley Associates

J-City
Tokyo, Japan

Two public spaces with Thomas Balsley sculptures provide two distinctive entrance environments and help to define the image for this new mixed-use project. Circulation paths are subtly indicated by a variety of elements that enliven these spaces for both passersby and building tenants. The main entrance plaza features a sculptural landform whose sloping stainless steel fountain and crescent shape attract visitors' attention to the front doors. This plaza is embellished with curving Corten sculptures and graphic walls whose cues have been taken from the book publishing heritage the neighborhood once nurtured. Retail cafes help activate this space throughout the week and the weekend. The project's residential units and conference rooms are entered through a terrace environment with lush gardens, fountains, and pergolas.

Above left: Stainless steel fountain sculpture where entry plaza meets public sidewalk.

Left: Graphic walls.

Below left: Sculpture with typographic motifs.

Above: Main plaza from above.

Left: Evening view from street.

Photography: Thomas Balsley (above, facing page top and center), Kokyu Miwa (all other).

Thomas Balsley Associates

Capitol Plaza
New York, New York

Left: Terrace with evening light.

Facing page, top left: Plaza passing through block.

Facing page, top right: Socializing at picnic tables.

Photography: Thomas Balsley (below and facing page below), Michael Koontz (all other).

The rezoning of the Sixth Avenue corridor in New York's Chelsea district provided for a through-block plaza whose success as a public space depends on sustained activity along its edges – similar to the traffic on a sidewalk. One edge of the plaza benefits from the new building's cafes and entrances, but the other edge required a different strategy. What was originally a 200-foot-long blank wall is now a new urban edge, carved out both as a narrow retail storefront and as a bright orange wall with oval penetrations, through which bamboo emerges. The plaza's contemporary design sensibility is a purposeful outreach to the neighborhood's creative professionals who work long studio hours and shoppers who flock to the neighborhood's unique retail "bazaar" environment. A wide range of seating and socializing choices, ranging from raised bar tables with swivel stools and benches with laptop tablettes to urban picnic tables, attracts working and conferencing well beyond the normal lunch peak periods.

Left: Boldly colored wall commanding attention from street.

Right: Raised terrace in bamboo glade.

Thomas Balsley Associates

Pacific Design Center
West Hollywood, California

Left: Fountains and gardens in front of the "Green" building, an annex to original "Blue Whale."

Below: New "Wave Park" in front of Blue Whale.

Below left: Three detail view of grassy amphitheater and undulating lawn panels.

Photography: Tom Hinckley (left and under), Jay Venezia (all other).

The five-acre setting of this Modernist landmark by architect Cesar Pelli — its main building known affectionately as the "Blue Whale" — has been transformed into a lively park-like landscape supporting the repositioning of the showroom complex as a multipurpose destination. Once a barren plaza, the space along Melrose Avenue, renamed "Wave Park" for it undulating panels of lawn, invites a variety of lounging and picnicking experiences. A destination café kiosk and terrace complement the new entrance and automobile arrival area. Red walls with recessed cobalt blue lights frame each lawn panel. A fountain plaza with terraced lawns and gardens has opened views and public access to the center. With the new building illumination and graphic sculptures, they create evening drama and a new public image for the facility.

Thomas Balsley Associates

Riverside Park South
New York, New York

The new urban development from 59th to 72nd street will include a new 27-acre waterfront park, giving westsiders direct access to their river for the first time. The first phase of the park, three acres along the Hudson River stretching from 65th to 70th Streets, provides a series of river-edge experiences involving an extensive network of boardwalks, overlooks, and plaza spaces at the ends of the cross streets. Riprap is used at the water's edge to blur the lines between river-edge grasses, public lawns, and the Hudson. This softer river edge, along with the low elevations of the board-walks, offers pedestrians more opportunity to get close to the water. Standing in dramatic contrast to these elements, an old railroad gantry tower has been stabilized and left in place. Dedicated bike and in-line skating paths connect Phase One of the park to the bike path system to the south. Elevated above the water's edge is a series of timber and steel overlooks providing viewing places and seating areas along the main walkway. Following the angled lines of the former railroad piers, the overlooks include interpretive signs telling the history of the site.

Above: Detail view of pier.

Right, top to bottom: Coastal grasses, with old railroad gantry in background; overlook terrace; aerial view of pier, cove, and gantry; boardwalks through grasses.

Photography: Michael Koontz.

Thomas Balsley Associates

World Trade Center Plaza
Osaka, Japan

Conceived as a water garden environment, this public space serves the Center as its front door as well as an outdoor extension of the winter garden's atrium and restaurants. Its terraces are surrounded by a lush landscape and a water feature whose raised basin is aligned with the visitor's sitting eye level and releases waves down its crescent slope. On the water basin's street edge is a water slide whose descent is interrupted by a grid of metal pipe protrusions. The plaza's dominant feature, the set of cone sculptures, has become the Center's iconic element. At first glance, they appear to serve only that purpose, but just beneath the surface, literally, are the mechanical rooms whose need for fresh air intake is accommodated by the cones' perforations. Emitting light and mist in the evening, these sculptures enrich the experience for the Center's workers and visitors.

Top: Aerial view.

Above left: Pool and cones at night.

Above: Plaza with building entrance.

Far left: Paths extending plaza experience.

Left: Raised basin and outdoor dining area.

Photography: Cervin Robinson.

Thomas P. Cox: Architects, Inc.

19782 MacArthur Boulevard
Suite 300
Irvine, CA 92612
949.862.0270
949.862.0289 (Fax)
info.oc@tca-arch.com
www.tca-arch.com

600 Wilshire Boulevard
Suite 1470
Los Angeles, CA 90017
213.553.1100
213.553.1111 (Fax)
info.la@tca-arch.com

Thomas P. Cox: Architects, Inc.

Botanica on the Green
Stapleton, Colorado

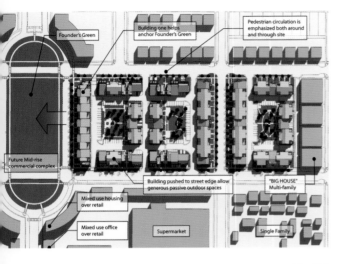

As part of a planned community on the site of the former Stapleton International Airport, this 244-unit project offers views of the Rockies along with the convenience of walking to stores, banks, and restaurants. Surrounded by a variety of commercial and residential building types, the development has been subtly adjusted from apartments at one end to townhouses at the other, all units offering private garages accessed from rear alleys. Architecturally, the project avoids the all-too-common vocabulary of the Denver region to announce a newer, non-traditional lifestyle that is directed toward young urban professionals. Assembled of crisp rectangular volumes, the buildings have numerous porches, balconies, and canopies that emphasize the amenities and individuality of the units. Directly adjoining this development is the 2.5-acre Founders' Green, the site of community celebrations and "under-the-stars" jazz concerts, wine festivals and a 2,000-seat amphitheater.

Left: Site plan, with Founders' Green at left.

Below left: Apartment units seen from Green.

Bottom left: Sheltered entries, porches, and balconies of townhouses.

Right: Row of apartment homes.

Opposite bottom: Row of townhouses.

Photography: Steve Hinds Photography, Dallas TX.

Thomas P. Cox: Architects, Inc.

Crescent Park Apartment Homes
Playa Vista, California

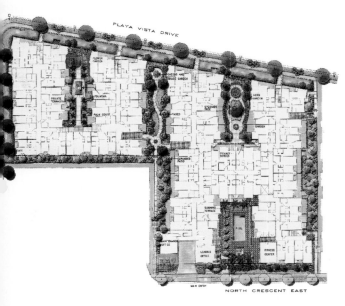

Left: Site and first residential level plan.

Below: Main front on North Crescent East, with pool court at center.

Below right: Portion of Playa Vista Drive front, with garden court at left.

Bottom right: Interior of leasing office.

Facing page: Exterior detail, with main entrance and pool court trellis.

Photography: Steve Hinds Photography, Dallas TX.

Located in Playa Vista, Los Angeles' first master-planned community in over 50 years, this 214-unit development was subject to many challenges in terms of zoning and design controls. Architectural styles were "dealt" to each developer to ensure design diversity in the community. This project was assigned the style of the pioneering California Modernist Irving Gill, whose work was notable for its smooth surfaces, sharp edges, and round arches. But while Gill's style exploited the characteristics of tilt-up concrete construction, this project had to recall his forms with wood and stucco. And since Gill never worked at the scale of this project, the building forms had to be broken down visually with advancing and receding planes and changes in color. The project includes four levels of apartments ranging from one-bedroom to two-bedrooms-plus den, notable for their 9-to-11-foot ceilings and high standards of fixtures and appliances. Shared amenities include a fitness center, spa and a business center with conference room. The distinctive garden courts and pool court provide views for residents and divide the complex into smaller-scaled volumes.

Thomas P. Cox: Architects, Inc.

Grand Avenue Competition
Los Angeles, California

TCA was a key participant in a runner-up team for the multibillion-dollar Grand Avenue Project, a redevelopment effort that is expected to link the civic and cultural districts of Los Angeles in a vibrant new regional center. The national competition for the project was open to any developer capable of proposing a 3.2-million-square-foot mini-city programmed to include entertainment venues, restaurants, retail, office buildings, a hotel, and new housing. TCA was a member of the Forest City Enterprises' team, which also included A.C. Martin & Partners and Calthorpe Associates. Housing was

TCA's major contribution of the team's proposal, which promised 4,700 units, including several high-rise apartment towers. A 16-acre "Great Park," stretching three city blocks from the City Hall to the cultural precinct along Grand Avenue, would have redeveloped an existing underused open mall, which is now hidden by an old county building. The project as a whole is expected to generate 16,000 permanent jobs and contribute $85 million annually in taxes. TCA is making other contributions to the revitalization of downtown L.A. with the renovation of the historic Subway Terminal

Building, for Forest City Enterprises, and an 850-unit high-rise mixed-use project for the Little Tokyo area for the Related Companies, the developer that won the Grand Avenue competition.

Left and top left: Residential towers with mixed-use bases.

Far left, top to bottom: View of "Great Park," with City Hall tower in foreground; Grand Avenue, with Chandler Pavilion in foreground, downtown skyline beyond; View of "Great Park," with City Hall in background.

Facing page: Plans and aerial visualization of competition proposal.

CATHEDRAL

GRAND AVENUE

TEMPLE STREET

Ahmanson
Theater

Mark
Taper
Forum

DWP

Dorothy
Chandler
Pavilion

A1

A2

Hall of
Records

Criminal
Courts

City
Hall

B1

B2

C

Bi-Party
Site

1ST STREET

HILL STREET

Disney
Concert
Hall

Q

W-2

County
Courts

W-1

Federal
Courts

BROADWAY

LA Times

SPRING STREET

County
Administration

2ND STREET

OLIVE STREET

L

Colburn
School

HOPE STREET

M-2

MOCA

CHINATOWN

CESAR CHAVEZ AVE

EL PUEBLO
DE LOS
ANGELES

SANTA ANA FREEWAY

TEMPLE ST

CIVIC CENTER
STATION

FIRST ST.

CROWN
HILL

HARBOR FREEWAY

SECOND ST.

OLIVE ST.

HILL ST.

BROADWAY

SPRING ST.

MAIN ST.

THIRD ST.

THIRD ST.

FOURTH ST.

HISTORIC
DISTRICT

FINANCIAL
DISTRICT

FIGUEROA ST.

HOPE ST.

GRAND AVE.

PERSHING
SQUARE STATION

FIFTH ST.

CENTRAL
CITY WEST

WILSHIRE BLVD.

SIXTH ST.

JEWELRY
DISTRICT

7TH / METRO
CENTER STATION

SEVENTH ST.

EIGHTH ST.

FLOWER ST.

NINTH ST.

FASHION
DISTRICT

OLYMPIC BOULEVARD

SOUTH PARK

OLYMPIC BLVD.

ELEVENTH STREET

PICO
STATION

HOPE ST.

GRAND AVENUE

TWELFTH STREET

PICO BOULEVARD

Thomas P. Cox: Architects, Inc.

Westgate – Pasadena
Pasadena, California

Left: Project plan in context of downtown.

Below: Entrance to pedestrian passage.

Bottom left: Pedestrian street with variety of housing types.

Bottom right: Residential units above street-level retail.

Development of this 12-acre site, adjoining the historic core of Pasadena, will reinforce the ambitious downtown revitalization effort. Today, the area consists mainly of abandoned industrial facilities and parking lots, acting as a barrier to pedestrian access to downtown from residential areas beyond. The design of the neighborhood includes 832 residential units, for both rental and for-sale, in a variety of 3-to-5-story configurations, with unit front doors typically off public streets or open spaces. Parallel parking on streets satisfies a fraction of the parking need, with the rest beneath the buildings. Pedestrian movement is encouraged by a system of paseos and courtyards penetrating the blocks. Retail components are included adjacent to existing downtown retail. This project has already been recognized by The Congress for the New Urbanism in 2005 when it received an Award of Excellence for The Neighborhood, the District, and the Corridor, and the American Institute of Architects, Orange County in 2004 for an Honor Award in Planning.

PROJECT CREDITS

Exceptional care has been taken to gather information from firms represented in this book and transcribe it accurately. The publisher assumes no liability for errors or omissions in the credits listed below.

180° DESIGN STUDIO

New Town Theater District
Client: Whittaker Builders, Inc.
Principal Consultants: 180° Design Studio, urban design, architectural design
Pickett Ray & Silver, engineers

New Longview
Client: Gale Communities, Inc.
Principal Consultants: 180° Design Studio, master plan, design charrette, architectural design (residential)
Patti Banks Associates, landscape
Zimmerman Volk Associates, housing market
Gibbs Planning Group, retail market
Swift & Associates, engineering design
Hamilton, Sterrett & Dooley, civil engineering
Allison Ramsey Architects, architectural design
Patrick Pinnell, architectural design

Crescent Creek
Client: Dial Realty
Principal Consultants: 180° Design Studio, master plan, architectural design
Missouri Valley Engineering, engineering
Patti Banks Associates, landscaping

Ottawa University Master Plan
Client: Ottawa University
Principal Consultants: 180° Design Studio, master planning

71st and Metcalf
Client: Dial Realty
Principal Consultants: 180° Design Studio, master planning

Union Hill Phase 3
Client: Union Hill Phase 3
Principal Consultants: 180° Design Studio, urban design, architectural design
Patti Banks Associates, landscape
Sullivan/Palmer, construction drawings

Beachtown Galveston Model Home
Client: Beachtown Galveston Village
Principal Consultants: 180° Design Studio, master planning, architectural design

Longfellow Court
Client: 180° Development, LLC
Principal Consultants: 180° Design Studio, master planning, architectural design

ALTOON + PORTER ARCHITECTS

Knox Shopping Centre
Client: AMP Henderson Global Investors
Principal Consultants: Altoon + Porter Architects, architectural design consultant
Hames Sharley International Ltd., associated architect
Bonacci Winward, structural/civil engineer
Simpson Kotzman Pty. Ltd., mechanical/electrical engineer
Tract, landscape architect
ARUP Fire, fire engineer
NDY Light, specialty lighting
Rawlinsons Pty. Ltd., quantity surveyor
Grogan Richards Pty. Ltd., traffic

C.J. Arms & Associates, hydraulics
Transportation Design Consultants Pty. Ltd., vertical circulation
ProBuild, general contractor

Victoria Gardens
Client: Forest City Development California, Inc.
Principal Consultants: Altoon + Porter Architects, architectural design
KA Inc. Architecture, executive architect
Field Paoli Architects, design architects
Elkus/Manfredi Architects Ltd, design architects
Thorson Baker & Associates, Inc., structural engineer
S.Y. Lee Associates, mechanical/plumbing engineer
Patrick Byrne & Associates, electrical engineer
MDS Consulting, civil engineer
SWA Group, landscape architect
Kaplan Partners Architectural Lighting, lighting designer
Redmond Schwartz Mark Design, environmental graphics
The Mobility Group, traffic engineer
Vratsinas Construction Company (VCC), construction manager
Forest City Construction Co., Inc., construction

Fashion Show
Client: The Rouse Company (project currently owned by General Growth Properties)
Principal Consultants: Altoon + Porter Architects, architectural design
Richard Orne, AIA, Orne & Associates, and Laurin B. Askew, Jr., FAIA, Monk LLC, conceptual design
Richard Orne, AIA, Orne & Associates, design manager for The Rouse Company
Ove Arup & Partners; ASI; SME Steel Contractors: structural
Tschuchiyama & Kaino, mechanical/plumbing
Patrick Byrne & Associates, electrical engineer
B&R Construction Services, electrical
G.C. Wallace, Inc., civil engineer
SWA Group, landscape architect
Rolf Jensen & Associates, Inc., fire & life safety code
RWDI, cloud canopy
Terracon Consultants Western, Inc., geotechnical engineer
Zipper Zeman Associates, Inc., geotechnical/environmental
Chew Specifications, specifications
Stantec Consulting, ADA
Shen, Milson, Wilke-Paoletti, Inc., acoustician
Enterscapes Entertainment, entertainment systems
Kaplan Partner Architectural Lighting; Lightswitch, decorative lighting
Gallegos Lighting Design, theatrical lighting
Central Parking System; Walker Parking, parking
Gorove/Slade Associates, Inc., traffic engineer
Sussman/Prejza Company, Inc., graphics/signage
Audio Visual (Structural); Vantage Technology Consulting Group, technology consultant
Ford Audio Video, audiovisual investigator
CM Resources, Inc., audiovisual consulting
Mendenhall Moreno & Associatesl, Inc., zoning
The Whiting-Turner Contracting Company, general contractor

ANNEX/5

Motorola Global Software Group
Client: Motorola
Principal Consultants: Annex/5, site master planning, architectural design, and documentation
Epstein Sp. z.o.o. structural and mep engineering

Planning Design of Haikou West Coast
Client: Planning Bureau of Haikou City, Haikou Municipal Government
Principal Consultants: Annex/5, detailed master plan and design guidelines
Epstein International (China) Co., Ltd.

Brighton Village
Client: Pyramid Group
Principal Consultants: Annex /5, master planning and architectural design of town center
CMX, civil engineer
Design Workshop (not shown), subdivision master planner

Serta International Center
Client: Serta, Inc.
Principal Consultants: Annex/5, site master planning, architectural design, construction documents
Epstein Engineering, structural, civil, mep
Jacobs/Ryan, landscape architect

AUSTIN VEUM ROBBINS PARTNERS

Allegro Tower Apartments
Client: Leo Frey
Principal Consultants: Austin Veum Robbins Partners, architectural design
Glotman Simpson, structural
McParlane and Associates, mechanical and plumbing
ILA Zammit, electrical
KTU&A, landscape
DPR Construction, general contractor

Egyptian Lofts
Client: Citymark Egyptian LLC
Principal Consultants: Consultants: Austin Veum Robbins Partners, construction administration, architectural design
Deneen Powell Atelier, landscape
Glotman Simpson, structural
Project Design Consultants, civil
McParlane and Associates, mechanical
Neal Electric, electrical
Megan Bryan Studio, interiors
Swinerton Builders, general contractor

Park Laurel on the Prado
Client: CLB Partners
Principal Consultants: Austin Veum Robbins Partners, full architectural services
Magnusson Klemencic & Associates, structural
Roel Construction, contractor

Smart Corner
Client: Smart Corner, LLC
Principal Consultants: Austin Veum Robbins Partners, full architectural services, site selection and feasibility
Davis Davis Architects, office building architects
Magnusson Klemencic & Associates, structural

McParlane & Associates, mechanical and plumbing
Kruse & Associates, electrical
Project Design Consultants, civil/survey/landscape
Hensel Phelps Construction Co., contractor

The Pinnacle Museum Tower
Client: Pinnacle International
Principal Consultants: Austin Veum Robbins Partners, full architectural services
Sterling Cooper & Associates, mechanical engineers
Glotman Simpson, structural engineers
Nemetz & Associates, electrical engineers
Schirmer Engineering, building code and fire safety consultants
P&D Consultants, civil engineers and surveyors

BEELER GUEST OWENS ARCHITECTS, L.P.

The Highlands of Lombard
Client: Lincoln Property Company
Principal Consultants: Beeler Guest Owens Architects, full architectural services
Virgilio & Associates, LTD, structural engineer
Lehman Design Consultants, mep engineer
V3 Companies, civil engineers,
Enviro Design, landscape architects

5225 Maple Avenue
Client: MAEDC
Principal Consultants: Beeler Guest Owens Architects, full architectural services
Brockette Davis Drake, Inc., civil engineer
Enviro Design, landscape architect
Brockette Davis Drake, Inc., structural engineer
BEI Basharkhah Engineering, Inc., mep engineer

Easton
Client: Phoenix Property Company
Principal Consultants: Beeler Guest Owens Architects, full architectural services
Jerald W. Kunkel Engineering, structural engineer
BEI Engineering, Inc., mep engineer
Enviro Design, landscape architects
Ferguson-Deere, Inc., civil engineer
North American Precast Company, garage consultant

The Davis Building
Client: Hamilton & Davis, L.L.P.
Principal Consultants: Beeler Guest Owens Architects, full architectural services
Parkin-Perkins-Olson, Inc., structural engineer
S Toab & Associates, mep engineer
J.A. Jones Construction, contractor

Union Station
Client: TKV Union Station, L.P.
Principal Consultants: Beeler Guest Owens Architects, full architectural services
Gannett Fleming, landscape architect
The Reynolds Group, Inc., civil engineer
O'Donnell & Naccarato, garage/foundation engineer
Sterling Engineering and Design Group, LTD., framing engineer
Schoor Depalma, traffic engineer
Basharkhah Engineering, Inc., mep engineer
Kathy Andrews Interiors, interior designer
Metropolitan Acoustics, LLC., acoustical consultant

CALLISON ARCHITECTURE, INC.

Ayala Center Greenbelt
Client: Ayala Land, Inc.
Principal Consultants: Callison Architecture, Inc., master planning, architecture, interior design, merchandise strategy, tenant strategy, environmental graphic design
GF & Partners, associate architects
Edward D. Stone & Associates, landscape design
ACL Asia, landscape design
Rey J. Calpo & Partners, mechanical engineer
DCCD Engineering Corp., electrical engineer
NBF Consulting Engineers, sanitary engineer and fire protection design
Davis, Langdon & Seah Philippines, quantity surveyor
Makati Development Corp., general contractor

Grand Gateway
Client: Hang Lung Development Co., Ltd.
Principal Consultants: Callison Architecture, Inc., master planning, architecture, interior design, environmental graphic design, leasing strategy, tenant criteria
Stamper Whitin Works, landscape architect
Horton Lees Lighting Design, Inc., lighting design
Frank C.Y. Feng Architects and Associates, Ltd., associate architect
Maunsell Consultants Asia, Ltd., civil/structural
Associated Consulting Engineers, mechanical/electrical
Levett & Baileyl, quantity surveyor
Fujita Corporation, contractor

Suwon Gateway Plaza
Client: Suwon Aekyung Station Development Co., Ltd.
Principal Consultants: Callison Architecture, Inc., master planning, architecture
Suh-han Architects & Engineering Inc., local architect of record
Magnusson Klemencic Associates, structural engineer
Hargis Engineering, Inc., lighting designer
Sean O'Connor Associates, lighting designer

Metropolitan Tower
Client: Continental Bentall, LLC
Principal Consultants: Callison Architecture, Inc., architecture
Cary Kopczynski & Company, structural engineering
Carter Burgess, mechanical engineering
KPFF, civil engineering
Sechrist Design Associates, interior design
Heier Design Group, landscape architecture
Mortensen Construction, general contractor

CANIN ASSOCIATES

Grande Lakes Resort
Client: Marriott International
Principal Consultants: Canin Associates, development approval, master planning in partnership with Site Concepts International
Site Concepts International, landscape architecture
Smallwood Reynolds Stewart Stewart, architects
Donald W. McIntosh Associates, Inc., civil engineers

Buena Vista
Client: Castle & Cooke Inc.
Principal Consultants: Canin Associates, master planning, landscape architecture, residential design
McIntosh & Associates, Inc., civil engineers

Solivita
Client: Avatar Properties Inc.
Principal Consultants: Canin Associates, entitlement acquisition, master planning, landscape architecture
Spillis Candela & Partners, Inc., architects

Promenade Town Center
Client: Crown Community Development
Lead Consultant: Canin Associates, master planning
URS Corporation, commercial development

CARTER & BURGESS, INC.,

North Hills
Client: Kane Realty Corporation
Principal Consultants: Carter & Burgess, Inc., master planning, architectural design, architect of record, mep, structural.
Mahan Ryhiel & Associates, Inc., landscape architect
The John R. McAdams Co., Inc., civil engineer
The Lighting Practice, lighting designer

Tha Walk
Client: Casino Reinvestment Development Authority (CRDA), Owner
The Cordish Company, Developer
Principal Consultants: Carter & Burgess, Inc., master planning, architectural design, environmental graphics, architect of record, mep, structural.
Pennoni Associates, Inc., civil engineer
Greenald-Waldron Associates, lighting consultant
J. Adamson Associates, landscape architect

Power Plant Live!
Client: The Cordish Company
Principal Consultants: Carter & Burgess, Inc., planning, program and environmental graphics design, project theme, tenant primary Identification, lighting, softscape, hardscape, wayfinding, project identification, furniture plan and plaza bar design.
Brown & Craig, Inc., architect of record
Stern & Associates, Inc., mep
Stone Mountain Lighting, lighting consultant
Century Engineering, structural
Hope Furrer Associates, structural

Citrus Plaza
Client: Majestic Realty Co.
Principal Consultants: Carter & Burgess, Inc., master planning, architectural design, environmental graphics, architect of record.
Ajit S. Randhava & Associates, structural
Environs, landscape architect
Commerce Construction LP, mep, design build

The Shoppes at Blackstone Valley
Client: WS Development/SR Weiner
Principal Consultants: Carter & Burgess, Inc., master planning, architectural design, environmental graphics, architect of record, mep, structural, landscape design.

Walkers Brook Crossing
Jordan's Furniture, Home Depot, Imax
Client: Dickinson Development, Developer
Principal Consultants: Carter & Burgess, Inc., master planning, architectural design, environmental graphics, architect of record, mep, structural.
VHB, civil engineer
Haley and Aldrich, geotech
Ernest Gould, site lighting

CHAN KRIEGER & ASSOCIATES

Beth Israel Deaconess Medical Center & Master Plan
Client: Beth Israel Deaconess Medical Center
Principal Consultants: Chan Krieger & Associates, architectural design, urban design, streetscape design
Rothman Partners, Inc., architect-of-record
Solomon + Bauer, interior architecture
Childs Associates, landscape architecture

City Hall Plaza Community Arcade and Government Center Master Plan
Client: City of Boston/Boston Redevelopment Authority, Trust for City Hall

Principal Consultants: Chan Krieger & Associates, master planning, urban design, architecture
LeMessurier Associates, structural engineering
LAM Partners, lighting design

Three Rivers Park
Client: RiverLife Task Force, Forest City Commercial Group
Principal Consultants: Chan Krieger & Associates, urban design, architectural design
Hargreaves Associates, landscape
Bohlin Cywinski Jackson, architecture and planning
Urban Instruments, architecture and public art
Economic Research Associates, economic development
Parsons Brinckerhoff Quade & Douglas, transportation and environmental planning

Fort Washington Way Highway Reconfiguration
Client: City of Cincinnati
Principal Consultants: Chan Krieger & Associates, urban and architectural design services
Parsons Brinckerhoff Quade & Douglas, lead engineer/project management
KZF Design, project architects
Hargreaves Associates, landscape architects

CHARLAN • BROCK & ASSOCIATES, INC.

Williams Walk at Bartram Park
Client: Daniel Corporation
Principal Consultants: Charlan • Brock & Associates, Inc., architectural design
KTD Engineers, mep
N.H. Joshi & Associates, structural engineer
Dix-Lathrope, landscape and land planning
Carnegis & Co., interiors

Aqua Condominiums
Client: Aronov Realty Management, Inc.
Principal Consultants: Charlan • Brock & Associates, Inc., architectural design and land planning
McNeil Engineering, Inc., civil engineer
Dix-Lathrope Landscape Architects, landscape architect
N.H. Joshi & Associates, structural engineer
KTD Engineers, mep
Florida Coastal Development Consulting, Inc., pool engineer
W.G. Yates Construction Co., general contractor

Uptown Maitland West
Client: Uptown Maitland West
Principal Consultants: Charlan • Brock & Associates, Inc., architectural design and land planning
Dyer Riddle Mills Precourt, civil engineer
Dix-Lathrope Landscape Architects, landscape architect
N.H. Joshi & Associates, structural engineer
KTD Engineers, mep
Kelsey Construction, general contractor

Rarity Pointe Lodge and Spa
Client: RPL Properties Inc.
Principal Consultants: Charlan • Brock & Associates, Inc., architectural design and land planning
Sterling Engineering, Inc., civil engineer
Hawkins Partners, Inc., landscape architect
N. H. Joshi & Associates, structural engineer
KTD Engineering Consultants, mep
Godfrey Design Consultants, Inc., interior design
Raleigh Design, interior design
Hardin Construction Company, general contractor
Lawler-Wood, LLC., developer

The Flats at Rosemary Beach
Client: Lowder Construction
Principal Consultants: Charlan • Brock & Associates, Inc., architectural design

Connely & Wicker, civil engineer
N. H. Joshi & Associates, structural engineer
KTD Engineering Consultants, mep
Lovelace Interiors Inc., interiors
Lowder Construction, general contractor

Cheval Apartments on Old Katy Road
Client: The Spanos Corporation
Principal Consultants: Charlan • Brock & Associates, Inc., architectural design and land planning
Carter-Burgess, civil engineer
Vernon G. Henry and Associates, Inc., land planner
K & W (Kudela & Weinheimer), landscape architect
N.H. Joshi & Associates, structural engineer
E.N., Inc., mep

CBT/CHILDS BERTMAN TSECKARES, INC.

Columbus Center
Client: Cassin-Winn Development Company
Principal Consultants: CBT/Childs Bertman Tseckares Inc., architects
Cosentini Associates, Consulting Engineers (mep, lighting, security, tele/data)
Harry R. Feldman, Inc., land survey
Haley & Aldrich, geotechnical
Judith Nitsch Engineering, Inc., traffic
BBG-BBGM, hotel
Central/Myers, parking
Pressley Associates, Inc., landscape architects
LeMessurier Consultants, structural engineering
Hughes Associates, Inc., code/life safety
Edgett Williams Consulting Group Inc., elevator
Cerami Associates, acoustical
Campbell-McCabe Inc., hardware
Zaldastani Associates, Inc., tunnel structure
Hatch Mott McDonald, tunnel engineering

North Point
Client: Spaulding & Slye Colliers & Guilford Transportation Industries, Developer/Development Manager
Principal Consultants: Kenneth Greenberg, Greenberg Consultants Inc., in association with CBT/Childs Bertman Tseckares, Inc., master planners
CBT/Childs Bertman Tseckares, Inc., architect, phase I team, parcel S residential building
Architects Alliance, architect, parcel T residential building
Michael van Valkenberg Associates, landscape architect, central park

The Residences at Kendall Square
Client: TP Kendall LLC
Principal Consultants: CBT/Childs Bertman Tseckares, Inc., architects
Cosentini Associates, consulting engineers
Bovis Lend Lease, general contractor

Rollins Square
Client: Planning Office for Urban Affairs / Archdiocese of Boston
Principal Consultants: CBT/Childs Bertman Tseckares, Inc., Architects
CBA Landscape Architects, landscape architect
Weidlinger Associates, structural engineer
Fitzemeyer & Tocci, mechanical engineer
Peter J. Roche, Real Estate and Community Development, development consultant
Suffolk Construction, general contractor

The Prudential Center Redevelopment
Client: Boston Properties
Principal Consultants: CBT/Childs Bertman Tseckares, Inc., architects
TMP Consulting Engineers, mep engineer

McNamara/Salvia, Inc., structural engineer
Vanasse Hangen Brustlin, Inc., civil & traffic engineer
Carr, Lynch and Sandell, landscape architect
Gordon H. Smith Corporation, exterior wall
LAM Partners Inc., lighting
Rolf Jensen & Associates, code
Cavanaugh Tocci Associates, Inc., acoustics
RTE Group, Inc., teleData
Selbert Perkins Design Collaborative, graphic design
Haley & Aldrich, Inc., soils engineer (geotechnical)
John Van Stone Fogg, CSI, specifications

COSTAS KONDYLIS AND PARTNERS LLP

Trump World Tower – 845 United Nations Plaza
Client: Daewoo-Trump
Principal Consultants: Costas Kondylis and Partners LLP, architectural design
Israel Berger & Associates, structural engineer
I.M. Robbins, mechanical engineer
Gordon H. Smith Company, curtain wall consultants
Brennan Beer Gorman/Monk Interiors, interior design (lobby)
Abel, Bainnson & Butz, landscape architect

The Heritage
Client: Hudson Waterfront Associates/Trump New World Project Management
Principal Consultants: Costas Kondylis and Partners LLP, architectural design
Rosenwasser/Grossman: structural engineer
I.M. Robbins, mechanical engineer
McGinley Design, interior design
Abel, Bainnson & Butz, landscape architect
HRH Construction, general contractor

Morton Square
Client: J.D. Carlisle Development Corp.
Principal Consultants: Costas Kondylis and Partners LLP, architectural design
Rosenwasser/Grossman: structural engineer
I.M. Robbins, mechanical engineer
Israel Berger & Associates, exterior wall consultants
Kondylis Design, interior design
Oehme, van Sweden & Associates, landscape architect
Philip Koether, interior design (lobby)
Tom Patti, glass artist

The Grand Tier
Client: Glenwood Management Corp.
Principal Consultants: Costas Kondylis and Partners LLP, architectural design
Rosenwasser/Grossman: structural engineer
I.M. Robbins, mechanical engineer
Saladino Group, Inc., interior design
Cosentini Associates, lighting design

CUNNINGHAM + QUILL ARCHITECTS PLLC

The Mather Building
Client: PN Hoffman Development
Principal Consultants: Cunningham + Quill Architects, architectural design
Ehlert/Bryan, Inc., structural engineers for senior center
Summit Engineers, Inc., mechanical, electrical and plumbing engineers for senior center
Best/Joslin, façade restoration consultant

Huntfield Master Plan
Client: Greenvest, LLC
Principal Consultants: : Cunningham + Quill Architects, master planning, urban design guidelines

Caton's Walk
Client: RB Associates
Principal Consultants: Cunningham + Quill Architects, architectural design
Ehlert/Bryan, Inc., structural engineers for senior center
Summit Engineers, Inc., mechanical, electrical and plumbing engineers for senior center

The Alta
Client: PN Hoffman Development
Principal Consultants: Cunningham + Quill Architects, architectural design
Ehlert/Bryan, Inc., structural engineers
GHT Limited, mechanical, electrical and plumbing engineers

National Cathedral School
Client: National Cathedral School
Principal Consultant: Cunningham + Quill Architects, master planning and site design

Park Hill Condominium
Client: PN Hoffman Development
Principal Consultants: Cunningham + Quill Architects, architectural design
Ehlert/Bryan, Inc., structural engineers
Bansal & Associates, Inc., mechanical, electrical and plumbing engineers

Fortnightly Neighborhood Master Plan and Herndon Senior Center
Client: Fairfax County Redevelopment Housing Authority Department of Housing and Community Development
Principal Consultants: Cunningham + Quill Architects, master planning, urban design Guidelines, Full Architectural Services for Senior Center
Oculus, landscape design for master plan and urban design guidelines
Ehlert/Bryan, Inc., structural engineers for senior center
Summit Engineers, Inc., mechanical, electrical and plumbing engineers for senior center
Riley & Rohrer, interior design services for senior center

DAHLIN GROUP ARCHITECTURE PLANNING

Black Diamond
Client: A. F. Evans
Principal Consultants: Dahlin Group Architecture Planning, urban planning, architectural design
Gates and Associates, landscape
Johnstone Moyer, construction manager
Main Street Property Services, retail consultant
Winzler & Kelly Consulting Engineers, civil engineer
Colour Studio, color consultant

Luxe Hills International Golf Community
Client: Wide Horizon Real Estate Development Company
Principal Consultants: Dahlin Group Architecture Planning, master planning, community building architecture, luxury estate villas
Nicolay Designs, landscape architects
JMP Golf Design Group, golf course architect

University Villages
Client: Marina Community Partners LLC
Principal Consultants: Dahlin Group Architecture Planning, master plan, urban design, residential architecture
MBH Architects, retail architects
RBF, civil engineer
The Guzzardo Partnership, landscape architect
Bob Schaffer, community outreach
Keyser Marston Associates, economic consultant
Zander & Associates, biology
Staub Forestry and Environmental Consulting, consulting forester and arborist

EIP, environmental consultant
McDonough, Holland & Allen PC, legal advisors
Lombardo & Gilles, legal advisors
Carol Lind, market research
Berlogar Geotechnical, soils/geologic engineer
Xenergy, sustainability

Coyote Valley
Client: City of San Jose
Principal Consultants: Dahlin Group Architecture Planning, lead consultant for plan, design guidelines
Ken Kay Associates, landscape architect, environmental footprint and landscape details
HMH Engineering, infrastructure design
EPS, economic consultant
Apex Strategies, community outreach

DAVID M. SCHWARZ

Ft. Worth
Sundance East
Client: Sundance East Partners
Principal Consultants: David M. Schwarz/Architectural Services, Inc., design architect
HKS, Inc., architect of record
Linbeck Construction Company, contractor

Ft. Worth
Sundance West
Client: Sundance West Partners
Principal Consultants: David M. Schwarz/Architectural Services, Inc., design architect
HKS, Inc., architect of record
Linbeck Construction Company, contractor

Ft. Worth
Nancy Lee and Perry R. Bass Performance Hall
Client: Performing Arts Fort Worth, Inc.
Principal Consultants: David M. Schwarz/Architectural Services, Inc., design architect
HKS, Inc., architect of record
Jaffe Holden Acoustics, acoustic/AV consultant
AltieriSeborWieber LLC Consulting Engineers, mep
Walter P. Moore & Associates, structural
Fisher Dachs Associates, theatre consultants
Linbeck Construction Company, contractor

Ft. Worth
Fort Worth Public Library
Client: City of Fort Worth
Principal Consultants: David M. Schwarz/Architectural Services, Inc., design architect:
Hidell Associates Architects (Interior), architect of record
Growald Architects (Exterior), architect of record
Huitt-Zollars, mep
Walter P. Moore & Associates, structural
Ratcliff Construction, contractor

Ft. Worth
Bank One Building
Client: Sundance Square Management, LLC
Principal Consultants: David M. Schwarz/Architectural Services, Inc., design architect
HKS, Inc., architect of record
Datum Engineering, structural
James Johnston & Associates, mep
Brockette Davis Drake, civil
FMG Design, Inc., graphics/signage
Linbeck Construction Company, contractor

Parker Square
Client: Five Star Development
Principal Consultants: David M. Schwarz/Architectural Services, Inc., design architect & master planner
Vidaud Associates (Bldgs. 8, 9), CSI (Bldgs. 3, 4), Five Star Development (Bldgs. 5, 6, 7), architects of record

Southlake Town Square
Client: Cooper and Stebbins
Principal Consultants: David M. Schwarz/Architectural Services, Inc., design architect & master planner
(Phase 1): Urban Architecture; subsequent phases: Urban Architecture*, Looney Ricks Kiss*, Bowie Griddley Architects*, Beck, architect of record:
* both Architect and Architect of Record responsibilities

West Village
Client: Phoenix Property Company and Urban Partners, Inc.
Principal Consultants: David M. Schwarz/Architectural Services, Inc., design architect & master planner
KSNG Architects, Inc., architect of record:
Dalmac Construction, contractor
L. A. Fuess Partners Engineers, structural

DOUGHERTY SCHROEDER & ASSOCIATES, INC.

Destin Commons
Client: Turnberry Associates, Legendary, Inc., and Retail Estate
Principal Consultants: Dougherty Schroeder & Associates, Inc. (full architectural services; architect of record)
Lee Richardson & Associates, landscape architect
Bliss Fasman, Inc., lighting design
Communication Arts, graphic design
Brady & Anglin Engineers, mep
Connelly & Wicker, Inc., civil engineer
Pruitt Eberly Stone, Inc., structural engineer
Tower Construction, general contractor

The Avenue East Cobb
Client: Cousins Properties Incorporated
Principal Consultants: Dougherty Schroeder & Associates, Inc. (design consultant to architect of record CMH, Inc.)
Post Properties, Inc., landscape architect
Ramon Luminance Design - Ramon Noya, lighting design
Hardin Construction, general contractor

Pinnacle Hills Promenade
Client: General Growth Properties, Inc.
Principal Consultants: Dougherty Schroeder & Associates, Inc. (full architectural services; architect of record)
Site Solutions, landscape architect
Bliss Fasman, Inc., lighting design
Huie Design, graphic design
Pacificom Multimedia, Inc., 3D graphic design
KLG Consolidated, mep
Shenberger & Associates, Inc., structural engineer
CEI Engineers. civil engineer
Spiker Baldwin, Inc., specifications

The Forum at Sunnyvale
Client: Forum Development Group
Principal Consultants: Dougherty Schroeder & Associates, Inc. (master planning & architectural design services)
Site Solutions, Inc., hardscape/landscape architect
BKF Engineers, civil engineer (retained by owner)
Standard Pacific, housing developer
MVE & Partners, Architect, housing design

Gulf Coast Town Center
Client: CBL & Associates Properties, Inc.
Principal Consultants: Dougherty Schroeder & Associates, Inc. (full architectural services; architect of record)
Site Solutions, landscape architect
Bliss Fasman, Inc., lighting design
Huie Design, graphic design
Brady & Anglin Engineers, mep
Shenberger & Associates, Inc., structural engineer

DUANY PLATER-ZYBERK & COMPANY

Tannin

Client: George Gounares
Principal Consultants: Duany Plater-Zyberk & Company, master planner
Caruncho, Martinez & Alvarez, residential and pool house architect
Khoury-Vogt Architects, town square designer
Michael Lykoudis, town center architect

Amelia Park

Client: Hometown Neighborhoods, Inc.
Principal Consultants: Duany Plater-Zyberk & Company, master planner
Oscar Machado, architectural and urban design consultant
Julie Sanford, town architect

I'On

Client: The I'On Company-Vince Graham, developer
Principal Consultants: Duany Plater-Zyberk & Company in collaboration with Dover-Kohl & Partners, master planner
Seamon Whiteside & Associates, civil engineer/ planner

Habersham

Client: Habersham Land Company- Robert Turner with Stephen Davis, developers
Principal Consultants: Duany Plater-Zyberk & Company, master planner
Steven Fuller Design Traditions, residential architect
Moser Design Group, residential architect
Historical Concepts, residential architect

Rosemary Beach

Client: The Rosemary Beach Land Company and Leucadia Financial Corporation
Principal Consultants: Duany Plater-Zyberk & Company, master planner
Keith LeBlanc Landscape Architecture, Inc., landscape architect
Aurora Civil Engineering, Inc., traffic engineer

Alys Beach

Client: Ebsco Gulf Coast Development
Principal Consultants: Duany Plater-Zyberk & Company, master planner
Khoury-Vogt, town architect
Glatting, Jackson, Kercher, Anglin, Lopez, Rinehart, traffic engineer
Moore Bass, civil engineering
Douglas Duany, landscape designer
James Wassel, renderer

ELKUS MANFREDI ARCHITECTS

35 and 40 Landsdowne Street

Client: Forest City Commercial Group, Millennium Pharmaceuticals Inc.
Principal Consultants: Elkus Manfredi Architects, master planning, architectural and interior design
AHSC-McLellan & Copenhagen, laboratory consultants
Halvorson Design Group, landscape designer
McNamara/Salvia, Inc., structural engineer
SEi Companies, mep engineer
Kaplan Architectural Lighting, lighting designer
Turner Construction Company, general contractor, 35 Landsdowne
Walsh Brothers Construction, general contractor, 40 Landsdowne

100 Cambridge Street/Bowdoin Place

Client: MassDevelopment/Saltonstall Building Redevelopment Corporation
Principal Consultants: Elkus Manfredi Architects, master planning, architectural and interior design

Sasaki Associates, associate architect
Brown, Richardson & Rowe, landscape designer
Daylor Consulting Group, Inc., civil engineer
LeMessurier Consultants, structural engineer
Vanderweil Engineers, Inc., mep engineer
Schweppe Lighting Design, Inc., lighting designer
Design, Inc., signage designer
Suffolk Construction Company, general contractor

ELS ARCHITECTURE AND URBAN DESIGN

California Theatre

Client: The Redevelopment Agency of the City of San Jose, Packard Humanities Institute
Principal Consultants: ELS Architecture and Urban Design, feasibility study, and architect
Weeks and Day, original (1927) architects
Rutherford & Chekene Consulting Engineers, structural
The Engineering Enterprise Consulting Engineers, electrical engineer
Guttmann & Blaevoet Consulting Engineers, mechanical
Brian Kangas Faulk, civil
Auerbach Pollock Friedlander, theatrical consultant
Auerbach Glasow, lighting consultant
Charles M. Salter Associates Inc., acoustical consultant
Davis Langdon Adamson, cost consultant
Hughes Associates, Inc., life safety consultant
TEECOM, telecom and security consultant
Top Flight, specifications consultant
Kate Keating Associates, Inc., signage consultant
James Goodman, decorative paint colors consultant
A.T. Heinsbergen with ELS Architects, interior furnishings and fabrics
Catalyst, landscape consultant
Rudolph & Sletten, construction manager
Swinerton Builders, general contractor

Church Street Plaza

Client: Arthur Hill & Co., LLC
Principal Consultants: ELS Architecture and Urban Design, master plan of district, design architect for Main Pavilion and parking structure
DeStefano + Partners, architect of record for Main Pavilion
Cooper Carry Architects, Hilton Hotel architects
OWP/P, 909 Davis (offices) architect
Walker Parking, parking structure architect
Nagel, Hartray, Danker, Kagan, McKay Architects, Borders Book Store architect
Optima, Inc., condominiums architect
Thorton-Tomasetti/Engineers, structural engineers
Environmental Systems Design, mep
Teska Associates, Inc, landscape
Bovis Construction Corp., general contractor

The Village at Merrick Park

Client: General Growth Properties, Inc.
Principal Consultants: ELS Architecture and Urban Design— concept master plan and architect for retail buildings and 2,000-car parking structure
SWA Group, landscape architect
Perkins & Will, office and residential buildings
Diedrich/NBA, Neiman Marcus store
Callison Architects, Nordstrom store
Sussman/Preja & Co., signage and graphics
Laurin B. Askew, Jr., of Monk LLC, client concept designer
The Lathrop Company, Turner Construction Company, contractor,

The City of Sunnyvale Downtown Design Plan

Client: City of Sunnyvale
Principal Consultants: ELS Architecture and Urban Design, urban design
Keyser Marston Associates, Inc., economist
Fehr & Peers Associates, Inc., transportation consultant
Architecture Models, Inc., model makers

FIELD PAOLI

Beverly Canon

Client: City of Beverly Hills, California
Principal Consultants: Field Paoli, Executive Architect
Jacques Verliden, Crate & Barrel architect
KPFF , structural engineer
Parkitects, parking consultants
Fong, Hart, Schneider Partners, landscape architects
W.E. O'Neil Construction Co., general contractor

On Broadway

Client: BHV Innisfree Ventures I, LLC
Principal Consultants: Field Paoli, architectural design
International Parking Design, parking structure
Freedman Tung & Bottomley, landscape architect
Architectural Lighting Design, lighting consultant
Fehlman Labarre, theater interiors

Victoria Gardens

Client: Forest City West Commercial Inc., Lewis Operating Co.
Principal Consultants: Field Paoli, master planning and concept design, building design
KA Inc., Architecture, executive architect
Altoon + Porter, executive design architect
Elkus Manfredi Architects, design architect
MDS Consulting, civil engineer
SWA, landscape design
Redmond Schwarz Mark, signage and graphics
City of Rancho Cucamonga Redevelopment Agency, city consultant

The Streets of Tanasbourne

Client: Continental Real Estate Companies
Principal Consultants: Field Paoli, conceptual design, architectural design
MESA Design, landscape
KPFF, structural engineer
Architectural Lighting Design, lighting

FXFOWLE ARCHITECTS, PC

The Helena Apartment Building

Client: The Durst Organization/Rose Associates
Principal Consultants: FXFOWLE ARCHITECTS, PC, architecture and sustainable Design
Flack + Kurtz, mep
Severud, Structural
Dagher Associates, living machine

The New York Times Building

Client: City Ratner Companies/The New York Times
Principal Consultants: FXFOWLE ARCHITECTS, PC, architecture
Renzo Piano Building Workshop, architecture
Flack + Kurtz, mep
Thorton Tomasetti, structural
Gensler, interiors
HM White Site Architects, landscape

Whitman School of Management

Client: Syracuse University
Principal Consultants: FXFOWLE ARCHITECTS, PC, architecture
Severud, structural
Flack + Kurtz, mep

Lincoln Center Redevelopment

Client: Lincoln Center for the Performing Arts
Principal Consultants: FXFOWLE ARCHITECTS, PC, architecture
Diller Scofidio + Renfro, architecture
Arup, mep

Tianjin Tower
Client: undisclosed
Principal Consultants: FXFOWLE ARCHITECTS, PC, architecture

Dosflota Multipurpose Complex Master Plan
Client: US CapitalInvest Bancorp
Principal Consultants: FXFOWLE ARCHITECTS, PC, architecture and urban design

Renaissance Place Redevelopment Plan
Client: Conroy Development Company
Principal Consultants: FXFOWLE ARCHITECTS, PC, architecture and urban design

GLATTING JACKSON KERCHER ANGLIN LOPEZ RINEHART, INC.

Hollis Garden
Client: City of Lakeland
Principal Consultants: Glatting Jackson Kercher Anglin Lopez Rinehart, Inc., park and public space planning, landscape architecture
Wallis Murphy Boyington Architects, Inc., architecture
Chastain-Skillman, Inc., engineer
Alex Piper, P.E., electrical engineer

Broad Street Park
Client: Baldwin Park Development Company
Principal Consultants: Glatting Jackson Kercher Anglin Lopez Rinehart, Inc., landscape architecture, urban design, environmental services, construction observation, relocation of trees
David G. Kittridge, PE, structural engineer
Prevost Irrigation Design, irrigation design
Hall Fountains, fountain mechanical

Park Avenue Streetscape
Client: City of Winter Park
Principal Consultants: Glatting Jackson Kercher Anglin Lopez Rinehart, Inc., planning, landscape architecture, transportation planning
Dover Kohl & Partners, urban design
GAI, civil engineer

The Heights
Client: Leslie Land Corporation
Principal Consultants: Glatting Jackson Kercher Anglin Lopez Rinehart, Inc., urban design, landscape architecture
Heidt and Associates, civil engineering
Fowler White Gillen Boggs Villareal & Banker, PA, legal counsel
Roberts Communication & Marketing, communications

GOODY CLANCY & ASSOCIATES

Fort Point Channel
Client: Boston Redevelopment Authority, Fort Point Channel Abutters Group
Principal Consultants: Goody Clancy & Associates, master planning
Vanasse Hangen Brustlin, Inc., watersheet permitting and quality
Vine Associates, marine infrastructure
FXM Associates, economic and market analysis
Byrne McKinney & Associates, implementation organization
Waterfront Center, charrette
Transportation Alternatives, water transportation

Assembly Square
Client: Assembly Square Limited Partnership (a collaboration of Gravestar, Inc. and Taurus New England Investments Corporation)

Principal Consultants: Goody Clancy & Associates, feasibility, architectural design, local permitting
Meredith & Grew, Inc., marketing
Atlantic Retail Properties, marketing
CLF Ventures Inc., environmental, transportation, community
Vanasse Hangen Brustlin, Inc., transportation, civil engineering
Carol R. Johnson Associates, Inc., landscape
Gibbs Planning Group, retail analysis
Connery Associates, fiscal impact
Reese Fayde & Associates, affordable housing
Woodard & Curran, environmental remediation
Gregory & Associates, legislative consultant
Holland & Knight LLP, legislative consultant
Nutter, McClennen & Fish LLP, legal counsel

North Allston Strategic Framework for Planning
Client: Boston Redevelopment Authority
Principal Consultants: Goody Clancy & Associates, planning
Volmer, transportation
Byrne McKinney Associates, real estate economics
Community Design Partnership, implementation strategies

LESSARD GROUP INC.,

Trump Plaza
Client: Cappelli Enterprises, Inc.
Principal Consultants: Lessard Group Inc., architect
HRH Construction, general contractor
Kellard Engineering, civil engineer
Tadjer-Cohen-Edelson Associates, Inc., structural engineer
SESI Consulting Engineers, P.C., geotechnical engineer
Edwards & Zuck, mechanical engineer
Cerami & Associates, acoustical
Lessard Commercial Inc., interiors
Desman Associates, parking
Lerch, Bates & Associates, elevators
Israel Berger & Associates, exterior envelope/fenestration/water proofing/roof

Springfield Town Center
Client: KSI Services, Inc.
Principal Consultants: Lessard Group Inc., architect
Sasaki & Associates, landscape

Canton Crossing
Client: KSI Services, Inc.
Principal Consultants: Lessard Group Inc., master planning
Whitney Bailey Cox & Magnani, LLC, civil engineer

National Harbor
Client: The Peterson Companies, K. Hovnanian Homes and McDaniels Homes
Principal Consultants: Lessard Group Inc., architect-in-charge, master planning, planning analysis and feasibility study, including building layout, density study and massing/height considerations
Tina Woods Smith, survey engineer
KTA Group, Inc., mechanical engineer
Tadjer-Cohen-Edelson Associates, Inc., structural engineer
Lawrence G. Perry, AIA, fair housing
Applied Fire Protection Engineering, code
Wyle Laboratories, acoustical engineer

LOONEY RICKS KISS ARCHITECTS

Jefferson at Providence Place
Client: JPI Development Partners, Inc.
Principal Consultants: Looney Ricks Kiss Architects, design architect, interior design, land planner
William F. Jervis, architect of record
Carol R. Johnson Associates, landscape architect
O. Ahlborg & Sons, Inc., builder

FedExForum
Client: Memphis Public Building Authority
Principal Consultants: Ellerbe Becket in association with Looney Ricks Kiss Architects, architecture
Looney Ricks Kiss Architects in collaboration with John F. Williams Architects, Inc., interior architecture
Looney Ricks Kiss Architects in collaboration with Bounds and Gillespie Architects, garage architecture
Looney Ricks Kiss Architects in collaboration with Self Tucker Architects, exterior skin architecture
Looney Ricks Kiss Architects, urban design, graphic design and theming
Ellerbe Becket, structural engineering, mechanical engineering, electrical engineering
Burr & Cole Consulting Engineers, structural engineering
ABS Consultants, structural engineering
Office of Griffith C. Burr, mechanical engineering, plumbing
Gala Engineering, mechanical engineering, plumbing
Shappley Design Consultants, fire protection
Liles Engineering Design Consultants, electrical engineering
Dunning-Martin Engineering, electrical engineering
PDR Engineers, civil engineering
Tetra Tech, civil engineering
Toles & Associates, infrastructure/civil engineering
Jackson Person & Associates, landscape architecture
Clark + Dixon Associates Architects, historic building survey
EnSafe, environmental consulting
Lerch Bates & Associates, Inc., vertical circulation
Walker Parking Consultants, garage consultant
M.A. Mortenson, general contractor

Ave Maria Town Center
Clients: Barron Collier Companies in partnership with Ave Maria University
Principal Consultants: Looney Ricks Kiss Architects, town core and Main Street planning; design of various town center mixed-use buildings
Wadsworth-O'Neal Engineering, Inc., mep and fp engineering
Liebl & Barrow Engineering, Inc., structural engineering
Bruce Howard Associates, landscape architecture
Wilson Miller, Inc., civil engineering, entitlements/site engineering
Williamson & Associates, waterproofing consultants
WJHW, acoustical consultant
Illuminating Concepts, exterior lighting designer

Ross Bridge Village Center
Client: Daniel Corporation
Principal Consultants: Looney Ricks Kiss Architects, master planning, architectural design
Holcombe, Norton & Pritchett, Inc., planning and landscape architecture
Walter Schoel Engineering Company, Inc., civil engineering
Lane Bishop York Delahay, Inc., structural engineering

Thornton Park
Client: name withheld
Principal Consultant: Looney Ricks Kiss Architects, architectural design
Alliance Structural Engineering, structural engineering
TLC-Engineering for Architecture, mep engineering
HDR, traffic engineering

GAI Consultants, civil engineering
Universal Engineering Services, geotechnical
Dix Lathrop & Associates, landscape architecture
Hardin Construction, contractor

MBH ARCHITECTS

West Hollywood Gateway
Client: J.H. Snyder
Principal Consultants: Principal Consultants: MBH
Architects, Executive Architect, tenant architect for
Best Buy and Target, LOD exhibits, leasing plans,
design criteria book
ING Clarion, new owner
Jerde Partnership, design architect
Studio Mark, graphic design
Kaplan Partners, lighting design
EDAW, landscape architects
Swinerton Builders, general contractor

Marina University Villages
Client: Shea Properties
Principal Consultants: MBH Architects, architectural
design, concept design, site planning, schematics,
design development
Guzzardo Partnership, landscape
RBF, civil engineering

The Town Center at Levis Commons
Client: Dillin Development, Hill Partners
Principal Consultants: MBH Architects, design
architect, design of master-planning, design of town
center
Collaborative Group, executive architect
LKL Engineers Limited, structural
Mechanical Design Associates, Inc., mechanical /
electrical
Fellar Finch, civil
Rudolph Libbe, cm
Mesa Design, landscaping
Kaplan, lighting design

200 Brannan
Client: Lennar Communities
Principal Consultants: MBH Architects, executive
architect and design architect for this building, master
planning of entire 4-building project with Kwan/Henmi
Architects.
Luk & Associates, civil engineer
Nishkian Menninger, structural engineer
MPA Design, landscape architect
Charles M. Salter & Associates, acoustical consultant
CM & D, construction management
Bovis Lend Lease, contractor

MCLARAND VASQUEZ EMSIEK & PARTNERS

Fruitvale Village
Client: Fruitvale Development Corporation
Development Partners: BART, City of Oakland
Principal Consultants: McLarand Vasquez Emsiek &
Partners, Inc., Urban Planning & Architecture
Fong, Hart Schneider Partners (prime landscape); Pattillo
& Garrett Associates, landscape
Luk, environmental consultant
EQE Structural Engineers, structural engineering
Design Electric, electrical engineering
Hickey, plumbing
Bay City Mechanical, Inc., HVAC
Michael Willis & Associates, space planners
James E. Roberts-Obayashi Corporation, contractor

The Promenade at Rio Vista
Client: PLC Greystone Apartments
Principal Consultants: McLarand Vasquez Emsiek &
Partners, Inc., Land planning & Architecture
Lifescapes International, Inc., landscape
DMC Engineering, civil
Group M Engineers, structural engineering
Helix Electric, Inc., electrical engineering
Parks Engineer, plumbing
LDI Heating & Air Conditioning, mechanical
Francis Krahe Associates, lighting lonsultan
Greystone Multi-Family Builders, Inc., contractor

Hollywood & Vine
Client: Legacy Partners and Gatehouse Capital
Principal Consultants: McLarand Vasquez Emsiek &
Partners, Inc., Urban planning & Architecture
Rios Clementi Hale Studio, landscape
Fuscoe Engineering, civil engineering
DCI Engineers, structural engineering
HKA Pacific Parking Consultant, parking
Roschen Van Cleve Architects, historical & hollywood
urban design consultant
Sussman Prejza, signage and graphics
Webcor Builders, contractor

Uptown Oakland Development
Client: Forest City Residential Development
Principal Consultants: McLarand Vasquez Emsiek &
Partners, Inc., Urban Design & Architecture; Peter
Calthorpe Associates, Urban Planners
Ken Kay Associates, master landscape planner
Korve, Inc., civil engineering
LSA Associates, Inc., EIR
KPFF Consulting Engineers, structural engineering
FARD Engineers, Inc., eechanical / electrical engineering
James E. Roberts-Obayashi Corporation, contractor

Douglas Park
Client: Boeing Realty Corporation
Principal Consultant: McLarand Vasquez Emsiek &
Partners, Inc., Urban planning & Architecture

Tralee
Client: Bancor Properties LLC
Principal Consultants: McLarand Vasquez Emsiek &
Partners, urban design, planning, architecture
The Guzzardo Partnership, Inc., landscape
Carlson, Barbee & Gibson, Inc., civil engineer

PAPPAGEORGE/HAYMES LTD.

The Glen Town Center
Client: Oliver McMillan, Kimball Hill Homes
Principal Consultants: Pappageorge/Haymes Ltd.,
planning, architectural design
Douglas Hoerr Landscape Architecture, landscape
Samartano & Company, structural
Cosentini Associates, mep
Cowhey Gudmundson Leder, civil

600 North Lake Shore Drive
Client: Belgravia Group Ltd. & SandZ Development
Company, Inc.
Principal Consultants: Pappageorge/Haymes, Ltd.,
architectural design
Samartano & Company, structural
Khatib & Associates, mep
Eriksson Engineering Associates, Inc., civil
Hitchcock Design Group, landscape
Wolf Clements & Associates, landscape

Block X
Client: The Thrush Companies
Principal Consultants: Pappageorge/Haymes Ltd.,
architectural design
Peter R. Krallitsch & Associates, structural
McClier Corporation, civil
Joe Karr & Associates, landscape

Museum Park
Client: A joint venture of The Enterprise Companies &
Central Station Development Corporation
Principal Consultants: Pappageorge/Haymes Ltd.,
architectural design
Samartano & Company, structural
Stearn Joglekar & Associates, structural
Rosenblatt Associates, mep
Cosentini Associates, mep
Eriksson Engineering Associates, Inc., civil
Daniel Weinbach & Associates, landscape
Joe Karr & Associates, landscape
Horvath & Reich, exterior wall
Jenkins & Huntington, elevator
Charter Sills & Associates, lighting

Kinzie Park
Client: The Enterprise Companies, The Habitat Company
Principal Consultants: Pappageorge/Haymes Ltd.,
architectural design
Peter R. Krallitsch & Associates, structural, townhouses
Chris P. Stefanos Associates, structural, midrise
GKC/EME, LLC, mep
Eriksson Engineering Associates, Inc., civil
Joe Karr & Associates, landscape

PERKOWITZ + RUTH ARCHITECTS

Bridgeport Village
Client: Center Oak Properties, LLC
Principal Consultants: Perkowitz + Ruth Architects,
schematic design, design development
Candera, lighting
Berger Partnership, landscape
Opus A & E, engineer

Mercantile West
Client: DMB Ladera, Westar Associates
Principal Consultants: Perkowitz + Ruth Architects,
architectural design and construction services
Land Concern, landscape
Lighting Design Alliance, lighting
ANF & Associates, engineer

Buena Park Downtown
Client: Festival Company, Pritzker Realty, Krikorian
Premiere Theatres
Principal Consultants: Perkowitz + Ruth Architects,
design through construction phase, including
documents and administration
EDAW, Inc., landscape architect
ANF & Associates, structural engineer

RETZSCH LANAO CAYCEDO ARCHITECTS

Royal Palm Office Building
Client: RLC Development, LLC
Principal Consultants: Retzsch Lanao Caycedo
Architects, design through construction administration
and construction management, interior design
Donnell Duquesne Albaisa, P.A., structural engineer
Thompson Engineering Consultants, mep engineer
EcoPlan, landscape architect
Icon Design Group, contractor

Cypress Park West, Phase II
Client: TIAA-CREF (Savannah Teachers Properties), CB Richard Ellis as agent for teachers
Principal Consultants: Retzsch Lanao Caycedo Architects, site planning, architectural design through construction administration for new building and parking structure
Johnson Structural Group, structural engineer
Thompson Engineering Consultants, mep engineer
Sun Tech Engineering, civil engineer
Red Eye Design, landscape architect
Phillips Fire, fire protection
Itasca Construction Associates, contractor

Fifth Avenue Place, Phase II
Client: Mocal Enterprises
Principal Consultants: Retzsch Lanao Caycedo Architects, site feasibility and schematic design through construction administration
O'Donnell, Naccarato, Mignogna & Jackson, Inc., structural engineering
Thompson Youngross Engineering Consultants, mep engineer
Caufield & Wheeler, Inc., civil engineer
A. Grant Thornbrough & Associates, landscape architect
Phillips Fire, fire protection
TBD, contractor

The Pointe at Middle River
Client: Brenner Real Estate Group
Principal Consultants: Retzsch Lanao Caycedo Architects, site planning and architectural design, design development, construction documents and construction administration
Donnell Duquesne Albaisa, P.A, structural engineering
Thompson Youngross Engineering Consultants, mep engineer
Sun Tech Engineering, civil engineer
EcoPlan, landscape architect
Phillips Fire, fire protection
TBD, contractor

RTKL

LaQua Tokyo Dome City
Client: Takenaka Komuten KK
Principal Consultants: RTKL Associates Inc., architecture
Takenaka, construction/structural engineering/landscape architecture
Takenaka and Kandeko, electrical engineering
Sangi Kogyo, TAK Evac Johnson Controls, mechanical/plumbing
Matsushita, lighting systems

Principe Pio
Client: Riofisa
Principal Consultants: RTKL Associates Inc., architecture
Estudio Fernandez del Amo, architect of record
IDOM S.A., mep engineering, structural engineering
Eralan, main contractor
Mero, Germany, glass subcontractor
Michael Schlaich, glass engineer

Downtown Brea Redevelopment District
Client: City of Brea and CIM Group LLC
Principal Consultants: RTKL Associates Inc., master planning, urban design, tenant design criteria, architectural guidelines, environmental graphic design, design review, signage presentation
Robin Faulk, events planning
Lauren Melendrez Associates and AHBE, construction documents
Olson Company, townhouse design

Zha Bei/The Hub International Lifestyle Centre
Client: Forrester Group
Principal Consultants: RTKL Associates Inc., architecture, environmental graphic design, master planning
SIADR (Shanghai Institute of Architectural Design and Research, local architect
WSP Hong Kong, Ltd. and SIADR, mep engineering, structural engineering
Chroma33, architectural lighting design

SASAKI ASSOCIATES, INC.

Addison Circle Park
Client: Town of Addison
Principal Consultants: Sasaki Associates, Inc., planning, urban design, landscape architecture, civil engineering
Jim Duffy, construction manager
Georgia Fountain Company, Inc., fountain design
Irritech Corporation, irrigation design
Campos Engineering, Inc., mep engineers
Gary Cunningham, Cunningham Architects, pavilion design

Thu Thiem New Urban Center
Client: Investment and Construction Authority for Thu Thiem
Principal Consultants: Sasaki Associates, Inc., planning, urban design, landscape architecture

Charleston Waterfront Park
Client: City of Charleston
Principal Consultants: Sasaki Associates, Inc., master planning, urban design, landscape architecture, civil/marine engineering
Holladay, Coleman and Associates, electrical engineers
David Carsen, structural engineer
LAW Engineering and Environmental Services, Inc. and MACTEC Engineering and Consulting, geotechnical engineers (In 2002, LAW merged with MACTEC.)
Edward Pinckney Associates, Inc., local landscape architects
CMS Collaborative, Inc., fountain mechanical/electrical design and engineering
Ruscon Construction Company, Inc., contractor

Detroit Riverfront Civic Center Promenade
Client: City of Detroit Parks Department
Principal Consultants: Sasaki Associates, Inc., planning, landscape architecture, civil engineering
The Albert Kahn Collaborative, client/architect
NTH Consultants, Ltd., environmental engineer
Tucker, Young, Jackson, Tull, Inc., civil engineer
Snell Environmental Group (SEG), surveyor

SEH (SHORT ELLIOTT HENDRICKSON INC.)

Mound Public Safety Facility
Client: City of Mound, Minnesota: Fire Station and Police Department
Principal Consultants: SEH (Short Elliott Hendrickson Inc.), feasibility study, community open house, architectural, landscape, site civil, mechanical, electrical
Bob Perzel, artist

Heart of Anoka Commuter Village Master Plan
Client: City of Anoka, Minnesota
Principal Consultants: SEH (Short Elliott Hendrickson Inc.), site inventory and analysis, master planning, transportation planning, civil engineering, public facilitation, landscape architecture
BRT Architects, architecture

Maxfield Research, Inc., real estate economics, market research

Loring Bikeway and Park
Client: City of Minneapolis, Minnesota
Principal Consultants: SEH (Short Elliott Hendrickson, Inc.), site analysis, preliminary and final bridge, trail and park design, public art consulting, public advocacy
Lisa Elias, decorative railing for Pocket Park

I-35W Access Project
Client: Hennepin County
Principal Consultants: SEH (Short Elliott Hendrickson Inc.), public facilitation, transportation planning, urban design, landscape architecture
HDR, engineering
Milo Thompson, architecture,
Gary Hallman, artist

Gateway Centre
Client: Gateway Centre, LLP
Principal Consultants: SEH (Short Elliott Hendrickson, Inc.), architectural design
Nicol Associates, Inc., structural
Innovative Mechanical Systems, Inc., mechanical/plumbing
Architectural Engineering Design Group, electrical

SWA GROUP

Lite-On Electronic Headquarters
Client: Artech Inc.
Principal Consultants: SWA Group, full landscape architectural design services for hardscape, softscape, and water elements
Innerscape design, local landscape architect for construction document production
Artech, Inc., building architect

PPG Place
Client: Hillman Properties, Inc.
Principal Consultants: SWA Group, urban design, landscape architecture
R.M. Gensert, structural engineer
WET Design, fountain consultant
IKM, Inc., architect/designer for renovation

Hangzhou HuBin Commerce & Tourism District Redevelopment Master Plan
Client: Hangzhou HuBin Commerce & Tourism District
Principal Consultants: SWA Group, urban redevelopment, master planning, Phase 1 design development, construction phase services
Jerde Partnership International, architecture, consultation on planning
ZSADI (Zhejing Southern Architectural Design Institute), architecture

Lewis Avenue Corridor
Client: City of Las Vegas
Principal Consultants: SWA Group, urban planning, site planning design, construction phase services (full landscape architectural services)
Russ Mitchell and Associates, irrigation
Poggemeyer Design Group, civil and structural
JBA Consulting Engineers, electrical
Fountain People, fountains
Comprehensive Planning Division, City of Las Vegas, planning

Santana Row
Client: Federal Realty Investment Trust (private)
Principal Consultants: SWA Group, full landscape architectural design services, including water features and construction administration

SB Architects (Sandy & Babcock), building architect
BAR Architects (Backen Arrigoni & Ross, Inc.), building architect
Steinberg Architects (The Steinberg Group), building architect
April Philips Design Works, additional landscape architecture design

SWABACK PARTNERS, PLLC

DC Ranch
Client: DMB
Principal Consultants: Swaback Partners, pllc, overall master plan, architectural guidelines, and special community features,
Various Structures by Multiple Architects

Biosphere 2
Client: Decisions Investments Corporation, CB Richard Ellis
Principal Consultant: Swaback Partners, pllc, conceptual planning and additional architectural facility alternatives

Scottdale Hangar One
Client: Scottsdale Hangar One
Principal Consultants: Swaback Partners, pllc, architects
Tihany International, interior design
Studio V, interiors technical support
Paul Koehler Engineers, structural
Lockwood Greene, mep
Automation IQ, automation technology
Steve Martino & Associates, landscape architecture

The Village of Kohler
Client: Kohler Co.
Principal Consultants: Swaback Partners, pllc, overall master planning, detailed site planning, architects for major buildings, special community features
Various Structures by Multiple Architects

Las Palomas
Client: Abigail Properties
Principal Consultants: Swaback Partners, pllc, site planning and architecture
Studio V, interior design
Forest Richardson, golf course architect

Marana Master Plan
Client: Town of Marana
Principal Consultant: Swaback Partners, pllc, landplanning, urban design, site design, design guidelines, architectural visioning, public process-participation, zoning documentation preparation

THOMAS BALSLEY ASSOCIATES

J-City
Client: Mitsui Fudosan Co. Ltd.
Principal Consultants: Thomas Balsley Associates, full landscape design services through documentation and construction over slab
Yamashita Sekkei, architect

Capitol Plaza
Client: Witkoff Group/Adell Corporation
Principal Consultants: Thomas Balsley Associates, full landscape design services through documentation and construction
Costas Kondylis & Associates, architect
Rosenwasser/Grossman, mep engineer

Pacific Design Center
Client: Cohen Brothers Realty Corp.
Principal Consultants: Thomas Balsley Associates, full landscape architectural design services through documentation and construction
Melendrez Design Associates, fandscape architectural construction documentation and construction services
Land Design Consultants, engineering services
Selbert Perkins Design, Graphic Consultant
Kaplan Partners Architectural Lighting, lighting designer
Crain & Associates, traffic engineers
Fluidity Design Consultants, Inc., water features

Riverside Park South
Client: Riverside South Planning Corp.
Principal Consultants: Thomas Balsley Associates, urban design/landscape architect
Skidmore, Owings & Merrill, urban planner
HNTB, engineering services
Olko Engineering, engineering services
Ysrael Senuk, P.C., engineering services
Philip Habib Associates, engineering services
Han-Padron Associates, marine engineering services
Parsons Brinkerhoff, construction manager
Lehrer McGovern Bovis, cost estimator/construction manager

World Trade Center Plaza
Client: World Trade Center Associates/Nikken Sekkei
Principal Consultants: Thomas Balsley Associates, full landscape design services through documentation and construction over slab
Nikken Sekkei, architects
Mancini Duffy, architects
LPA Inc., lighting

THOMAS P. COX: ARCHITECTS, INC.

Stapleton Town Green
Client: Forest City Properties
Principal Consultants: Thomas P. Cox: Architects, Inc., architect

North Crescent
Client: Playa Vista, Fairfield Residential
Principal Consultants: Thomas P. Cox: Architects, Inc., architecture and planning
ima+design, landscape architect
Style Interiors, interior design

Grand Avenue Competition
Client: Forest City Enterprises
Principal Consultants: Thomas P. Cox: Architects, Inc., architect
A.C. Martin, architect
Calthorpe Associates, planning
Civitas, landscape, landscape architect

Westgate-Pasadena
Client: Sares Regis
Principal Consultants: Thomas P. Cox: Architects, Inc., architect
Melendrez, landscape architect

313

Index by Project

Acknowledgments

The first edition of *Urban Spaces* was launched just about ten years ago. Over this decade we have had the privilege of showcasing the very best in urban design and development. This continuing series represents one of the most extensive pictorial collections of contemporary urban projects.

Our fourth edition of *Urban Spaces* is the result of the combined efforts and the cooperation of a talented group of professionals representing the best in their field.

The Urban Land Institute has again cosponsored the publication of *Urban Spaces*. The support and guidance of Rick Rosan, Rachelle Levitt, Gayle Berens, Karrie Underwood and Lori Hatcher were essential to publishing this series. Many thanks to this great organization for its continued interest in *Urban Spaces*.

John Dixon, once again, shepherded the editorial process. His descriptive prose and technical knowledge enhanced the presentation of the over 190 projects covered in the new edition. His skill in developing the essential elements of each project and interpreting the goals of the design firms expedited the exchange of copy and graphics and required a minimum of corrections and rewriting.

The imaginative and effective layouts of the images were produced by our expert designer and photo editor, Harish Patel, who was the point man in turning proofs around quickly and interpreting the proof marks and comments of the participating firms. He was ably assisted by our master of proofreading, John Hogan. Although we utilize all the state-of-the-art electronic communications and graphic systems, no software can substitute for the artistic ability required to create good visual design.

The production professionals at our printers, Gracie Xie and Avan Lee, are also to be thanked for their contribution to the production of this beautiful book. Their watchful eye and attention to detail through all the myriad printing processes ensured the timely completion of the book from disk through distribution.

Of course, there would not have been a fourth edition of *Urban Spaces* if it were not for the cooperation and interest of the architects, marketing executives and graphic directors representing the 37 firms featured in the new volume. We very much enjoyed working with them and became good phone friends and e-mail buddies.

Thanks again to all of you that made this possible.

Henry Burr
Publisher